INTERNATIONAL
TECHNICAL
COMMUNICATION

WILEY TECHNICAL COMMUNICATION LIBRARY

SERIES ADVISORS

JoAnn T. Hackos—Comtech, Denver, CO

William Horton—William Horton Consulting, Boulder, CO

Janice Redish—American Institutes for Research, Washington, DC

SERIES TITLES

JoAnn T. Hackos—Managing Your Documentation Projects

Larry S. Bonura—The Art of Indexing

Jeffrey Rubin—Handbook of Usability Testing: How to Plan, Design, and Conduct Effective Tests

Karen A. Schriver—Dynamics in Document Design: Creating Texts for Readers

Nancy L. Hoft—International Technical Communication

Ken Whitaker—A Guide to Publishing User Manuals

Jack DeLand—Mastering Win Help

OTHER TITLES OF INTEREST

William Horton—The Icon Book: Visual Symbols for Computer Systems and Documentation

Deborah Hix and H. Rex Hartson—Developing User Interfaces: Ensuring Usability Through Products and Processes

William Horton—Illustrating Computer Documentation: The Art of Presenting Information on Paper and Online

William Horton—Designing and Writing Online Documentation: Help

INTERNATIONAL TECHNICAL COMMUNICATION

How to export information about high technology

NANCY L. HOFT

John Wiley & Sons, Inc.

New York • Chichester • Brisbane • Toronto • Singapore

Publisher: Katherine Schowalter
Editor: Theresa Hudson
Managing Editor: Maureen B. Drexel
Interior Design & Composition: Benchmark Productions, Inc.

This text is printed on acid-free paper.

ISBN 0-471-03743-5

Printed in the United States of America
10 9 8 7 6 5 4 3 2 1

To my husband, John T. Devlin . . . Without you, this book could never have existed. Because of you, this book is written. With you, I want to travel the world.

· · · · · · ·

To my father, Robert D. Hoft, whose many international travels and subsequent tales sparked my passion to learn about other cultures in the world.

· · · · · · ·

To my mother, Patricia L. Hoft, whose love of entertaining allowed our family to meet and develop friendships with people from many other countries.

· · · · · · ·

To my brother, David R. Hoft, whose life embodies the realities of cultural diversity.

❧

ABOUT THE AUTHOR

Nancy L. Hoft is president of International Technical Communication Services, an independent consulting firm that specializes in the strategies required to develop effective world-ready information products. She is a frequent lecturer at conferences and teaches workshops on a variety of topics related to international technical communication.

As a technical communicator for more than a decade, Ms. Hoft has provided solutions to technical-communication problems—from writing technical manuals to creating home pages in HTML for the World Wide Web—for large and small companies all over the U.S. and in Europe. Some of her clients include Digital Equipment Corporation, The Boeing Company, Lotus, Sun Microsystems, and the World Health Organization in Geneva, Switzerland.

In 1992, she conceived and managed the first Seminar on International Technical Communication, which was sponsored by the Puget Sound chapter of the Society for Technical Communication (STC). The Seminar was such a success that it was responsible for the Puget Sound chapter's receiving the STC Chapter Achievement Award.

She serves as the manager of the STC's International Technical Communication Professional Interest Committee, which has over 500 members worldwide.

Ms. Hoft is a Novell Certified NetWare Engineer (CNE). She has a degree in English from the University of Connecticut, and has studied fine arts, technical communication, computer programming, and law at various universities throughout the U.S.

PREFACE

This book asks real questions—tough questions. For example, how do you assess the quality of an information product for an international audience? How do you analyze the information needs of users whose language and culture are different from your own? How do you identify cultural bias in your writing? How do you design a management strategy for international technical communication projects? How do you evaluate tools for international technical communication projects?

International Technical Communication: How to Export Information about High Technology is for anyone who develops information products for international use. It is a practical guide to the strategies, processes, and techniques for creating world-ready information products that are successful in today's global marketplace. Business case examples show you how many high-technology companies approach international technical communication.

This book focuses on developing the **skills** (communicating technical information to an international audience), the **processes** (an information development cycle for international product distribution), and the **product** (international technical information that is printed, graphic, or online).

WHO SHOULD READ THIS BOOK

This book assumes that you have practical experience in technical communication and that you are interested only in international issues and considerations. It deals with real business problems. While it offers ample information for academic consideration and further exploration, it is written primarily for practicing professionals. For more background information on any topic, see the references at the end of each chapter.

International Technical Communication can help:

- **Writers** to identify cultural bias in their writing, create core information for reuse, write with translation and the international user in mind, work with translators, and choose and use tools with international features.

- **Editors** to identify cultural bias, edit for translatability, and develop international technical communication standards and guidelines.

- **Technical translators and localization managers** to understand the technical communication process and learn to work with technical communicators.

- **Technical publications managers** to create an international management strategy for information products that works for their corporate environments and their budgets (large or small).

- **Trainers and technical-communication professors** to educate technical communicators by designing and delivering seminars and undergraduate or graduate courses about international technical communication.

- **Graphics professionals** to create appropriate graphics, choose appropriate colors and file formats, and design a page layout that supports translation spread and culturally sensitive content.

- **User interface designers** to develop product interfaces that are flexible, culturally appropriate, and intuitive.

- **Quality assurance, human factors, and usability professionals** to assess the quality, usability, and appropriateness of international information products.

- **Marketing professionals** to prepare more effective marketing and advertising material when selling internationally.

- **Cross-cultural communication consultants** to understand the technical communication process and consult with high-technology companies more effectively.

- **MIS and engineering managers** to design better product interfaces and work with professional writers to create suitable error messages, online help systems, and user documentation.

- **International managers and international business leaders** to create proactive internationalization strategies that integrate the technical-communication process with all other business processes at the enterprise level.

- **International distributors** to understand the value of international information products and to advise companies whose products they distribute on methods for cost-effective internationalization and localization.

- **Students** to learn about the process of creating technical communication for an international audience.

SOME NOTES ON CONTENT

I wrote this book because I could not find a collection of sensible and cost-effective approaches to creating effective international technical communication. Most of the information that does exist is grossly incomplete or written for big companies with access to a wealth of resources. The information that does exist also tends to focus on only translatability issues, which, as you will see as you read through this book, is only a small part of international technical communication.

The content of the book is the result of my research, work, and experience in international technical communication over the past decade. I have culled the most practical information from an assortment of sources in technical communication, software engineering, international management, human factors and usability engineering, linguistics, and cross-cultural communication. I have tried to refer to very recent works. Most of my references are from 1990 to the present, and some are so recent that they are drafts of chapters or papers from books that had not yet been published at the time I received them.

I have also consulted with many people throughout the world and offer solutions here based on real-world experiences. Some solutions are specifically oriented toward small and mid-sized companies with small budgets, while others are oriented toward large companies with generous talent and financial resources.

HOW TO PROFIT FROM THIS BOOK

You can read the chapters sequentially, or only the chapters that are relevant for your current needs. However, you should at least read Chapters 2 through 4, since they introduce core ideas and terminology that are used throughout the rest of the book.

Consider taking the time to read the other chapters—collectively, they offer both a thorough understanding of the many issues that exporting introduces and a comprehensive set of guidelines for addressing them. For example, many technical communicators struggle to improve their processes because they lack the management support they need. Many chapters here provide ideas for collecting statistical data that can help you win that management support and move on to the next level of maturation.

Another chapter of interest is Chapter 13, "Assessing Quality." It shows you how to prepare for ISO 9000 registration and the legal requirements that affect international technical communication.

The last chapter, Chapter 14, "Toward Concurrence," offers ideas for integrating international efforts throughout a corporation to reduce redundancy and inefficiency and to promote a consistent focus on quality and usability.

Appendix A offers a collection of worksheets that can help you organize and manage the information and processes presented in this book.

It will take time to fully integrate these ideas into your existing processes. There are many short-term solutions that you can apply immediately. There are just as many long-term solutions for you to consider as your approach to international technical communication matures.

SOME CONCEPTS

- **Technical communicators:** Anyone who develops information products.

 - **Information products:** This is an umbrella term that encompasses printed user guides, technical reference manuals, online manuals, context-sensitive help, online tutorials, multimedia presentations (audio, video, animation, imaging, text), training materials, the user interface (icons, menus, dialog boxes), error messages, illustrations, marketing communication, business proposals, technical and functional specifications, and so on.

- **Source information, source language, source product:** Each of these describes some facet of the original work that reflects the cultural context and language of its creator. For example, technical writing created in France for a French audience is source information in the source language that describes how to use the source product.

- **Target information, target language, target country, target audience, target user:** These phrases are used to distinguish between the original work or the native audience and those which are different because of exporting. For example, if a German company exports to Japan, the source language is German and the target language is Japanese. Information can be customized for a source audience in Germany and a target audience in Japan.

- **Variants:** I often use this word to describe products that have been altered in some way from either the source product or some internationally generic product.

- **World ready:** This phrase describes anything—people, processes, and products—that is designed to adapt to cultural, technical, and linguistic differences quickly, easily, and economically.

M I S C E L L A N Y

If you have questions, ideas, or suggestions for future editions of this book, send them to me at International Technical Communication Services (ITCS), RR2 Box 493 Moran Road, Temple, NH 03084-9761 USA. You can also send your comments to me electronically at itech@mv.mv.com.

Send inquiries on workshops, seminars, and consulting services offered by ITCS to the addresses above.

ACKNOWLEDGMENTS

Many people contributed to this book, either directly or indirectly. I am very grateful to these individuals, each of whom has provided me with a rich and priceless education in either writing a book or some facet of international technical communication.

John Hedtke, Washington, who has written many books and who told me more than a year ago about the impact that writing a book has on your life. Oh, how correct he was!

Janice King, Marketech, Washington, who has provided me with helpful advice and encouragement for many years, and who has been a particularly good friend during the writing of this book.

Terri Hudson, my editor at John Wiley & Sons, with whom I have had many long and fun telephone conversations, and who has been very helpful and understanding through this entire process. The rest of the staff at John Wiley & Sons, who have been very professional and as concerned about my book as I have been.

Marcia Sweezey, internationalization consultant, New Hampshire, who shares my passion for international technical communication, and who was a formal reviewer of this book. Marcia is a coauthor of the *Digital Guide to Developing International User Information.*

Jan Ulijn, Eindhoven University of Technology, The Netherlands, who was a formal reviewer for this book. Jan has published some fascinating research that explores technical writing, culture, psycholinguistics, and international negotiation. His comments and research have been useful to me.

Jon Lavine, senior editor, Berlitz Translation Services, New York, who has provided me with brilliant and acutely perceptive feedback on every chapter in this book.

Dick Crum, senior editor, Berlitz Translation Services, California, whose sincere interest in learning about the challenges of technical writing is so contagious that it sparked my sincere interest in learning about the challenges of technical translation. Dick has been instrumental in laying the foundation for interaction among technical writers and technical translators.

Chauncey Wilson, human factors consultant, Massachusetts, who provided insightful comments throughout this book and supplied me with many good sources for additional information. He also contributed a lot of useful information to the chapter on quality.

Elaine Winters, a cross-cultural communication consultant and multimedia specialist, California, who offered some good suggestions regarding cultural information and multimedia.

John Kohl, SAS Institute, North Carolina, who has been researching translatability issues for years. John reviewed the chapter on writing issues and provided many helpful comments.

Many people from International Language Engineering (ILE) Corporation, Colorado, provided me with a somewhat technical education in the internationalization and localization of software. They include: Bernard Gateau, president; Dina Bennet, vice president; M. Raymond Jason, project engineering department; and Walter Smith, technical publications manager.

In addition to the individuals previously mentioned, the following people provided me with very helpful comments on the chapter on translation. How much I learned! Theodora Landgren is the President of Bureau of Translation Services in Haddonfield, New Jersey. Robert Bononno, owner of Techline in New York City, is a technical translator and teaches translation at New York University. Walter Popp is a technical translator and localization consultant in La Roque d'Anthéron, France.

Penny Wilson, intellectual property attorney for American Superconductor Corporation, Massachusetts, who read over references to standards and related legal issues and provided valuable feedback.

John Brockmann, University of Delaware, Delaware, who provided some commentary for the chapter on design issues.

Three authors shared with me drafts of their work, which were helpful: Will Doherty, Localization Services Manager, Sybase, "Document Globalization:

Process and Guidelines"; and Susan L. Fowler and Victor R. Stanwick, "International Software," from *The GUI Guide*.

Bob Walker, audio engineer and MIDI musician, New Hampshire, who gave me a crash course in audio engineering and who makes great home brew. Susan Walker, a professional writer and photographer, who provided moral support.

Keith Beal, software engineer extraordinare, Custom Microprocessor Software Systems, New Hampshire, who provided some commentary and whose intellectual curiosity makes his software so very clever and so very usable.

JoAnn Hackos, president, Comtech Services, who, if I could choose a mentor in this profession, it would be her. JoAnn has been helpful and supportive of my endeavors throughout my career, and for this and more I am sincerely grateful.

Michael Anobile, director, Localization Industry Standards Association, Switzerland, who has been supportive of this book by supplying me with copies of LISA Forum proceedings and the LISA newsletter. Based on these and Michael's leadership, LISA has great potential.

Robert Bringhurst, WordPerfect Corporation, Utah, who shared an approach to core documentation that he used at WordPerfect.

Ralph Calistro, Northern Telecom Canada, Ontario, who spent some time with me discussing his research on Controlled English.

The Society for Technical Communication (STC), which has provided me with a wonderful arena in which to explore many of the ideas in this book, network with many of my colleagues throughout the world, and for encouraging the development of international technical communication. Three colleagues whom I met because of STC and who, unbeknownst to them, inspired some ideas in this book: Norio Kobayashi, Seishosha Company, Ltd., Japan; Fred Klein, University of California at Los Angeles, California; and Brigitte Beuttenmüller, Tekom, Germany.

Peter Gelpi, Operations Manager, Aldus Corporation, whose approach to internationalization and localization is still the most creative I have encountered.

Arthur Braunstein, Director, AT&T Business Translations, whose business sense is truly a great contribution to this arena.

Lori Lathrop, Lathrop Media Services, Colorado, who created the index to this book.

There are several people who influenced this book before it was ever conceived. They include the speakers and contributors to the Seminar on International Technical Communication that I conceived and managed in Seattle, 1992, with the sponsorship of the STC; and, the managers I interviewed for an article I wrote in 1991 for the *Puget Sound Business Journal* on internationalization and localization.

Dr. S. Mandil, Dr. George Dorros, Mr. Pascal Diethelm, and Mr. C. Dumas, with whom I worked at the World Health Organization in Geneva, Switzerland, which is where I began to appreciate the need for a book like this.

And my whole family, who have been so supportive of this project. My husband, John Devlin, who is a project manager for an electronic publishing company, took over most of our household responsibilities so that I could focus on this project. He also very patiently read every draft of every chapter even when he would rather have been playing in his gardens.

CONTENTS

1

BE AWARE OF TRENDS IN INTERNATIONAL COMMUNICATION AND THE OPPORTUNITIES AND THE SKILLS YOU NEED TO ADDRESS THEM.

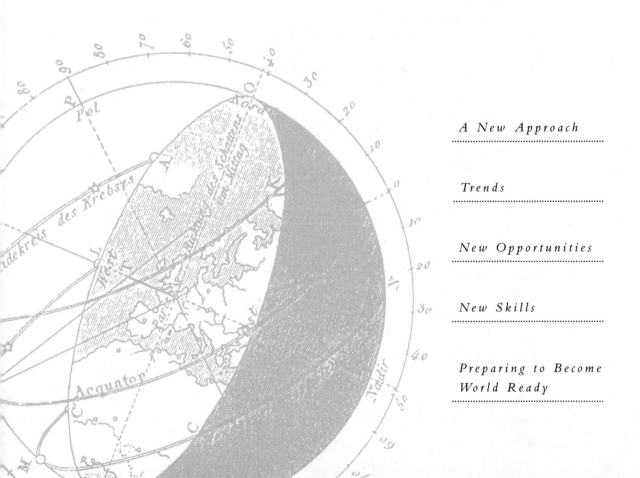

T H E   N E X T   G E N E R A T I O N   ⬤1

As more and more high-technology companies export their products, they are pressuring technical communication into its next generation: *international technical communication*. International technical communication is the development of information that can be exported to any country in the world. International technical communication can be used by any audience that is culturally, linguistically, and technologically variant from the audience in the source country.

International technical communication requires a significant extension of technical communication as we know it today. It dictates a completely different approach to developing information, new tools, and new methods for its design and testing. In short, we need to reengineer technical communication for international use.

- Where technical communication added value to a product, international technical communication is a user requirement.

- Where technical communication explained how to use high technology, international technical communication bridges cultural differences and national boundaries.

- Where technical communication required writing skills, international technical communication requires multicultural and multilingual awareness.

- Where technical communication relied on text, international technical communication explores other methods of communication, like auditory and visual communication.

- Where technical communication referred to users, international technical communication refers, selectively, to target users.

- Where technical communication sought common ground, international technical communication seeks diversity.

- Where technical communication assumed a domestic focus, international technical communication regards the source country and all target countries as international variants.

- Where technical communication depended on input from subject-matter experts in the source country, international technical communication requires the input of subject-matter experts from around the world.

- Where technical communication was user centered, international technical communication is world ready.

- Where technical communication reacted to business needs, international technical communication perceives global requirements.

A NEW APPROACH

A new approach, an effective one, is required to address the challenge and complexity of international technical communication. An effective approach filters choices so that you can make decisions with foresight, focus a team's efforts, and develop information that embraces diversity.

An effective approach allows international technical communication to balance these often contradictory goals: economy (business needs) and cultural understanding (user needs). Figure 1.1 illustrates an effective approach.

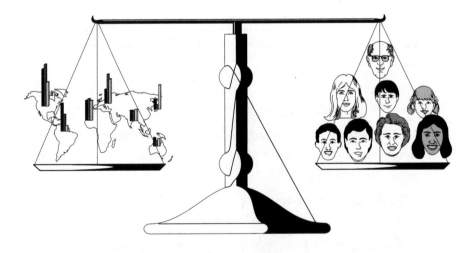

FIGURE 1.1: **An effective approach to international technical communication balances economy (business needs) with cultural understanding (user needs).**

BUSINESS NEEDS

Corporate objectives and the strategies chosen to meet those objectives offer technical communicators only one-half of the equation for creating an effective approach. Some corporate goals and strategies that technical communicators need to consider are:

- Be profitable

- Contain costs

- Be the first to market in a particular area of the world

- Export products simultaneously around the world

- Cultivate consumer loyalty

- Achieve quality certification

- Satisfy national and international legal requirements

- Minimize product liability

USER NEEDS

The other half of the equation for creating an effective approach is developing a cultural understanding of the people who need to learn how to use high-technology products. Users' needs differ not just because of their computing skills, but because of cultural differences. Some of the cultural differences that technical communicators need to consider include:

- Language

- Learning style

- Communication style

- Visual literacy

- Technical literacy

- Computer literacy

TRENDS

Here are some of the trends relating to international technical communication since 1990 that attempt to address business needs and user needs:

- Technical communicators who communicate information about high technology respond to international pressures more slowly than their counterparts in software engineering. Many software products have already been completely re-engineered to accommodate the cultural, linguistic, and technological diversity of international audiences. Very few technical communication products have been adapted at all, let alone re-engineered, for the challenges that international business introduces.

- Technical communicators who write source information in English experiment with restrictive grammars, often referred to as *Controlled English*. Restrictive grammars address the needs of machine translation and of readers for whom English is a second language. Restrictive grammars are spoken of in only business terms. Benefits to the reader remain to be proved empirically.

- Visual information replaces much written information. Visual information reduces the need for translation. But graphics often assume a level of visual literacy that is not universal. Visual information can make cultural assumptions that are inappropriate or offensive. Reliance on icons and related conceptual images can mislead as much as a poor translation.

- Online information replaces much printed documentation. Online information is affected by the same technological restraints for customization as software. The technological restraints are significant. Also, online information makes cultural assumptions about work environments. In many countries, users share a single workstation, making time sharing and learning a logistical problem.

- Non-traditional disciplines contribute information assisting in global success. Cultural anthropology, cross-cultural communication, linguistics, and professional technical translation are all disciplines that are relatively new contributors to the success of high technology.

- High-technology companies invest in machine-translation software. Currently machine-translation software must be used in conjunction with restrictive grammars. A central goal of machine-translation software is to minimize the need for post-editing of the target language by a professional translator. To date, machine-translation products have not attained this goal. Machine-translation software also suffers from being cost prohibitive for most companies.

- High-technology companies realize the benefits of hiring professional technical communicators to develop information about their products. In most countries in the world, technical communication is not yet a recognized specialty, a focus in universities, or a true profession. Engineers and administrative assistants currently write the information that is exported with products. Companies realize that quality product information is not just a competitive advantage but is a fast-developing user requirement. In some cases it is a legal requirement.

- High-technology companies develop training materials and tools that simplify customization for software engineers who develop software on their respective proprietary computing platforms. Companies like Microsoft, Apple, IBM, and Novell are ensuring that software running on their computing platforms is world ready. These same companies have yet to provide information for the technical communicators who write about these software products.

- High-technology companies focus on synchronizing time-to-market of all product variants in order to accommodate user demand. High-technology products provide target users around the world with a competitive edge. Users from target countries demand equal access to high-technology products that users in the source country receive automatically. Users from the target countries demand high-technology products that are technologically, culturally, and linguistically customized to their needs.

- Simultaneous release of high-technology products sacrifices quality. Many companies do not thoroughly test all variants of the product and its documentation. Problems missed in the source product are repeated in all target variants. Short product-development cycles contribute to these problems. The amount of target variants, often for five or more countries, requires significant funding and time to test thoroughly.

- Standards, both national and international, assist in creating high-technology products that are world ready. High-technology companies form consortia to develop ways of bridging technological incompatibilities around the world. There are no standards that help technical communicators bridge the diverse information needs of an international audience.

- Liability law matures in many countries, rendering customization that affects a user's health and safety particularly susceptible. Any technical information that a user reads, be it a label on hardware or a user's guide, must be translated and thoroughly tested to reduce liability.

NEW OPPORTUNITIES

International technical communication introduces challenges that open opportunities. Here are some new opportunities for those who are interested in helping technical communicators balance business needs and user needs:

- Technical communicators need tools that interface well with the tools of translators. To date, there are none available.

- Technical communicators need tools that support multilingual and multicultural information management. To date, none exist.

- Technical communicators need clip art that is representative of people, environments, and technology in target countries around the world. To date, no one clip-art package is available to address these needs.

- Technical communicators need access to cultural information about target users, their information needs, and their learning styles. To date, very little research is being done in this area.

- Technical communicators need reliable and uniform usability testing methods for all language and cultural variants. To date, many methods are cost prohibitive.

- Technical communicators need reliable subject-matter experts in all target countries who can assess the quality of the translated and localized product information for use in the target countries.

- Technical communicators need training in existing approaches to developing international technical communication. To date, there are very few universities supporting such an effort.

- Technical communicators need criteria to evaluate the quality of information for all languages and cultural variants. To date, quality evaluation is culture bound.

- Technical communicators need information designs that can accommodate cultural and linguistic diversity. To date, information design adds to the cost of customization because it cannot accommodate diversity efficiently.

- Technical communicators need a universally understood collection of symbols. To date, icons require explanation or modification.

- Technical communicators need processes that are proven to help them meet quality and time-to-market expectations. To date, few case studies for technical communicators have been published.

- Technical communicators need statistical data from all over the world that quantifies processes, methods, and quality assessments for international technical communication. To date, there is no collaboration within or across national borders in support of this effort.

- Technical communicators need standards that guide them in the development of technical information for target countries. To date, there are none. National standards are preferable, since they can help technical communicators address the information needs of a target audience more specifically.

NEW SKILLS

Technical communicators need new skills to develop international technical communication that balances business needs and user needs. Some of these new skills are listed here. Technical communicators need training in the following areas:

- Developing and using cultural models so that they can perform international user analyses

- Developing cross-cultural communication and language skills to work well in multicultural and multilingual teams

- Understanding the technological complexity of developing high-technology products for the world to perceive changes in the product information that they develop

- Cultivating long-term relationships with technical translators in all target countries to discover ways of improving the source information for translatability

- Performing cultural edits of source information to eliminate cultural bias

- Recognizing business strategies so that they can align their processes to them

- Developing financial models so that they can create processes that are economically sound

- Developing metrics that collect the statistical data they need to assess the effectiveness of their processes

- Modifying existing tools to implement multilingual and multicultural information

- Developing criteria to measure the quality of source and target product information

PREPARING TO BECOME WORLD READY

International Technical Communication: How to Export Information about High Technology is a comprehensive guide that provides the information you need to develop the skills identified here. The following chapters explain the trends and explore the new opportunities identified above. Table 1.1 maps these skills to chapters in this book.

TABLE 1.1: **New Skills and the Chapters in This Book That Show You How to Develop Them**

SKILLS	CHAPTERS
How to develop the most effective strategy for managing international technical communication projects	2, 3, Appendix A
How to identify and develop information for reuse	7
How to identify international resources that can help you gather information on a target country	4, 5, Appendix C
How to analyze the audience in a target country and how to apply that information to international technical communication	4, 5, Appendix B
How to identify cultural bias in technical writing and what to do about it	5
How to write in your native language to optimize translatability	5, 6, 7, 9
How to create a glossary for translators	8
How to choose and work with translators	8
How to have translated information reviewed for accuracy and appropriateness	8
How to design information that considers cultural differences and translation	6

TABLE 1.1: *Continued*

SKILLS	CHAPTERS
How to create multilingual online information that is not hampered by technological problems	10
How to test the quality and usability of source and target product information	13
How to investigate and prepare for legal requirements in the target country	4, 13, Appendix C
How to prepare for ISO 9000 registration	13
How to choose tools that facilitate international technical communication	12
How to create multimedia presentations that accommodate cultural, linguistic, and technological differences	10, 11, 13
How to create graphics that consider translation and cultural issues	11
How to choose colors that minimize misunderstanding	11
How to develop and share information throughout a corporation to direct the product team toward developing quality, world-ready products from the start	14

2

SUCCESSFUL INTERNATIONAL HIGH-TECHNOLOGY COMPANIES APPLY THESE FOUR APPROACHES WHEN CREATING EFFECTIVE INTERNATIONAL TECHNICAL COMMUNICATION.

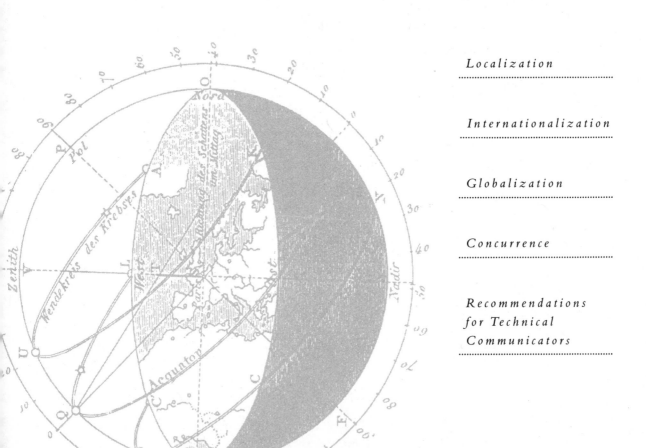

Localization

....

Internationalization

....

Globalization

....

Concurrence

....

*Recommendations
for Technical
Communicators*

....

APPROACHES TO INTERNATIONAL TECHNICAL COMMUNICATION ②

Many companies have discovered approaches to creating international products that address incompatible expectations and needs fairly successfully. These approaches can be generalized to include localization, internationalization, globalization, and concurrence. Applied to the creation of information products, these approaches offer effective ways of balancing economy and cultural understanding.

LOCALIZATION

Looking at the literature, we find a variety of definitions of *localization*. Synonyms for localization include *customization*, *adaptation*, and the abbreviation *L10N*.[1] Dave Taylor in *Global Software* defines localization as "the process of infusing a specific cultural context" into a product.[2] In *Developing International User Information*, Digital Equipment Corporation defines localization as "the process of adapting a product to suit the language, conventions, and market requirements of a locale other than the one for which the product was originally developed."[3] And Microsoft Press, in *Computer Dictionary*, defines localization as "the process of altering a program so that it is appropriate for the area in which it is used."[4]

Here is the definition of localization used in this book:

Localization is the process of creating or adapting an information product for use in a specific target country or specific target market.

Localization requires adapting an information product so that it can be used by people of a particular cultural context, locale, and area. There are different degrees of localization. *General localization* focuses on superficial cultural differences. *Radical localization* focuses on cultural differences below the surface, those that affect the way users think, feel, and act. Choosing between the two is a business decision based on balancing the economic goals of a company with a cultural understanding of the target users.

General localization accommodates superficial cultural differences like language, currency formats, date, and time formats. General localization would require a translation of the information product from the source language into French with perhaps some minor modifications to date, time, and currency formats. It is possible that the French could be further modified to reflect subtle linguistic differences among France, French-speaking parts of Canada, or in all countries in which French is a primary or secondary spoken language. The list of countries in which forms of French are spoken includes France, French-speaking areas of Canada, Tunisia, French-speaking areas of Switzerland, Belgium, Algeria, Mauritania, Madagascar, Morocco, the Ivory Coast, Mozambique, Haiti, French Polynesia, and French Guyana.

In another example of general localization, the source country is Japan and the target countries are all English-speaking countries. To create a localized product, the Japanese technical communicators might adapt their user manual to accommodate only the British and the American spellings of words. If the target market for the Japanese product is larger in the U.S. than in Great Britain and other English-speaking countries that use British English (India and Hong Kong, for example), then it would be more prudent for the Japanese to choose to write in American English and adapt their information products to the American user, despite their selling the product in all English-speaking countries. The information products would need to incorporate currency, date, and time formats, in addition to other superficial cultural differences like addresses, telephone numbers, and so on.

With *radical localization*, the approach is quite different. It incorporates cultural differences that affect the way users think, feel, and act, above and beyond the superficial differences cited previously. For example, the cultural differences incorporated in the information product would address learning styles and culturally specific examples. In some companies, the difference is so radical that it results in multiple information products.

In a simple example of radical localization, the source country is the U.S. and the target country is Great Britain. To create a localized product, the American user manual needs to be adapted so that it uses the British spellings of words, British idioms and expressions, currency amounts in the British pound sterling, and measurements expressed in metrics, to name a few of the changes. A further distinction would involve adapting to the reading and learning styles of the British users. Consider a tutorial for children ages seven to ten on how to analyze newspaper articles. The tutorial should imitate the British teaching style for children of that age group. The tutorial should also include examples from the British press, since British journalism is stylistically different from American journalism.

Note that in this example, localization did not include what we traditionally think of as language translation. The spelling of some words like *color* and *colour* is different, but some companies do not consider this translation. Digital Equipment Corporation stresses that localization may or may not include language translation. Some products' features may be adapted (localized) for the legal, market, and technological requirements of a target market, but the written information remains in English.[5]

B E N E F I T S   O F   L O C A L I Z A T I O N

- **Localized products improve sales.** Localization is marketing. As an approach, its primary purpose is to improve sales to a particular country or user group. Of all the approaches to creating a localized information product, general localization is the easiest to apply and implement because its focus is narrow and superficial. It is easy to research and apply superficial cultural differences.

- **Localized products overcome cultural differences.** A simple example is to look at the design of automobiles. Automobile manufacturers who sell cars in the U.S. and many parts of Europe and Asia build cars that have the steering wheel on the left side of the car. Automobile manufacturers who sell cars in England, Japan, Australia, Indonesia, and New Zealand build cars that have the steering wheel on the right side of the car.

Another example of how the localization approach is used to overcome cultural differences is to look at the wood products industry. In the 1950s, Japan, whose natural wood resources are limited, approached both the U.S. and Canada in search of a supplier for wood products. Japan had one requirement: that wood be cut according to Japanese building tradition. To accommodate this request, the suppliers in the chosen country would have to create special tools for cutting the wood into sizes and shapes specific only to Japan. At the time, it seemed improbable to some suppliers that Japan would become a major world economy. So, thinking shortsightedly, the Americans chose to turn down the request, not wanting to get involved in localization. Canada, on the other hand, accepted the challenge and adopted the localization approach to create wood products for Japan. Many years later, a look at Canada's income from its localization of wood products makes American wood products suppliers cringe. In this case, localization overcame the cultural differences between Canada and Japan.[6]

- **Localized products overcome inherent product resistance.** While related to improving sales, this reason for the localization approach is defensive in nature. An example of this is McDonald's creation of a vegetarian burger for people in India. McDonald's, whose main menu item is an all-beef hamburger, the Big Mac, wanted to expand its business to India to increase its presence and sales in that region of the world. However, not all people in India eat beef (inherent product resistance). To overcome the inherent resistance to its staple product, McDonald's applied the localization approach and adapted its product for use by a specific target group, consumers in India, by creating a vegetarian burger.[7] In this instance, localization combined economy (India has the second largest population of any country in the world and is a huge consumer market) with cultural understanding (many Indians are vegetarians, so the Indian Big Mac is meatless).

- **Localized products are stratagems for being the first to market or for entering a niche market.** Aldus, an American company, introduced its flagship desktop-publishing product PageMaker in countries where desktop publishing did not exist. Aldus's approach to localization had the specific goal of having PageMaker be the first to achieve a worldwide desktop publishing market. This was a risky move since it seemed that Aldus was throwing away money to sell such a small number of copies of a new kind of product while its success was still being tested in the U.S. Aldus succeeded in building a large market presence in these countries as the desktop publishing market slowly grew in the U.S. as well as in Europe. Aldus had 100 percent of the desktop publishing market in many countries by the time the desktop publishing market expanded, and it continues to maintain this market share in many countries in the world despite the presence of competing products. Aldus attributes its success to radical localization.[8]

PROBLEMS WITH LOCALIZATION

For all the good it accomplishes, the localization approach is not without its problems. Localization introduces three problems that cannot be avoided.

1. **Localization is expensive.** Localization inevitably adds to the cost of a project. Product re-engineering is often required, especially for radical localization. Translation, while not always necessary, is typically part of localization. Translation of the source text into one target language can range in cost from $50 USD to over $200 USD per page translated; most user manuals are a minimum of 200 pages, making the minimum cost of localization $10,000 USD. Often localization projects require translation into more than one target language (English to German and Japanese, for example). The cost of doing international business is expensive, too. Telephone calls, faxes, postage, shipping charges, licensing fees, export and import taxes, and international travel charges add up to a significant sum. In Europe and Canada, for example, airline travel is often so expensive that many companies are forced to minimize air travel. These examples are only *some* of the charges companies can expect to incur when doing business internationally and creating a localized product for one or more target markets.

   Despite the financial investment, localization offers companies around the world a means of entering a market in another country. Many companies earn over 50 percent of their revenue from international sales. This reward more than makes up for the financial investment in localizing a product.

2. **Localization increases the time it takes for a product to be introduced in an international market.** Re-engineering and translation alone can add months to a product's development cycle. Also, contacts in other countries may not have the same idea of expediency that your company does. U.S. companies are often faulted for wanting to move too quickly in their business dealings. Countries in the Middle East, however, believe in developing a solid relationship with business partners before making any deals. This relationship building can often take months or years, much to the frustration of companies with the opposite inclination. As I hope this book will impart *ad nauseam*, time-to-market issues and most other obstacles to localization can be minimized through sufficient planning and research.

3. **Localization introduces additional legal issues.** This final problem that localization introduces may not be avoidable in spite of sufficient planning and research. The Boeing Company, a major airplane manufacturer based in Seattle, Washington, localizes the features it includes in all the airplanes it builds for each of its clients, many of whom are airlines from other

countries. Boeing does not have any of the maintenance manuals that explain how to repair the particular airplane translated for its offshore customers. Translating the maintenance manuals is the choice and sole responsibility of the customer who buys the airplane. Boeing does not translate the maintenance manuals because of the liability Boeing would assume if the translation was incorrect or misleading. If a bad repair is made to an airplane based on inaccurately translated instructions, and if the airplane consequently malfunctions, Boeing might be liable for any damages and injuries incurred as a result of the inaccurate translation. As Marcia Sweezey, an internationalization consultant, comments, "The decision to translate should not be made at the level of the information function. Whether to translate is a serious business decision with legal implications."[9]

Liability, while not a visible problem today, is becoming more apparent as countries change their import requirements, making translation of certain kinds of product information mandatory. A 1993 *Law Department Spending Survey* of 201 major companies indicated that 50 percent of all companies surveyed expected their legal needs to increase around international issues. This was the second-highest rated category of 16 categories listed in the survey, topped only by environmental legal issues (rated number one by 68% of respondents).[10]

Many countries in the European Union are requiring that product documentation be written in the official language of each country. Information regarding the safe use of a product is an example of the kind of information that needs to be translated into the language acceptable to the user. These requirements may soon change how companies exporting to the European Union localize their products.

Localization is an effective approach if the number of target countries or target user groups is small. Localization is effective if a company lacks a business need for expanding the export of its product beyond a few target countries.

Localization is also the approach of choice for companies new to international technical communication. As mentioned in the beginning of this chapter, creating international technical communication is an iterative process. It often requires years of experience before localization reaches a point of satisfaction for all affected. The localization approach provides a rich opportunity to learn how to create effective technical communication without incurring great risk, financial or otherwise. It does so by allowing you to focus on the needs of one country or target user group whose cultural expectations and needs may be incompatible with your own. In this way, you can learn how to accommodate these differences through writing and through the managerial and production processes required to create a localized information product. By starting small, you will know what you need to do when your company expands its international presence.

INTERNATIONALIZATION

Many companies perform localization by adapting a product that was created specifically for its domestic market. A product created for its creator's domestic market is often embedded with the cultural markings of the creator's cultural context. Localizing a domestic product for a different cultural context can be an arduous editorial process since it is hard to find and adapt all cultural references in the product.

In the software industry, for example, the domestic cultural context is often embedded in the software code itself. Thus, any localization will require recoding and possibly re-engineering to get the product to accommodate the cultural context of a target country or target market. To see how this problem becomes exaggerated when localizing one little feature for many target countries or target markets, consider the simple example of putting a list of names into alphabetical order for several language versions of an American product.

An American software product that outputs a list of names in alphabetical order collates the names in the order of letters in the English alphabet. But in Spanish the order of letters is different from that of English. If a software product is written for a domestic audience of Americans, then there is a good chance that the code for collating a list of names is written with the American alphabet in mind. If the American product is localized for the Spanish market, then the code will have to be reworked to employ the collating sequence for letters in the Spanish alphabet.

Consider some other languages and the collating sequences for their alphabets. "The character *Ä* or *ä* is sorted as equivalent to *A* or *a* for the German language, but for Swedish and Finnish the character is treated as distinct from *A* or *a*, and must appear after *Z* in the collating sequence."[11]

And how about Arabic, Hebrew, Chinese Hanzi, or Japanese Kanji? They are all different, the ideographic languages, Chinese Hanzi and Japanese Kanji, being by far the most complex to work with when implementing collating sequences. For example, Digital's VMS computer operating system can collate Chinese Hanzi using three methods: by radicals, number of strokes, or by phonetic sequence (based on their romanized (western) spelling).[12]

If the American code for collating has to be modified time and time again for each new language, then localization becomes a tedious editorial task that ceases to be an efficient and effective balance of economy and cultural understanding.

The point here is that it is much easier to localize a product that is not embedded with the cultural context of its creators. The product (for example, the software code) must be generic enough to accept many variations, many cultural contexts. This approach is called *internationalization*. Internationalization is sometimes referred to as a "separation of form from function" and "creating a core product." It is also known as *I18N* (first and last letters in English, plus the amount of the number of characters between them).

Taylor defines internationalization, which he asserts is the opposite of localization, as "the preparatory stage where products have their embedded culture and language extracted and generalized."[13] The result of internationalization is "a sort of generic package, with an appendix or attachment that details all the culturally specific items."[14] To Taylor, good product design assumes that localization will occur. He shows, in many examples of software code, that the most effective way to create a product for internationalization is to modularize it so that all cultural context is separated from the core information. By comparison, "localization is the completion stage, where the [internationalized] product is fine tuned for the specific market niche that is targeted."[15]

Digital Equipment Corporation defines internationalization as a two-step process that includes product localization. Internationalization is a "process that includes both the development of an international product and the localization of the international product for delivery into worldwide markets."[16] An international product consists of four components, one of which is a generic component and the other three of which are market-, user-, and country-specific components that are subsequently localized.[17] Like Taylor's approach to internationalization, Digital's approach recommends separating the core information from the target market's culturally dependent elements by using a modular design. Note that both of these definitions enhance the definition of localization. Localization, as these definitions suggest, is most effectively performed on an internationalized product. In the context of international technical communication, here is the definition of internationalization used in this book:

Internationalization **is the process of re-engineering an information product so that it can be easily localized for export to any country in the**

world. An internationalized information product consists of two components: core information and international variables.

Core information is invariant information that can be reused. Core information can come from several information sources. Printed manuals, online help text, training materials, graphics, multimedia, sound and video segments are all examples of potential core information. Digital refers to a similar concept as *core text*, which is defined as "information that remains the same for an entire family of products or for the same product used in different operating environments."[18] Chapter 7 discusses core information in great detail.

International variables are the localizable elements. International variables identify superficial and deep cultural differences. In the example of the user manual for a software database product, the international variables can influence the page design, the writing style, the cultural content of graphics and of examples, and the language in which the localized product is printed. The international variables can also identify the units of measurement, and the time, date, and currency formats.

Internationalization involves isolating and researching these international variables to discover where in your information product general localization needs to be performed.

There are many international variables that this book investigates concerning international technical communication. The superficial international variables that this book investigates are:

- Political
- Economic
- Social
- Religious
- Educational
- Linguistic
- Technological

This book investigates deeper cultural differences by using the international variables identified in four models of culture. Chapter 4, "Performing an International-User Analysis," looks at the models of culture presented by Edward T. Hall, David A. Victor, Geert Hofstede, and Fons Trompenaars. The international variables in Trompenaars's model, for example, include:

- Universalism versus particularism

- Individualism versus collectivism

- Neutral or emotional

- Specific versus diffuse

- Achievement versus ascription

- Attitudes to time

- Attitudes to the environment

Trompenaars uses these seven international variables to describe how a group of people solves problems, which is how he defines culture.[19] Infusing an information product with cultural information derived from studying Trompenaars's international variables would inevitably lead to radical localization.

BENEFITS OF INTERNATIONALIZATION

By identifying the core information and separating it from the international variables, you can significantly minimize the localization effort of an information product. Consider the implication of this statement, "Core text was used in about 30 percent of the hardware user information sets translated at Digital in 1990."[20] This means that 30 percent of the information can be used repeatedly, even its previously translated versions, over time, which saves money on translation costs. Reducing the amount of information to localize can also decrease the time it takes for a localized product to reach its target market.

Identifying the core information eliminates cultural bias in the information product. As shown in the example about collating sequences for putting a list of names in alphabetical order, the cultural context of the creators can permeate every aspect of a product—in this case, an information product. Consider a user manual that contains an extended example of how to do a household budget using spreadsheet software. The currency used in the example needs to change for each country, as well as the amounts used for line items in the budget. The amounts may not even correlate to a strict conversion of the source currency to the target currency, since the cost of living in each country can differ significantly. Therefore, you may need to do some research on how much various items cost in a target country. Consider, too, the line items. What is considered a household budget item in one country may not be appropriate in another. It is also possible that a household budget is considered inappropriate as an example in a country because the target country considers a household budget to be private information. Making a household budget public in a document may be considered offensive, or at least in poor taste.

In another example, an online tutorial may show how to create an organizational chart. The tutorial will require major revision for each target country. Forms of address, titles, common names, and corporate hierarchies vary significantly from country to country.

By separating this culturally dependent information from the core information, localization can become a less intensive, more manageable, and more measurable effort.

Identifying international variables makes it easier to adapt each information product to a target market and a target audience. By performing an international user analysis using the international variables as categories, you can discover where in your information product localization needs to be performed. The result of performing an international user analysis for each target country or target market may indicate that the following elements of technical communication vary from cultural context to cultural context:

- Colors
- Currency format
- Date format
- Time format
- Units of measurement
- Graphics
- Writing style
- Product packaging

Internationalization makes it much easier to divide the localization tasks among an international team. The task of preparing the core information for inclusion in the internationalized version of a user manual, for example, is accomplished very quickly. For example, you could create a document template for user manuals that already contains core information. The international team can be assigned various international variables to research with respect to the target countries or target markets. Research done to investigate the international variables for a particular target country can then be reused for any subsequent product localization for that country. This minimizes the localization effort as well as focuses it. Once the research is complete, the data collected can be further categorized before localization. Digital, for example, groups its research into three categories: country-specific information, market-specific information, and user–interface information.[21]

All information products should be developed with internationalization in mind. It is significantly more difficult to internationalize an existing product than it is to internationalize a new product. The reasons for this range from the problems associated with deeply engrained cultural bias in the source product to the problems of integrating the cultural complexity of the target country or target market into its localized variant. Internationalization gets easier over time and with experience.

However, the internationalization approach is a business necessity for companies who export worldwide. It is a sensible step for companies that currently localize, since it plans specifically for the localization process. Localization, as mentioned in the previous section, can be expensive and require time and resources that may undermine a company's desire to localize. Planning for it can ensure a balance between economy and cultural understanding.

G L O B A L I Z A T I O N

While a very good approach, internationalization still requires a minimum of two steps: internationalization of the product and then localization of the international product for each target market. Localization still requires additional effort, time, and money for each product variant, even though it is a very successful approach for expanding a business.

When internationalization and localization are used to expand business to dozens of target countries, they cease to provide a balance between economy and cultural understanding because the localization investment will eventually erode a healthy return on that investment. For example, while many companies enjoyed revenues of over 50 percent from international sales in the late 1980s and early 1990s, they witnessed the shrinking of those profits in 1993. Here are some headlines from *The Boston Sunday Globe* on July 4, 1993:[22]

Struggling Europe is little help in pulling U.S. out of recession
Bad News Threatens U.S. Export Gains
Anemic Europe

Japan has been struggling economically, too. The three major trading zones in the world have been in a slump together. If these countries are in recession, it makes it difficult for companies to export and sell their products to consumers in those countries. How, then, can companies justify the cost of internationalization and localization if the return on their investments shrinks daily?

The ultimate, ideal solution is to create a global product, one that can be used by anyone, anywhere, without modification, rendering internationalization and localization unnecessary.

What is a *global product*? Strictly speaking, a global product is something that has universal appeal and that can be understood and used by anyone, anywhere.

The Ancient Greeks talked of the four elements as being universal—earth, air, fire, and water—and indeed, all people in the world are familiar with these. Human emotions and basic human needs might be considered universal; Shakespearean plays, Ancient Greek and Roman mythology, and other classic writings from around the world, particularly religious documents, are filled with examples of human universals.

But are there man-made global products, products whose universal appeal transcends the human condition? Global products do exist . . . more or less. For example, it could be argued that a paper clip, a pencil, a nail, and a safety pin are universal products. Strictly speaking, the pencil is only a global product if everyone in the world accepts it and uses it. But is there a need for pencils in the middle of the Sahara desert, or on a remote island still populated by an ancient tribe? No, not yet. Do these extreme examples render these products non-global, despite their being accepted and used by so many with much success?

Global is a relative concept that is defined by the success of products that can be used in multicultural and multilingual environments without modification. Thus, the definition of global product, and consequently, globalization, narrows.

Microsoft Corporation has a different definition of a global product. It defines a global product as having:

- A core worldwide feature set

- Market/country specific localization as appropriate

- Interoperability between the various language versions

Microsoft adds that a global product does not have to have exactly equivalent features in all countries.[23] This definition, though, is no different from a definition for a product that has been internationalized and subsequently localized. There is little in the way of universalism in this definition. There is little that is global in this definition of a product.

Digital defines *global product* as "a product that functions properly in a usage environment that includes users throughout the world."[24] This definition does address the sense of universal appeal in the word *global* and is therefore a more accurate definition of a global product.

For the purposes of this book, here are definitions of *global product* and *globalization*.

A *global product* is one that can be used successfully in several target markets without modification of any kind.

***Globalization* is the process of creating a product that can be used successfully in many cultural contexts without modification.**

Perhaps a synonymous idea for globalization is that it is the process of creating a universally *intuitive* product.

Some signs are universally intuitive or are becoming universally accepted. Traffic signs, signs for the rest room, bus and train signs, and safety signs tend to be universal, although variants do exist. Figure 2.1 provides some examples of global products.

FIGURE 2.1: **Examples of global products and signs that can be considered universal.**

Some efforts have been made, particularly in the airline industry, to create more complex global products. The safety information card that you find in the seat pocket in front of you on an airplane is an attempt at creating a more complex global product. Most safety information cards are written in at least three or four languages and are illustrated for universal understanding, whether you can read any of the languages provided or not. However, there have been many complaints about how the safety information cards lack universal appeal and intuitiveness. Perhaps this is why many airlines now show videos of the safety information and supplement these videos with demonstrations by flight attendants.

Jon Lavine, a senior editor at Berlitz Translation Services, remarks that global symbols, like those illustrated in Figure 2.1, are successful because they convey a single message. The safety information cards, on the other hand, fail because they try to convey too many messages. He cites the additional example of graphical user interfaces that have very busy compositions. There are many software products that have a graphical user interface consisting only of icons. The icons can represent many actions and ideas and cause the graphical user interface to suffer because of this.

Lavine adds that this "failed global appeal" may be related to the media used to convey the message. For example, the video of airline safety information is successful while the card with similar content is not.[25]

So while globalization in its purest sense does not really occur, it can be achieved to the degree that the intended message is understood by more people than a localized message.

In an effort to balance the need for economy and cultural understanding, all information products should strive for globalization to minimize localization. Some companies, Aldus in particular, have experimented with globalization. In their documentation and even in their advertisements, they try to use examples in several languages and from several cultural contexts. By doing so, Aldus is able to minimize the localization effort that much more.[26]

Globalization is achievable to some degree, but only by way of performing a thorough user analysis, building an international team that is truly representative of all the target markets, and doing multinational usability studies on all information products, each of which is explored in detail in this book.

CONCURRENCE

To combat some of the problems inherent in the internationalization and localization approaches, many companies are now focusing on *concurrent engineering*. Concurrent engineering is the latest attempt at making internationalization and localization affordable and effective approaches. It can be defined as:

> . . . a systematic approach to the integrated, concurrent design of products and their related processes, including manufacture and its support. This approach is intended to cause the developers, from the outset, to consider all elements of the product life cycle from concept through disposal, including cost, quality, schedule, and user requirements.[27]

Concurrent engineering offers a corporate methodology for controlling internationalization's and localization's less attractive virtues, such as expense, time to market, and liability. A technique that is already being used to achieve concurrent engineering is called *enabling*, which is the implementation of internationalized software such that it is localized automatically. To implement and automate the localization of an international product is a significant achievement. Read any software developer's guide to internationalization and you will understand the complexity referred to here.

For example, most software companies struggle with Asian languages because of the large number of characters that form these languages. Asian languages are also called *multi-byte languages* because of the way that each character is physically stored in the computer. To illustrate how complex a problem the implementation and automation of just Asian languages is to software developers, consider this: "Perhaps the greatest challenge with multi-byte languages is that of input. For example, Japanese has over 50,000 glyphs in their language which not only presents a great challenge for displaying them, but the even greater challenge of how do users enter information?"[28]

Other difficulties are apparent in the quest to find a software development language that can support the idiosyncrasies of localization, like inputting information in a language like Japanese. Unicode, X/Open, the American National Standards Institute (ANSI), the International Organization for Standardization (ISO), and other standards organizations are struggling to find solutions to localization.

Aldus offers a new twist to the problem of enabling. Being one of the first companies to try localization and internationalization, Aldus initially had to create its own tools to implement localization. Now, there are many more tools available to software companies developing product variants. For example, both Microsoft and Apple computing platforms, on which Aldus's products depend, offer internationalization and localization toolkits that make it easier for companies like Aldus to create international products. Aldus is now having to re-engineer its products to stay current with tools for localization, despite the irony of its having been one of the first software companies to localize its products at all.

The software industry has *almost* perfected enabling. We see examples of this at Aldus, Apple Computer, Lotus Development Corporation, Hewlett-Packard, Microsoft Corporation, Sun Microsystems, Borland, Digital Equipment Corporation, and IBM, to name only some of the leaders in this area. All of these companies now have formal, documented standards for localizing and internationalizing their products, which are publicly available in user manuals, often called something like *Guide to Internationalization*.

These companies have enabled their products to the point where localization and internationalization happen concurrently for all product variants, solving the problem of time to market, among others. Combined with the virtues of enabling, concurrent engineering can help companies create products for simultaneous worldwide distribution. Simultaneous release of a product with variants for over a dozen target countries is a reality.

Consider the enabling of a product like Microsoft Word for Windows, version 2.0. You can use the Format Language command to have MS Word automatically check the spelling of words in the selection by using one of the foreign language dictionaries. Version 2.0 supports 16 languages, three of which are variants of English (Australian English, British English, and American English). Other Microsoft products are equally enabled. Language orientation and feature localization are user controlled, and can be changed almost instantly.

Other companies, like Microsoft, offer this capability to users as well. Data I/O, a company in Bothell, Washington, which manufactures electronic systems and software products that use programmable integrated circuits, provides customers with the option of using its products in English or in their native language. They do this by shipping the product with a supplemental disk that contains the target language version of the help screens.[29]

In a presentation made at the Society for Technical Communication's 40th Annual Conference, WandaJane Phillips, a computer documentation specialist at the

International Development Research Centre in Ottawa, Canada, described how their technical communication department is trying to enable its documentation. Their approach is to enable a glossary of terms for translators and, subsequently, translate the source document.

> Because our product is used in so many different languages, terminology in the source language (English) is important. We selected terms and defined them. The information is stored in a database. We control the original texts, assist translators, build a glossary (paper and online), and create indexes (paper and online)....[30]

The database creates the glossary that is included in the manuals and in the online documentation. It is also used for the printed index and for the online search capabilities of the online document.

But in all of these examples, there is still minimal enabling. While some companies are starting to enable their documents by using tools like the Standardized General Markup Language (SGML), an ISO standard for creating and designing large documents, most companies enable their documents for output, not input. Products like Microsoft Word, WordPerfect, Ventura Publisher, and Aldus PageMaker are used to design the appearance of the document when it is complete. These products offer a variety of functions that make the creation of the document easier. But few companies use these products as localization tools that can supply localized content to a document (input) before document production. And while it is not easy to use these tools in this manner, it is also not impossible. (Chapter 12 covers this topic in more detail.)

This book extends the definition of concurrent engineering to offer another approach to international technical communication called *concurrence*. Concurrence affects not only software engineering, but technical communication, training, marketing, sales, customer support, and all the other departments that are involved in the creation and export of international products.

Here is the definition of concurrence that is used in this book:

Concurrence is the simultaneous occurrence of processes with shared goals that operate at the enterprise level.

Concurrence elevates internationalization and localization to positions of prominence and visibility in a corporation—the enterprise—to minimize the redundancy of localization and maximize the economy of internationalization. Concurrence achieves these goals through the strategic thinking of the international team and the tools it uses to implement and automate various processes. Concurrence capitalizes on each international team member's need for access to the same information and the same tools when creating international products.

The team identifies the characteristics of the core product (recall that Microsoft's definition of a global product referred to a *core worldwide feature set*). It then strives to maximize the core product in all components of the international product, from the software, for example, to the user guide, marketing material, training material, sales material, and so on. Everyone tries to draw from the same core set of information. In a true concurrent enterprise, information sharing is done electronically, through a wide area network using groupware.

The team then identifies the international variables. Again, the team strives to maximize the use of the international variables in all the components of the international product. Automation, information sharing, and groupware make concurrence possible here, too.

Concurrence requires a re-engineering of the enterprise, and not just a re-engineering of a software product or an information product. Refer to Chapter 14 for more information on concurrence.

RECOMMENDATIONS FOR TECHNICAL COMMUNICATORS

Apply this formula for success:

- Identify core information and internationalize.

- Identify international variables and localize.

- Strive for universal appeal and intuitiveness with globalization.

- Develop, implement, integrate, and automate concurrently by sharing information with members of the international team.

END NOTES

[1] The abbreviation L10N uses the first and last letters of the English word *localization* and inserts the amount of the total number of characters in between them.

[2] Dave Taylor, *Global Software*, p. 34.

[3] Scott Jones, Cynthia Kennelly, Claudia Mueller, Marcia Sweezey, Bill Thomas, and Lydia Velez, *The Digital Guide to Developing International User Information*, Digital Press, 1992, p. 2.

4 *Computer Dictionary,* Microsoft Press, 1991.

5 Electronic dialog with Marcia Sweezey, internationalization consultant, via the Internet, February 1, 1994.

6 A presentation by Greg Schellberg of the Evergreen Partnership, Women in International Business Conference, February 28, 1991, Bellevue, Washington, USA.

7 Valerie Reitman, "India Anticipates the Arrival of the Beefless Big Mac," *Wall Street Journal,* Wednesday, October 20, 1993, p. B1.

8 Nancy Hoft, "Preparing for the Inevitable: Localizing Computer Documentation," *SIGDOC '91 Conference Proceedings,* p. 37, based on interviews with Peter Gelpi, Operations Manager, Aldus Corporation.

9 Electronic conversation on the Internet with Marcia Sweezey, February 2, 1994.

10 From a chart labeled "Growth Chart," *Wall Street Journal,* February 4, 1994, p. B7. The survey was conducted by Price Waterhouse Law Firm and Law Services Group.

11 Cynthia Hartman Kenelly, *The Digital Guide to Developing International Software,* Digital Press, 1991, p. 31.

12 Ibid., p. 33.

13 Taylor, p. 34.

14 Ibid., p. 29.

15 Ibid., pp. 30, 33.

16 See entry in the glossary section of *Digital Guide to Developing International Software.*

17 See Chapter 2, *Digital Guide to Developing International Software,* for more information.

[18] See entry in the glossary, *Digital Guide to Designing International User Information*.

[19] Fons Trompenaars, *Riding the Waves of Culture*, Nicholas Brealey Publishing, London, 1993.

[20] *Digital Guide to Developing International User Information*, p. 30.

[21] Ibid., pp. 8–12.

[22] *The Boston Sunday Globe*, pp. 25–26.

[23] Ulrich Henes, "Building a case for (and against) localization: How Symantec, Apple, Lotus, and Microsoft decide when to localize," *Software Publisher*, July/August 1994, p. 32.

[24] See entry in the glossary, *Digital Guide to Developing International Software*.

[25] Telephone interview with Jon Lavine, February, 1994.

[26] Based on interviews with Peter Gelpi at Aldus. See also page 32 of *Global Software* for an illustration of a multilingual advertisement by Aldus.

[27] Donald E. Carter and Barbara Stillwell Banker, *Concurrent Engineering: The Product Development Environment for the 1990's*, IDA Report R–338, 1992.

[28] Taylor, p. 201.

[29] Nancy Hoft, "Preparing for the Inevitable: Localizing Computer Documentation," *SIGDOC '91 Conference Proceedings*, p. 40, based on interviews with Mark Kuenster, the Product Manager for Software Products, in 1991.

[30] WandaJane Phillips, "Creating Texts for an International Audience: 2 important issues," handout at the Society for Technical Communication's 40th Annual Conference, June 1993, Dallas, Texas.

MANAGE SO THAT YOUR TEAM CAN SUCCEED.

3

LEARN THE COMPONENTS OF A SUCCESSFUL

INTERNATIONAL-MANAGEMENT STRATEGY THAT

PERCEIVES INSTEAD OF REACTS TO CHANGE

AND DIVERSITY.

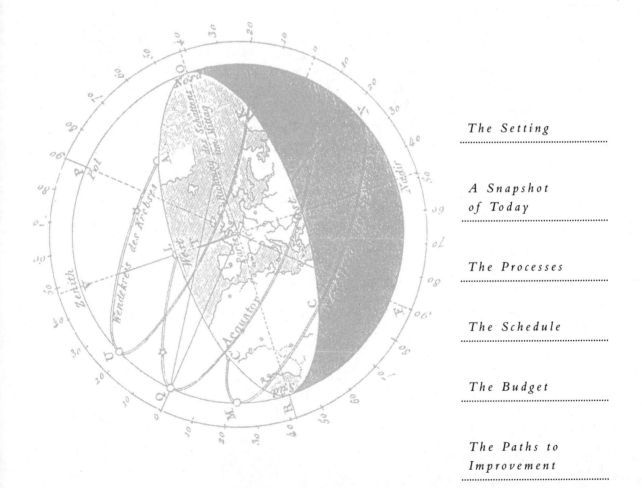

M A N A G E M E N T   I S S U E S

(3)

Τhis chapter identifies the processes that need to be in place to develop effective international technical communication. Effective international technical communication balances *economy* (business needs) with *cultural understanding* (user needs). Only by achieving this balance can you ensure quality-oriented processes.

There is a misconception that one perspective (business needs or user needs) is the correct perspective and that the other perspective is wrong. Polarity is not the solution, harmony is; one perspective cannot exist without the other, as they are symbiotically entwined.

International technical communication prepared exclusively for business needs would necessarily produce sterile and oversimplified information to address translatability problems. International technical communication prepared exclusively for user needs would necessarily be too expensive to develop and maintain. In addition, there remains little evidence in the research suggesting that either perspective is better or more effective than the other.

This rift is real and should influence the foundation of your management strategy. Allowing this rift to grow is asking to build walls instead of asking to build bridges. In seeking the balance of the two perspectives, you will build bridges.

This chapter provides ideas on how to cull the information you need to get management support for improving these processes over time.

THE SETTING

I once had a manager who told me that he did not want our technical communication department to write "award-winning, quality publications." He wanted us to write quickly and get our publications finished. We tried to convince him that we were not asking to add months to our deadlines. We wanted to change the way that we developed our source material and we wanted management support for those changes. We felt that quality-oriented processes would allow us to develop technical publications of a very high, award-winning quality without adding much delay to the schedule.

"No," was the answer we received.

Shortly thereafter, I left the company, unable to come to terms with the ethical dilemma with which I had been presented: sacrifice my professional standards and develop mediocre publications just to write them and meet a deadline.

Many years later, I can say that I have seen this incident repeated in my career and in the careers of others many times. I recently attended a Forum of the Localization Industry Standards Association (LISA) in Boston (August 1994), and heard the same ethical dilemma debated by high-level managers from the U.S. and Europe. During this debate, the attendees were asked to raise their hands if they felt that time to market was more important than quality. About two-thirds of the people in the room raised their hands, making it clear that quality would be sacrificed if deadlines were not met.

As I reflect on that manager, I remember that he was quality oriented. He had a technical background and was an excellent troubleshooter, technician, and technical trainer. It has always baffled me that someone who is a perfectionist in some areas can be so willing to accept mediocrity with complacence in other areas.

The manager did not understand technical communication, our processes and needs, and simply did not want to learn. He recognized the need for technical publications—after all, computers are not that intuitive. He did not understand editorial checks, technical and management reviews, usability testing, and production processes. He considered all the processes and check points that we wanted to add as time wasters and money wasters.

I still believe that quality technical communication can be achieved by establishing clear processes. I have seen it done. I have experienced the luxury of working for companies that insist on this.

The reason I tell this story is that international technical communication truly exacerbates these problems. Mistakes and technical inaccuracies in the source product—information about high technology—are repeated over and over again in all target languages. The poor quality product is then exported to all target countries. Feeble processes become all too apparent in an international arena.

Managers like the one I describe have even less empathy for technical communication problems when they have to deal with international issues. This is a very real situation for many companies in many countries. Add to this internal strife third parties like distributors and translation companies and the problems become more and more entrenched. Nobody seems to win, least of all the user.

But I have also come to understand what is on the other side of the fence, as it were. I have interviewed many international managers at all levels of organizations and attended many conferences and seminars at which these managers voice the problems they face when they go international. In order to stay alive as a business, you have to meet market-driven deadlines and do so within conservative budgets. This is reality. This makes sense.

So how do you reconcile these differences? Can they be reconciled?

The key to reconciling these differences is to develop clear and concise processes that involve many parts of the organization. This is how you address management problems like the one just described, and this is how you survive going international. Chapter 14 discusses an approach called *concurrence* that accomplishes this.

A SNAPSHOT OF TODAY

All processes described in this chapter require that you thoroughly understand how information about high technology is developed by your team today. All partners (translation companies, distributors, internationalization and localization consultants) with whom you choose to work will ask you questions about your current situation. Plan and do this analysis now so that partners can better assist you tomorrow.

Document *everything*. You can later use this snapshot to your advantage to leverage your progress and successes.

Another advantage to documenting everything that you do today is that you will be forced to think objectively about these processes. Be both prepared for and open to eliminating processes that run counter to your international goals. Your ability to be flexible and objective will be thoroughly tested as you develop a strategy that allows you to meet the business expectations with which you have been presented by your management.

If your documentation department is large, you should consider that documenting this snapshot will take some time. Your department may already have this information well documented, making this task very easy. Collect any existing information.

If you are committed to aligning your department with business objectives for internationalization, you should set a deadline of a maximum of one month for receiving reports on how information is developed today in your department. There is no reason to spend more time on this process than that. A one-to ten-person department can easily be analyzed in one or two days. The smaller your department is, the less time this will take. My experience has been that the longer that this analysis takes, the less likely it is that the analysis will be completed at all.

Table 3.1 identifies the major areas that contribute to a snapshot of how your department develops information about high technology today. These topics are representative of the topical queries that partners will make. The Suggestions column identifies the kind of information that you should gather and document for your snapshot.

TABLE 3.1: **Topical Outline for a Snapshot of Your Current Situation**

SNAPSHOT TOPIC	SUGGESTIONS
Tools	■ Identify your computing platform(s) (UNIX, DOS, Windows, Macintosh, and so on). ■ Identify all tools that technical communicators in your department use. Categorize this information; for example, graphics tools, word processing tools, online documentation tools, and desktop publishing tools. ■ Identify the version numbers of all tools. ■ Identify the hardware that technical communicators in your department use and its capabilities (Sun SparcStation, IBM-compatible 486 PC with 8 MB of memory, and so on). It is important to have ready information on the hard disk capabilities, RAM, and processor speed. This information may be important if you intend to purchase multilingual software. ■ Identify known limitations of the tools that are used to develop information in the source language.
Roles and Responsibilities	■ This can be as simple as an annotated organization chart or as complex as a set of job descriptions.
Editorial Guidelines	■ Most technical communication departments have already published editorial guidelines. In some departments, this is a formal book that professional editors refer to when editing draft copy. In other departments, this is a verbally agreed upon set of guidelines that has never been documented, or that changes from project to project. Editorial guidelines are very important and are extremely

TABLE 3.1: *Continued*

	helpful to translators. If you have yet to document these, this is a very good time to begin.
Formatting Guidelines	Most technical communication departments use a standard template or collection of formatting styles for each type of document that they publish. These formatting styles are often documented in a standards manual for the department.
	Some departments have not created a set of guidelines for formatting styles. In these cases, however, formatting conventions areoften found in the front matter of most manuals in a section typically called "Conventions Used in This Manual." All information on the formatting styles that your department uses to format information is very useful to translators who must reproduce the format in the target language. Consider creating templates or at least collecting the "Conventions" section of all manuals published recently.
	If your department publishes online information or multimedia productions, collect information on the formatting conventions used as well for the same reason.
Review Cycle	Diagram the review cycle by which most, if not all, information is reviewed. It is important to identify the departments responsible for review and where they are physically located (France, the U.S., Canada, Japan). Also specify the amount of time given to each department to review the information. If you provide the reviewers with any criteria by which they review the information, document this or collect typical review instruction sheets.
	In some cases, reviews already take place in other countries; in other cases, reviews are done by the engineering and marketing departments, which are just down the hall from your department. The players in your review cycles and their locations have a significant effect on the amount of time required for information to be reviewed. This information will be important when scheduling an international project.

In addition to taking a snapshot of how the technical communication department does its business, you should consider collecting information on how your company conducts its export business.

- Research the channels that your company uses to export its products. This information may prove useful, since you might be able to use these channels to do in-country reviews of translated information.

- Collect information on who in your company is involved in the export of products and their responsibilities. These individuals and departments may become your strongest allies as you change the way that your department develops information. (Refer to Appendix C, "Resources in International Technical Communication," for ideas on where to look in your organization.)

- Evaluate your company's internal abilities to handle the localization of technical information: localization, in-country review of translated information, and testing of translated information. What volume can these resources handle and within what time frame? What languages can these resources handle? What do these resources cost?

- Review your company's strategic goals. Align your strategy with these goals. These goals should provide the justification you need as you develop a strategy for handling international technical communication projects. Chapter 14 provides some ideas.

- Look at how and when usability testing is conducted, and which target countries are regularly involved in these tests.

- Review the processes by which product development teams communicate. For example, is communication mostly verbal and informal? Are regular meetings held? Look at the flow of information in your company.

THE PROCESSES

International technical communication requires additional processes in order for it to be effective. In many cases, these processes modify current processes. These changes can be significant, depending on how you proceed and the strategy you choose to implement. If the changes are significant, you need to consider how your team will respond to them. You will need their support, in addition to the support of your management, if you want your strategy to be a success.

The following processes encompass an entire technical communication development cycle. Their descriptions are not meant to provide you with an introduction to managing documentation projects.[1] These processes focus on the significant differences between a domestic and an international development strategy. It will be left for you to decide how to modify your current processes to adapt to the challenges introduced when your information is exported to many countries.

Because international technical communication projects can be very complex, this section provides you with a global view and filters out much of the detail in favor of identifying all the parts. Only a brief description of each process is provided here, although it is described in detail in various chapters in this book. References to the appropriate chapters are provided for your further study. In this way, you can fully understand the scope and considerations of the task before you, and you will be well briefed to create a management strategy.

BUILDING A TEAM

As with all projects, you need to know who is on the project team and what each person's responsibility is. The difference with international technical communication projects is that they usually require more team members, more responsibilities, and new communication skills and channels.

Of these team members, some may work for your company, while others work independently or for another company. These team members can also be many time zones away, in one or more countries, where their native languages and business protocols are very different from your own and from each other's. This makes project coordination more difficult, and opens the possibilities for serious communication breakdowns.

For all of these reasons, you need to specify roles and responsibilities and define communication channels very early in the project. Here are some ideas for minimizing confusion and communication problems. Not all projects will require all of the team-building ideas that I provide here. The large and complex projects, though, should implement all the recommendations identified here.

- Stagger work hours to accommodate time differences if real-time communication is required on a regular basis.

- Choose team members who are interested in cultural diversity and who are flexible. Team members should also be sensitive to the business concerns of the project: schedule, budget, and business objectives. Be a model for team members. At all times encourage new ways of thinking, but be firm and focused about business objectives. Be open to change.

- Be clear as to what information about the project is proprietary and what information can be shared freely with external team members on the project. Consult your management and possibly corporate attorneys on this matter. Signing an agreement of non-disclosure may be required.

- Organize a team meeting early in the project. Allow translators to meet the writers, editors, trainers, and engineers with whom they will be communicating throughout the project, either in person or electronically. Consider inviting members of management and have them discuss the strategic importance of the project or product to reinforce the business issues. Also consider asking translators to brief the team on the cultures and language considerations for target countries and the translation process. In this way you manifest the idea that all team members contribute something to the success of the project and everyone learns something. While in-person meetings are preferable and more effective, you can also accomplish this via a video conference to save some money. At the team meeting, review roles and responsibilities and channels of communication.

- Arrange training for the translation team. Many companies have found that providing translators with training about the product early results in translation of a higher quality and improved communication.

- Pay particular attention to the cross-cultural differences of the team members and advise individuals accordingly. These differences are often the basis of communication problems that arise during the project.

- Provide all team members with the names, contact information, locations, and roles of each member of the team. Be clear about whether translators can contact engineers directly, or whether they should first contact an intermediary. If you use an intermediary, be clear about whom translators can contact if the intermediary is unavailable. Make sure there are backups. Choose intermediaries who can answer basic technical questions, and who possess good people skills and cross-cultural communication skills. An intermediary can track issues to a conclusion, help develop metrics and baselines, and prevent different answers from being given to the same question.

- Choose target language reviewers early and provide them with specific editorial criteria. Set clear criteria for how technical and style conflicts between translators and target language reviewers will be addressed.

- Start a translation glossary early. Have the translations of glossary terms approved by target language reviewers early.

- Consider having a draft chapter translated into all of the target languages early so that target language reviewers can approve translation style and tone. Translators should be allowed to comment on overt translatability problems in the source language document that, if addressed early on, might contribute to higher-quality translations. This approach also serves to test sensitive communication channels before you begin relying on them to meet deadlines. This approach eliminates later surprises that can be time consuming and costly to rectify.

- Clearly identify deliverables for each team member.

- Clearly define the criteria for quality. Let team members know up front what is expected of them and how their deliverables will be evaluated. Let team members know how the success of the project will be evaluated.

See Chapter 8, "Working with Translators," and Appendix C, "Resources in International Technical Communication," for further discussion of the issues.

PERFORMING AN INTERNATIONAL USER ANALYSIS

This is a critical process that for many reasons should be considered an ongoing activity and not one that begins and ends with a particular project. If your team is asked to work on one international project, more will follow. If information is exported to two target countries today, it will be exported to four or five tomorrow. Be prepared and invest in learning about users and their cultural contexts. All of this knowledge contributes to cultivating a global attitude, which international managers agree is the best strategy going for a company that exports its products and information worldwide.

Other advantages to performing an international user analysis are: determining whether localization, and hence translation, is unnecessary for certain countries; and determining the media to use to present the information (printed manuals, online documents, CD-ROM productions, standup training, video, and so on). Marcia Sweezey, an internationalization consultant, adds, "You can also use this practice to track changing user requirements. For example, your Hong Kong users might require English-language documents today. After 1997 they may require both English and Chinese."[2]

- Consider international user analyses as ongoing secondary projects for your team. Assign one or more team members the secondary project of performing an international user analysis on a particular target country. Do the same for all target countries of immediate strategic importance to your company.

- Use this activity as a way to bring a sense of fun and interaction to the team.

- Allow members of your team to become target country liaisons. Consider offering monthly lunchtime seminars featuring the knowledge that your team members have accumulated by performing international user analyses. Advertise these seminars throughout the company so that all departments affected can attend, learn, and enjoy. Focus on one target country at a time. Have team members develop user profiles to hand out as long term reference material to other employees in your company. Schedule these meetings when visitors from the target countries will be able to attend and include them in the festivities.

- If these activities are successful, consider organizing a conference internal to your company that is focused on educating employees about users in target countries. Work with your management to involve many other departments in the company. Use this as an opportunity to leverage the research your team has developed. Make sure that all attendees leave with materials your team has developed.

See Chapter 4, "Performing an International-User Analysis," and Appendix C, "Resources in International Technical Communication," for further information.

INTERNATIONALIZING SOURCE INFORMATION PRODUCTS

International project managers concur that preparing products that are world ready is the most successful international strategy in terms of cost, time, and quality. This is the focus of internationalization. Internationalization is often discussed with reference to products only and rarely with respect to the source information products. It is time to change this and to start adopting good internationalization design practices in the development of source information products.

All source information should be written as if it is a core product on which all variants will be based. The goal is to minimize the amount of localization required, but not to forget that your domestic market is just as important as your international markets. If market demands require some degree of localization, then these changes should be easy to make, regardless of differences in language and culture.

The following topics identify methods and techniques that aid in developing internationalized information products. Incorporate these, on an ongoing basis, into your management strategy.

- Establish formal, written, and easily accessible guidelines and standards for international technical communication. Educate all members of your team on their existence and content, and be willing to update and modify them regularly. Share these with translators.

- Develop templates for creating internationalized information products that are easily adapted for target market demands.
  See Chapter 7, "Creating Core Information," Chapter 9, "Writing Issues," Chapter 12, "Tools Issues," and Chapter 14, "Toward Concurrence."

- Eliminate unnecessary information and redundancy to minimize the amount of information that needs translation. This saves money and time.
  See Chapter 7, "Creating Core Information," Chapter 8, "Working with Translators," Chapter 9, "Writing Issues," and Chapter 10, "Online Issues."

- Perform a cultural edit of source information to eliminate cultural bias in the internationalized information product. Develop guidelines for doing this and provide training.
  See Chapter 5, "Identifying Cultural Bias," and Chapter 7, "Creating Core Information."

- Invest in identifying and maintaining core information to maximize the reuse of information.
  See Chapter 7, "Creating Core Information."

- Research the use of a restricted grammar. This is an approach adopted by some companies whose translation needs are voluminous.
  See Chapter 9, "Writing Issues."

- Research the use of machine translation. This approach is generally successful only when it is used in conjunction with a restricted grammar.
  See Chapter 8, "Working with Translators," and Chapter 9, "Writing Issues."

ASSESSING THE TOOLS

You need the right tools to implement your internationalization plan. There are many factors to consider, and a full assessment of all tools is important.

- Pursue tools standards within your organization to encourage the ease of information reuse. Cross-platform information sharing is often too cumbersome because of complicated file-format translations.

- Be willing to sacrifice the short term issue of the cost of tools for the long-term goal of ease of localization.

- Minimize internal tools customization. Customized tools require maintenance, support, and training, and may complicate localization.

- Consider the complexities of multilingual updates and favor products with revision tracking capabilities.

See Chapter 10, "Online Issues," Chapter 12, "Tools Issues," and Chapter 14, "Toward Concurrence."

LOCALIZING INTERNATIONALIZED INFORMATION PRODUCTS

Localization should be easy, affordable, and produce high quality, usable variants of the source information products.

- The degree to which you localize source-information products is determined by the balance of user needs and business needs. Get management approval for the degree to which you localize the target variants to distribute accountability.

- Simultaneous release of target variants complicates localization, because the time pressures are significant for achieving high-quality results. The better the internationalized information product, the less of an issue this becomes.

- Depending on the product and the target industry in which the product is used, there may be international, national, or industry-specific standards or laws that target variants must adhere to. Research standards early in the project. Keep a log of all standards that you discover and develop channels inside your company or through professional organizations or national standards associations for keeping up-to-date on any changes to them.

See Chapter 4, "Performing an International-User Analysis," Chapter 10, "Online Issues, Chapter 11, "Graphics Issues," Chapter 12, "Tools Issues," Chapter 13, "Assessing Quality," Chapter 14, "Toward Concurrence," Appendix B, "Sample International User Analysis," and Appendix C, "Resources in International Technical Communication."

REVIEWING AND TESTING SOURCE INFORMATION AND TARGET VARIANTS

- Consider that if the domestic market for your company's product is small or shrinking, then the success of the target variants is critical to the success of the product.

- Consider that if the source information is inaccurate or misleading then the target variants will also be inaccurate or misleading, perhaps more so. Correcting these kinds of problems is not the responsibility of translators, but is the responsibility of the source information development team and its information reviewers and testers. Emphasize this fact to all writers, editors, reviewers, and testers of the source information.

- Reviewing and testing the source information does not guarantee that the target variant will be of a high quality. To ensure quality (accuracy, accessibility, completeness, and so on) the target variants must also be tested.

- Develop clear review and testing criteria for the source information and its target variants and provide all reviewers and testers with these criteria. Share this information with translators early in the project so that they are aware how their work will be evaluated. Allow translators to make suggestions and changes to your review and testing criteria. Your criteria could be impossible to meet given the current project schedule and resources and therefore unrealistic. Be fair to your translators and trust that they want to provide you with high-quality translations.

- Arrange to do testing in the target countries. If this is too expensive to do for all international projects, consider investing in this kind of testing for major projects. You can also hire students who are native to the target country but who currently live in the source country to do less expensive testing. (However, be wary of what traits students might lack, like business insight and intuition.) You can also contact visitors' centers or put ads in the paper, and screen respondents as you search for target country nationals who meet your user-profile criteria.

See Chapter 4, "Performing an International-User Analysis," Chapter 8, "Working with Translators," and Chapter 13, "Assessing Quality."

PUBLISHING THE INFORMATION

Electronic publishing's target-language capabilities are limited by the multilingual capabilities of your computing platform and publishing software.

- Research font styles and their availability in all target languages both for printing and online display early in the project. Minimize the use of customized fonts, since they will need to be modified to incorporate target-language characters. This is very expensive and time consuming.

- Clearly identify who is responsible for the electronic publishing or desktop publishing of target-language variants. Clearly specify what tasks this involves: converting files to different file formats or outputting camera-ready copy or film. Many companies hire translation companies to provide this service, since they have already invested in target-language publishing tools. Other companies search around the world for cheaper multilingual publishing solutions, and often have manuals printed in more than one location depending on volume, the location of distribution centers, and special printing needs.

- Research the packaging of target-language variants early in the project. Packaging is often completely localized for each target country. Involve marketing and sales people early.

- Consider whether you will use recycled materials for packaging.

- If your target-language variants are exported with the product, like a laser printer, consider the amount of time that customs in the target countries requires to approve the shipment and factor this into your schedule.

See Chapter 6, "Design Issues," Chapter 10, "Online Issues," Chapter 11, "Graphics Issues," and Chapter 12, "Tools Issues."

PERFORMING A POST-PROJECT ANALYSIS

The best way to learn how to improve your processes is to take the time to critically evaluate their successes and failures after they have been used in real time, when you have the opportunity to be objective and thoughtful. Too few companies invest in this inexpensive but very valuable self-assessment technique.

- Involve the entire project team! This is not just a management technique, which is often how it is treated. Each team member's input is valuable.

- Solicit feedback from people outside your department: engineering, marketing, sales, testing, and so on. Solicit feedback from the translators and target-language reviewers. Solicit feedback from your management.

- Consider hosting a post-project gathering, preferably off site. Provide lunch or other refreshments. Spend an afternoon in an open exchange of feedback. Set ground rules that solicit feedback in a constructive fashion and that allow all team members an equal opportunity to voice their opinions. Have an agenda to guide the discussion. Consider asking team members to reflect on any cultural differences they encountered during the project, and engage others in a discussion of how to address these differences in the future. Share the feedback you received from people outside your department. At the end, summarize the feedback as lessons learned.

- Demonstrate your interest in improvement to your team and to your management by making some of the changes recommended at the post-project gathering.

- Prepare a post-project report. JoAnn Hackos provides a useful outline for this in *Managing Your Documentation Projects*.[3]

- The Localization Benchmarking Special Interest Group of the Localization Industry Standards Association (LISA) published a *Post Mortem Template* in the presentation handouts of the LISA Forum held in Runnymede, England (January 31–February 1, 1994). The categories and representative descriptions, which the template recommends should compare Language A to Language B, and so on for additional target languages, include:

  - **Size** (budget, forecast, shipped, and worked on). Number of words in documentation, number of words in help, number of words per screen in computer-based training.

  - **Timeliness.** Actual versus planned absolute release date, actual Delta versus planned Delta.

  - **Cost versus forecast and budget.** Overall project cost per word, cost per word of documentation, cost per word of software.

  - **Quality.** Number of bugs found during localization per bug in the source software, number of bugs broken down by type, software quality rating, documentation quality rating.

  - **Throughput metrics.** Number of works of software that are localized per man-month, number of help pages localized per man-month, number of pages of documentation released per editor-man-month, percentage reuse documentation pages, percentage reuse help pages, number of bugs found per testing man-month.

■ **Rework.** Number of words per page of help reworked, number of words per page of documentation reworked.

THE SCHEDULE

Scheduling international technical communication projects is becoming more of a challenge as more companies strive for the simultaneous release of the source product and all its target variants.

You probably already have metrics established for project estimating, or at least have some guidelines for doing so. There are no published estimates for most of the ideas for processes I recommend in the previous section, so you will have to develop estimates as you go and maintain them over time to render them more accurate. In general, most of the ideas I provide in the previous section are designed for an initially intensive time investment that decreases significantly afterward.

Arrange with your team to have them track their time on specific tasks that you identify in advance. In this way, you can begin to see where most time is spent and where your scheduling estimates are inaccurate or accurate.

Consider that translation companies offer you estimates based on receiving bug- and error-free source information. (If they have worked with you in the past, they can provide better estimates based on experience.) If they are hired to local-ize software and translate the user interface, help screens, and so on, they often encounter bugs that need to be corrected in the source software. Sometimes these software fixes require an update to the documentation and possibly to the help text and error messages. All these changes cause delays.

What is offered here are some of the known scheduling considerations that are not typical for a domestic project. You will need to add these to your domestic schedule.

TRANSLATION

There is a saying about translation scheduling that can be misleading, but it is not necessarily incorrect: "It takes as long to translate the source information as it did to create it." Jon Lavine, a senior editor at Berlitz Translation Services, comments, "This saying is misleading, because translation is not a black box. Translators have to pause, as do technical communicators, to consider the best ways to present information. Technical communicators have done the background work already. However, the more complex the job and the broader the scope, the longer translation takes."

As with all publications estimating, you need to start with an estimated page count. JoAnn Hackos, author of *Managing Your Documentation Projects*, states that the standard for developing source technical information is about five to seven pages per day.[4] Most companies that I have worked with (Digital, Sun, Lotus) have a lower standard writing output, typically one to three pages per day. Compare these figures to the following translation metrics.

- The United Nations' quota for a translator's output is three pages per day.

- Robert Bononno, a freelance translator and professor of technical translation at New York University, reports that "a more accurate estimate would be five finished pages in an eight hour day. . . . Add to this any time required for formatting (tabular material and charts as formatting, as well as equations, etc., should also be included), graphics, camera-ready copy, and you reduce the output even further."[5]

When you consider these sources and their estimates, you should not be surprised to learn that most companies are unable to export to all target countries simultaneously. Hatsi Delori, the manager of translations at the Unisys International Engineering Center in Brussels, Belgium, reports:

Currently Unisys experiences considerable lag times that vary between three to eighteen months from the English ship date. Country organization and resources, local language resources, and the extent of localization content in the product factor into the lag times.

In Western Europe, for example, the Norwegian, Finnish, and Danish language versions are shipped within three weeks of the English ship dates. These products consist of a diskette with localization enablers for the keyboard, and character set changes, but no translated documentation. The British English, Italian, and Swedish releases take from two to four months to ship, but the localization content consists of re-packaging and re-linking. All of the French and German products are localized. These are shipped up to six months after U.S. release dates, as are the Dutch products with less localized content. But due to the lack of resources, Portuguese and Spanish products wait more than a year to be sold.[6]

Regarding when to begin translating the source information, most companies recommend that you wait until you have a fairly stable draft of the source information. Most often this is the second draft of the source information, but this will depend on the strategy you choose, the reliability of products, and the development environment within which you work, among other factors.

REVIEWING THE TRANSLATED INFORMATION

Begin with the amount of time that you typically schedule for reviewing the source information. Jon Lavine recommends that you double this amount of time for reviews of translated information. The cause of this time doubling is that the reviewers need to refer from the translation to its source information in order to do a complete and thorough review of the translation.[7]

CULTURAL CONSIDERATIONS

Cultures value time differently. In some cultures, time is a major consideration, "of the essence." In other cultures, time is not a consideration. This value difference can be particularly frustrating to both cultures, especially in deadline-driven environments. Consider the cultural values of your project team as they relate to time and factor in a buffer for this into your project schedule.

SYBASE'S DOCUMENT LOCALIZATION PROCESS

Will Doherty, the manager of localization services at Sybase, Inc., describes the localization process for documentation at Sybase.[8] See Table 3.2.

TABLE 3.2: **Schedule Outline at Sybase, Inc., for Localizing Documentation**

PHASE	STEPS AND THEIR DESCRIPTION
0	■ Complete project planning and preparation.
	■ Make sure that source-language document writers have prepared properly internationalized documentation.
	■ Generate target language glossaries.
	■ Achieve reviewer consensus on the target-language glossaries.
	■ Train translators on technical topics and tools related to the document translation project.
1	■ Obtain and translate the documentation to produce a first-draft translation.
	■ Perform a stylistic and technical edit on the first-draft translation.

TABLE 3.2: *Continued*

- Distribute and get review feedback on the first-draft translation.

- Update the target-language terminology list.

2
- Obtain, translate, and incorporate any changes from the source-language documentation in the target-language documentation.

- Evaluate and incorporate appropriate changes from the review of the draft translation.

- Send the new draft out for editing, proofreading, and technical review.

- Repeat the steps in Phase 2 until all changes from the source-language document are included and all relevant review comments are evaluated.

THE BUDGET

Establish department budget charge numbers to track costs in detail. Work with your finance department for ideas as to what to track and how to set up budget charge numbers.

Make sure that all translation costs are not part of your department's budget. These costs should be treated as separate cost centers, because they are separate activities that are often performed by contracted translation companies. Including them in your budget will make your budget highly visible and particularly vulnerable to cost reduction since translation is so expensive.

Remember that the cost of localization increases proportionally each time a target language is added.

As with scheduling, there are only a few known estimates for costs as they relate to international technical communication.[9]

TRANSLATION

Translation rates vary around the world. In Europe, translation is typically billed by the line. In the U.S., translation is typically billed by the word. All over the world, translation rates vary according to the difficulty in finding qualified translators who are fluent in both the target and source languages, and who are knowledgeable in the subject matter. The more obscure or difficult the two languages, the more costly the translation.

In the U.S., on average, a page of 250 words (no graphics or desktop-publishing necessary) in the source language that is translated costs approximately $50 USD. If you add in graphics (callouts and captions need translating) and desktop publishing, the same translated page can cost $75 USD or more. Translation firms typically adjust their rates based on the potential for a long-term relationship, the target language, and the volume of work.

Susan Fowler and Victor Stanwick, the authors of *The GUI Guide*, report one U.S. company's itemized translation rates in 1990:

- Glossary compilation, translator training, software translation, and formatting averaged $40–$60 USD per hour.

- Documentation, billed on a per-word basis, ranged from $50-$150 USD per page (typically 250 words).[10]

Consider, too, that changes made to the source information late in the translation process are billed at a higher rate. This should not be a surprise to anyone who has made editorial changes (author's alterations) to typeset copy late in a printing cycle. Few if any localization projects are flawless, so consider adding a line item to your budget that addresses this contingency.

H I D D E N   C O S T S

There are some hidden costs that join international technical communication projects. These are just a few of them.

- Time spent managing additional staff (translators, reviewers, and so on)

- Communication costs (faxes, international telephone calls)

- Training costs for source teams to learn how to facilitate internationalization and localization

If this is the first time that your team has worked on an international project, if it is the first time that your team has worked with a particular translation company, or if any of the major processes are new or significantly delayed, schedule all processes generously. They will take longer than normal as your team adapts to these changes

L O T U S   D E V E L O P M E N T
C O R P O R A T I O N ' S   L O C A L I Z A T I O N   C O S T   P R O F I L E

Kevin Cavanaugh, the director of international product management at Lotus Development Corporation, provided this localization cost profile at the Localization Industry Standards Association's Forum in Boston (August 1994):

- Engineering, 20 percent (of total localization costs)

- Documentation Staff, 10 percent

TABLE 3.3: **Word-Count Comparison of a Typical Software Project to One at Novell**

TRANSLATION CATEGORY	TYPICAL INDUSTRY PROJECT	TYPICAL NOVELL PROJECT
User Interface	30,000 words translated	> 300,000 words translated
Online Help	50,000 words translated (can be shared with documentation)	> 300,000 words translated
Documentation	100,000 to 200,000 words translated	1,800,000 words translated

- Documentation Services (translation, for example), 25 percent
- Quality Assurance, 45 percent

Based on audience response, Lotus's cost profile, which focuses on quality assurance, differs significantly in philosophy from the cost profile of most companies in attendance at the Forum. Most companies in attendance indicated that most of their cost goes into engineering and documentation services.

The cost profile that you develop will reflect, as does Lotus's, the balance of user needs and business needs at your company.

NOVELL'S TRANSLATION VOLUME

José deHoyos, the manager of corporate translation services at Novell, must budget for extraordinary translation volumes. Table 3.3 compares the typical project word count to Novell's word count.[11]

THE PATHS TO IMPROVEMENT

There are many steps you can take to further improve the processes that you establish for creating high-quality international technical communication. Here are some of them.

- Create process checklists.
- Invest in team training.
- Develop localization cookbooks for each target country or each target language.
- Identify and maintain metrics, and start doing cost/benefit analyses.
- Develop multilingual document databases for information reuse.
- Invest in tools that facilitate the automation of localization.

- Establish long-term relationships with translation companies so that they will begin investing in you. For example, translation companies can begin saving your previous translations in databases so that they can re-use translated information, reducing the time-to-market and possibly the cost of translation.

- Prepare processes with established quality standards in mind, like the ISO 9000 series. These processes require rigid documentation of all processes and work flows.

END NOTES

[1] For an excellent and thorough introduction, refer to JoAnn Hackos's book, *Managing Your Documentation Projects*, John Wiley & Sons, Inc. New York, 1994.

[2] Correspondence from Marcia Sweezey, October 20, 1994.

[3] Hackos, pp. 586–590.

[4] Ibid. See pp. 168–170.

5 From review comments made by Robert Bononno on Chapter 8, "Working with Translators," dated September 28, 1994.

6 Hatsi Delori, "Centralizing Internationalization and Localization at Unisys Corporation," *Global Talk*, Vol. 3, Fall 1994, p. 1. This is the newsletter of the International Technical Communication Professional Interest Committee of the Society for Technical Communication.

7 Telephone interview with Jon Lavine, September 14, 1994.

8 From a draft of paper by Will Doherty entitled "Document Globalization: Process and Guidelines," that he presented in Bejing, China, in fall 1994.

9 For an interesting set of cost-justifying figures from four major U.S. software companies regarding localization, see Ulrich Henes, "Building a Case for (and against) Localization: How Symantec, Apple, Lotus and Microsoft decide when to localize," *Software Publisher*, July–August 1994, pp. 28–35. Note, however, that these figures are sales and marketing projections and offer no information specific to technical communication costs.

10 Susan Fowler and Victor Stanwick, from a draft of Chapter 6, "International Software," from their book *The GUI Guide*, Academic Press Professionals, Cambridge, Massachusetts, 1994, p. 46.

11 From the presentation handouts at the Localization Industry Standards Association's Forum in Heidelberg, Germany (April 21–22, 1994).

To create world-ready information products, you need to know about target audiences. Use international variables and models of culture as tools for collecting cultural data about obvious cultural differences, unspoken rules, learning styles, and behavioral differences. Synthesize cultural data for meaningful internationalization and localization.

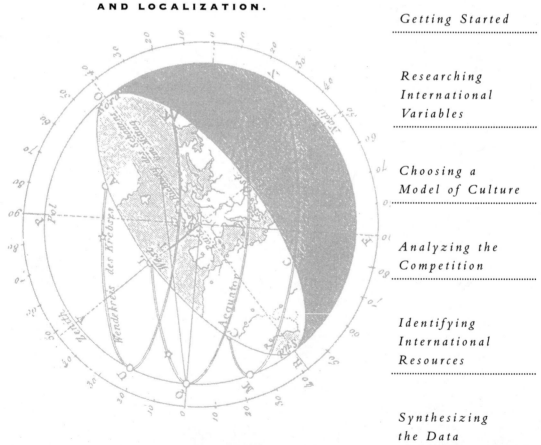

Getting Started

Researching International Variables

Choosing a Model of Culture

Analyzing the Competition

Identifying International Resources

Synthesizing the Data

PERFORMING AN INTERNATIONAL-USER ANALYSIS

4

As instructors of technical communication courses and as human factors and usability specialists emphasize, "Know your audience!" This cornerstone of effective technical writing and product design becomes overwhelming when your audience spans the globe. An audience for international technical communication will consist of individuals with contradictory expectations, a broad range of educational backgrounds, and limited access to the technology on which your company's product depends. Factor in the ever-changing political and economic climates in countries around the world, and you have a recipe for chaos.

Effective international technical communication must minimize this chaos if it is to balance economy (business needs) and cultural understanding (user needs). To minimize this chaos, you need to perform an international-user analysis.

The international-user analysis presented in this book focuses on finding ways to understand how the information needs of a user in one country differ from the information needs of a user in another country. We begin by looking at obvious differences like language, and work our way deeper into exploring the ways that a group of culturally related users think, feel, and act in different situations. With this knowledge, we can begin to understand what kind of information a target audience needs and how best to present that information for maximum comprehension. We can also begin to explore the learning styles and behavioral differences of target audiences that are so necessary to understand when creating useful information products.

An international-user analysis consists of five steps, which are illustrated in
Figure 4.1:

1. Research international variables

2. Choose a model of culture

3. Analyze the competition

4. Identify international resources

5. Synthesize the data

After completing these five steps, you will be able to:

- Select international variables that best suit your business needs.

- Identify international resources.

- Collect cultural data from international resources.

- Assess cultural similarities and cultural differences.

- Apply cultural data to a model of culture.

- Develop a cultural profile of target users.

- Determine the degree of localization required.

- Apply cultural data to information products.

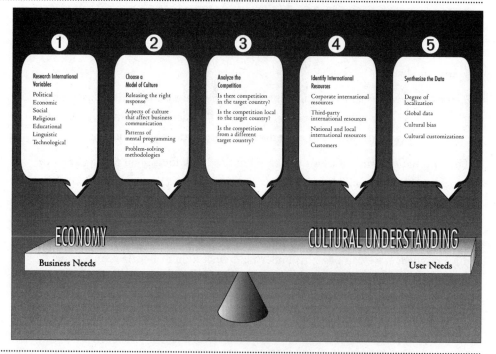

FIGURE 4.1: **A model for performing an international-user analysis.**

GETTING STARTED

There are two tools that you can use to make collecting cultural information about your target users easier. They are the Iceberg Model, which provides a useful metaphor to help in your research, and the International Variables Worksheet, which offers an at-a-glance table that you can use to fill in the cultural information that you collect.

THE ICEBERG MODEL

The iceberg provides a useful metaphor for describing the cultural characteristics of a target audience. Only 10 percent of an iceberg is visible above the surface of the water, while the remaining 90 percent is below the surface and thus not visible. Just as only 10 percent of an iceberg can be seen, only 10 percent of the cultural characteristics of a target audience are easily visible to an observer.[1] The Iceberg Model, which is illustrated in Figure 4.2, will provide you with a mental image that can help you understand the cultural data you collect while researching international variables and building models of culture.

Iceberg model

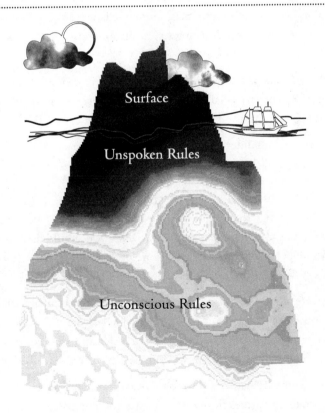

FIGURE 4.2: **The Iceberg Model.**

The Iceberg Model identifies three categories of cultural characteristics:

- **Surface.** The cultural characteristics at this level are visible, obvious, and easy to research. Examples include the superficial international variables identified in Chapter 2. They include number, currency, time, and date formats, language, and so on.

- **Unspoken rules.** The cultural characteristics at this level are somewhat obscured. You generally need to identify the context of the situation first in order to understand what the unspoken rules are. Examples include business etiquette and protocol.

- **Unconscious rules.** The cultural characteristics are not part of conscious awareness and are difficult to study for this reason. Examples include non-verbal communication, a sense of time and physical distances, and the rate and intensity of speech.

The Iceberg Model can be used as visual aid when determining the degree of localization that is required for an information product. For instance, general localization focuses on the superficial cultural characteristics. Radical localization can go deeper and explore learning styles (unconscious rules), group dynamics (unspoken rules), and so on.

The Iceberg Model is referred to throughout the remainder of this chapter to help you group international variables, or, conversely, to choose international variables that help you study a particular layer of a target culture.

To begin researching international variables, we start at the surface layer of the Iceberg Model and then work our way down to the layers below the water line.

H O W T O D O C U M E N T D A T A W H E N R E S E A R C H I N G I N T E R N A T I O N A L V A R I A B L E S

When collecting data on international variables, you should document your findings in a simple table like the abridged one presented in Table 4.1. (Refer to Appendix A for the expanded international variables worksheet.)

1. Create a one-page, at-a-glance table of the international variables you choose to use. (See Table 4.1.) The table lets you objectively compare, contrast, and synthesize the data with localization and internationalization in mind. Alternatively, create a similar table using spreadsheet software.

2. Divide the data area of the table in two, horizontally. Use this division to separate similarities from differences as you compare the target country to the source country.

Technical projects

3. Always put the name of the target country and the target language on the worksheet.

4. You can also put a date on the worksheet to keep track of its revisions. Try to keep the data in the worksheet current.

5. Consider having the members of the international team and some of your international resources in the source and target countries review the data in completed worksheets. They might identify inaccurate or missing data. (You may find that they want to borrow the worksheets to help them in their projects.)

6. As you create more worksheets, one for each target country, you can review the differences and similarities of many countries. Take these worksheets and tape them to a wall to create a storyboard.

TABLE 4.1: **A Worksheet for Collecting Data for International Variables**

TARGET COUNTRY: LAST REVISED:

TARGET LANGUAGE:

8 x 2

	POLITICAL	ECONOMIC	SOCIAL	RELIGIOUS	EDUCATIONAL	LINGUISTIC	TECHNOLOGICAL
SIMILARITIES							
DIFFERENCES							

7. Look for ways to minimize the localization effort, maximize the globalization effort, and find ways to enable your information products.

Constant updating

The secret to performing a thorough international-user analysis, though, is updating the data you collect. Performing an international-user analysis only once for users in Japan, for example, is insufficient. Users' needs and expectations change, as does your understanding of their needs and expectations. You do your users a disservice if your understanding of their needs does not mature as quickly as their understanding of your products.

Localization Cookbooks

Imagine how helpful a document on the needs and expectations of Japanese users, with respect to your company's products, would be to other departments in your company. At a seminar in Seattle, Washington, in 1991, Jeremy Butler, then vice president of international and OEM sales at Microsoft Corporation, described how Microsoft creates *Localization Cookbooks* for each of its target markets.[2] The *Localization Cookbooks* contain product engineering issues, documentation and packaging issues, and translation dictionaries. The cookbooks are shared within the company and can significantly speed up localization efforts of a given product. The cookbooks also train employees to think and design with internationalization and localization in mind so that localized products enter the target market more quickly.

An international-user analysis, then, can contribute significantly to reduce the localization learning curve, cost, time to market, and duplication of effort. An international-user analysis increases efficiency and effectiveness. Chapter 14 explores the use of *Localization Cookbooks* in more detail.

RESEARCHING INTERNATIONAL VARIABLES

This book explores seven international variables that you can use to collect cultural information for the surface layer and the unspoken rules layer in the Iceberg Model. Each international variable addresses an area of cultural diversity among nations and not among individuals. You can also use these international variables to address cultural diversity among markets if this distinction makes more sense in your company.

The seven international variables discussed here are:

1. Political differences and similarities

2. Economic differences and similarities

3. Social differences and similarities

4. Religious differences and similarities

5. Educational differences and similarities

6. Linguistic differences and similarities

7. Technological differences and similarities

Consider creating additional international variables that make more sense in your environment. For example, if your company manufactures medical instruments, consider adding a category called *Health*. Use this category to research perceptions of health, nutrition, and health care in the target countries, for example. If your company manufactures automobiles, consider adding an international variable called *Transportation*. Use this category to explore modes of transportation, users' preferences for transportation, accessibility of transportation, and so on. The international variables presented here are conducive to most high-technology environments, but they are neither definitive nor exhaustive. Add and delete international variables as needed to explore visible cultural differences and unspoken rules that pertain to your industry and information products.

POLITICAL DIFFERENCES AND SIMILARITIES

The government and laws of a country affect the lives of your target users significantly. Understanding the political differences and similarities between the source country and the target country offers insight into:

- **Trade issues.** Consider how your company must conduct business in and create products for export to the target country

- **Legal issues.** Understand how laws regarding intellectual property law affect the design of a product and the content of legal statements in information products

- **Political tradition and symbolism.** Consider how political traditions and symbolism can influence the content of examples and graphics in information products

Trade Issues

Export and import restrictions change constantly between nations and among groups of nations. These restrictions can affect how information concerning the safety and health issues for product use is presented.

The European Union, for example, issued a directive (Council Directive 90/270/EEC) for video display terminals (VDTs) that renders mandatory minimum requirements affecting: "equipment (display screens, keyboards, work surfaces), environment (space, lighting, reflections and glare), and operator/computer interface."[3] Technical communicators who write installation and operation guides for VDTs that are exported to any of the twelve member countries of the European Union must be familiar with the directive for VDTs. The expectations of product safety for using a VDT must be addressed in all accompanying product literature. If technical communicators who write these manuals are not familiar with this directive, they may place their companies at legal risk.

When researching the political international variable, refer to the relevant standards organizations listed in Appendix C to find out if there are mandatory requirements or voluntary standards with which you need to be familiar. It would be impossible to list them in this book, since they change too often, are product or industry specific, and vary from country to country. In the International Variables worksheet you create for each target country, document the mandatory requirements and voluntary standards that affect the products on which your international technical communication project is focused. Review these with the members of the international team to determine how they should be addressed in the information products. Monitor the requirements and standards and keep your worksheets current.

Legal Issues

There are three categories of legal issues that concern technical communication: product liability, intellectual property, and truth in advertising/fraud standards.

Product liability. Technical communicators who create information products for products that affect the health and safety of consumers need to be concerned with relevant laws and standards in the target country. Labeling and warnings are of particular concern. In answer to the question "What does product liability have to do with EC [European Community, which is currently referred to as the European Union] standards?" the U.S. Department of Commerce states: ". . . it is widely believed that a manufacturer who has met all the legal requirements in EC directives, has certified to any existing EC-wide standards, and has placed all the adequate warnings and labels on a product will have a stronger defense in any possible liability suit."[4]

Contact the appropriate individuals in your organization for more information and document your findings in the International Variables worksheet for the target country.

Intellectual property. Companies in high technology are especially concerned with laws regarding copyright, trademark, and patent infringement in the target country. *Pirating,* which is the illegal duplication of a product like computer software or hardware, is a common problem in many countries. For these reasons, many companies have included special security precautions in the design of their products. (However, courts are currently cracking down on these techniques, since they can disable the software once it is in a paying customer's hands.)

At CeBit '92, the world's largest computer trade show, held every year in Hannover, Germany, Microsoft continuously showed a video of an industrial-sized magnet wiping the data off hundreds of thousands of illegal software disks that had been confiscated. The large crowd in front of the video monitor was completely shocked at the directness of the message in the video. Microsoft has hotlines around the world and offers rewards to people who provide information regarding the illegal use of their products.

While technical communication cannot control piracy, it can serve as a medium for encouraging responsible product use. Confer with members of the international team and with the legal resources you have at your disposal for ideas. All efforts to minimize piracy of your company's products make your company that much more likely to succeed.

Another intellectual-property concern is how the trademark, copyright, or patent of a product is referenced in technical communication products. There is no such thing as global international protection against intellectual-property infringement. Trademarks, copyrights, and patents have to be registered in individual countries (the European Union is trying to adopt directives to avoid this in its member countries), which costs companies quite a bit of money both initially and over time. A product may have intellectual-property protection in one country but not in another.

Confer with members of the international team and with legal resources for direction on how to address these issues. Document all of your findings on the International Variables worksheet for the target country.

Truth in advertising/Fraud standards. Some countries, like Germany, have stiff penalties for inflated or misleading claims about a product. Germany also has rigid requirements for comparing one company's product to that of a competitor. Be sure that all product claims are supported by adequate evidence. Disclose all testing conditions in the main text of information products or in footnotes.

Again, contact the appropriate people and seek their advice on how to avoid problems. Document relevant standards in the International Variables worksheet for the target country.

Political Tradition and Symbolism

Political tradition differs all over the world. It is important to understand at least some rudimentary details of the target country's political tradition, because it will help you understand how people respond to authority. For example, in the U.S., an historically democratic country where anyone over the age of 18 has the right to vote for the country's leaders, people consider the overt questioning of authority normal behavior. This is not the case in China, where socialist/communist ideology encourages people to accept, unquestioningly, the decisions made by the government. This sort of response to authority can make a big difference in how you present training material. It can also make a big difference in how people are portrayed in illustrations.

Here are some examples of what to research about the political tradition of a target country:

- **Forms of government.** Some common types are democracy, socialism, autocracy.

- **Voting rights.** Can people vote? Who can vote? When do people vote? Are voting practices just and fair, or are they often violent and unrepresentative affairs?

- **Politically significant dates.** In the U.S., the 4th of July, also known as *Independence Day*, is a politically significant date on which most American companies are closed. Referring to this date in an example that is read by an American audience might send different or at least additional messages to your American readers. To readers from India, this date has no political relevance. Another example of a politically relevant date is July 14th, Bastille Day, which commemorates the fall of the Bastille in France, and is a national holiday.

Important political symbols to consider include:

1. **Flags.** The design, symbolism, and colors of a national flag can have significant meaning in a target country. The design of a flag usually reflects important political beliefs of a country. The old Soviet flag showing the hammer and the sickle reflected the working masses that were so much a part of the communist political tradition in the U.S.S.R. Research the symbolism of the colors of a flag. If the political tradition in a target country is strong, the colors in its flag may have greater meaning for your target audience. Consider the flag itself. At the groundbreaking ceremonies for Hitachi Automotive Products (a Japanese company) in the state of Kentucky (U.S.), the Governor of Kentucky gave a Japanese executive a Kentucky flag. The Japanese businessman, after displaying the flag to the crowd, carelessly but innocently dragged the flag on the ground. The audience was offended. In the U.S., flags are not supposed to be dragged on the ground. In Japan, the way you treat a flag is different and it is acceptable to drag a flag on the ground.[5]

2. **National documents.** Are there national documents that have particular significance? For example, in the U.S., the Declaration of Independence, the Constitution of the United States, and the Bill of Rights are significant national documents. Understanding these documents to even a small degree provides insight into the American political system and American values.

3. **National symbols.** The target country may also have national symbols, like a national flower or animal. You can use these symbols to your advantage or disadvantage in a localized information product, depending on how well you have done your homework.

ECONOMIC DIFFERENCES AND SIMILARITIES

The economic realm focuses on the overall economic status of a country, how target users are ranked economically within the country, and what their perception of wealth is. For instance, there is an economic difference between people in Poland and those in Canada. The users in both countries have a marked difference in purchasing power that should be reflected in information products exported to both countries. Being aware of these economic differences and similarities can contribute to more effective international technical communication.

In your International Variables worksheet, document details like how much common material goods cost, using your own currency, in the target country. Some examples include a competitor's product, your company's product, the price of technology on which your company's product depends (a laser printer for electronic-publishing software, for instance), the cost of renting an apartment, and the average grocery bill.

Then compare the cost of living and the average gross income in the target country to your own. The comparison of these numbers will give you a sense of the economic climate in the target country, your target users's perception of wealth, and their purchasing power.

For example, in the U.S., we take for granted the bargain stores that are found in many areas of the country. Americans have the luxury of finding the same product for a greatly reduced price if they shop at different stores. This is not the case in Japan, where bargain stores are considered a cultural threat to store owners whose shops have been in existence for generations.

If your company's product is an off-the-shelf product, like a commercial software product, you need to understand and appreciate the cost of the product as it relates to other items. You also need to understand how the cost of a product relates to the average gross income. What kind of an investment are consumers making when they buy your company's product?

In the U.S., we have a variety of price tiers for purchasing commercial software, for example. We can pay the retail price, which is high, or we can go to a bargain computer store and pay a discounted price. We can get an even lower price if we order the product through the mail. Because we can bargain hunt we are more likely to be less loyal to a particular manufacturer's products than people in Japan, for example.

Knowing this information may be justification for a more radical localization effort or conversely, a general localization effort, depending on the buying habits and purchasing power of the target audience and the business needs of your company. In the example above, it would be prudent to perform radical localization for your Japanese users, since their buying habits (loyalty) would justify the effort. In the U.S., however, where buying habits tend to be less predictable, a more general localization effort might suffice.

SOCIAL DIFFERENCES AND SIMILARITIES

The social realm focuses on how target users interact at a formal and informal level and what their expectations and needs are. *Social* should be viewed from both a business perspective and a family perspective, since in most countries business and family life are separated; different rules and expectations exist in both realms, even within the same country. Both sets of rules and expectations influence an individual. Here are some facets of the social international variable that you should collect data on and add to the International Variables worksheet for the target country.

- **Age.** This factor can help focus research on other international variables, like education.

- **Business etiquette.** Knowledge of business etiquette helps facilitate interaction with members of the international team, and provides insight into proper and improper examples and graphics for international technical communication.

- **Family and social interaction.** Learning about social structures provides understanding of value system, tradition, and cultural expectations.

- **Discrimination and prejudice.** Knowledge of what is taboo offers insight into "caution" topics that are guaranteed to offend.

- **Popular culture.** Try to gain insight as to what is popular and what is traditional in a target culture.

Age

Clearly there is a difference in information products made for children ages seven to ten and adults ages 30–45. If the age range of the target users is not obvious, sometimes the marketing and sales people in your company can provide this information.

Once you know the age range of the target users, you can focus the research of the other international variables to get more specific data to add to your International Variables worksheet.

Business Etiquette

Business etiquette varies sometimes dramatically from country to country. It even varies from industry to industry. There are many books available that provide information on how to do business in a given target country.[6] These books are often sufficient. However, the best teacher is a colleague with lots of business experience who is from the target country, and who now lives and works in the source country, preferably for your company. This person has already made the transition to another cultural context and is sensitive to the differences and similarities in how business is conducted in both countries. Your next choice is to interview a businessperson who does a lot of business in the target country, but who is from and currently lives in your country.

Being familiar with business etiquette in the target and source countries is an invaluable asset. It offers insight into the unspoken rules layer of the Iceberg Model. When you communicate with members of the international team who are from the target country, you need to minimize the communication problems that inevitably exist (language barriers and cultural differences). Good business etiquette can minimize these problems.

Business etiquette may also feature in your information products, either overtly or implicitly. When you show a graphic of people interacting in a business scene, you imply some form of business etiquette. Shaking hands may imply closing a deal in one country but not in another, for example. On the implicit level, consider the example of collating names in Japan. These are properly done by rank in a Japanese company, not in alphabetical order as is the case in the U.S.

Family and Social Interaction

This is a broad category, which could inspire a long essay. Instead, here are a list of questions that you should consider researching and adding your findings to the International Variables worksheet. Each of these questions enriches your understanding of the visible culture and the unspoken rules of a target audience.

- What is the predominant way of life in the target country? Is it predominantly an agrarian, industrial, or urban society?

- Do people tend to live in houses or apartments? What is the physical layout of their housing? Is physical space at a premium, or is it amply distributed?

- What are some traditions in the target country? Has popular culture replaced them, and if so, how?

- What do people eat in the target country? What is their concept of nutrition?

- Are families extended or nuclear? Are families matriarchal or patriarchal? Do people have large or small families?

- What is considered proper etiquette for major social events, like weddings, funerals, and births? Can tradition and proper etiquette tell you anything about colors, symbols, and cultural expectations?

Discrimination and Prejudice

Discrimination and prejudice exist in every country in the world. In some countries they are more pronounced. To use an American expression, "Don't pour salt on an open wound." What is perceived as unacceptable in one country may be expected in another. Knowing this information ahead of time can help you avoid embarrassing mistakes.

In the U.S., for example, it is best to be sensitive to portrayals and discussions of women or African-Americans, which, if handled insensitively, can suggest discrimination and prejudice. Portraying and discussing women and African-Americans in graphics or written examples without considering the significance of these subjects in the U.S. is taking the serious risk of greatly offending many people. Obviously this is detrimental to your goal of creating effective international technical communication.

Do your homework and know what forms of prejudice and discrimination exist in the target country. Add these insights to your International Variables worksheet.

Popular Culture

The relationship between popular culture and tradition offers interesting information about how a culture changes. For example, MTV is a popular cable television station that shows music videos. It originated in the U.S., but is now locally produced in over 20 countries in Europe, South America, and Asia. It is a form of entertainment for younger people. MTV is often criticized and said to be creating a generation whose attention spans are short, and who need visual and auditory stimuli. Two or three generations ago, people read books or listened to the radio for entertainment. These differences are affecting information products around the world. Multimedia and video are becoming more popular media for technical information because of the change in the way that people get information. As these young people age, they will expect to learn from media like those they grew up with.

RELIGIOUS DIFFERENCES AND SIMILARITIES

There are countries in the world where religion plays such a major role in the majority of people's lives that it must be considered when performing an international-user analysis.

It is important that you familiarize yourself with the significance of religion in the target country. Do some research on fundamental religious beliefs of the target religion, and be aware of major religious icons and the significance of various colors. Are there foods or behaviors that are forbidden in the target religion? For example, pork is forbidden in some religions, while lamb and fish are eaten on special occasions in others. Know what the major religious documents are. Document all of this on the International Variables worksheet.

EDUCATIONAL DIFFERENCES AND SIMILARITIES

The educational realm focuses on how target users learn and what expectations they have based on what they already know. Educational systems vary widely around the world and so does the value people in a target country place on education. In Japan, the U.S., Germany, and many other European countries, education is paramount. Knowing this is learning that much more about the target country and the cultural expectations of your target users. Here are some facets of the educational international variable that you should research and document on the International Variables worksheet for the target country.

- **Literacy.** This determines whether it is more or less effective to introduce text-intensive information products.

- **Common body of knowledge.** This helps you define what your target audience already knows.

- **Learning style.** This helps you understand how people learn in a target country, which is what they are doing when they use your information products.

Literacy

Most countries calculate their literacy rate, which is the percentage of the population who can read and write. Literacy is defined differently from country to country. For this reason, literacy figures are often inflated, but they can be useful. A good source for getting this information quickly is by referring to *Culturgrams*, which are published by Brigham Young University. *Culturgrams* are short introductions to a country, its culture, and salient facts of doing business in the country; each *Culturgram* specifies the official literacy rate of the particular country.

Literacy is a significant concern, since literacy skills are often mandatory for using information products. Literacy is a growing concern in the U.S., for example. The U.S. is considered quite literate. However, in a recent survey sponsored by the U.S. government called the *National Adult Literacy Survey*, "twenty-one to 23 percent—or some 40 to 44 million of the 191 million adults in this country—demonstrated skills in the lowest level of prose, document, and quantitative proficiencies."[7] The findings of this survey have grave implications for technical communicators whose audience might include some of the American population referred to in this quotation.

Common Body of Knowledge

Another useful set of information to be familiar with is the common body of knowledge in the target country. For example, if most people have at least seven years of education, you should research what kind of information people with seven years of education in the target country can be expected to know.

In France, for example, the educational system is so structured that a child in Paris learns exactly the same information as a child in Nice.[8] Being familiar with this information is useful for technical communicators who localize information products for France. You will be able to make safe assumptions about your users' common body of knowledge.

A good resource for gathering this information is a college professor who teaches education courses. Most professors of education read about trends in education in other countries, and are the best resource for quick access to this kind of information. If you are interested in taking your research a bit further, you can ask these professors for names of studies and professional journals that cover this topic.

Another good resource for this information is a national-level education body in the target country. In the U.S., for example, the U.S. Department of Education can offer statistical data as well as national standards and mandates for education at all levels.

Learning Style

The learning style in a target country is an important factor to consider, even though it is more difficult to research. Knowing more about how people expect to learn new information can be a great asset, especially if your technical communication products include tutorials and course materials.

Jakob Nielsen, a human factors and usability specialist, provides a good example of how assumptions about learning style can fail in one country but succeed in another. He describes a French hypertext product called *LYRE*, which teaches poetry. LYRE lets students analyze the poem from the perspective that the teacher defines, but prohibits students from adding their own perspectives of the poem. Nielsen comments:

> This is obviously socially acceptable in the Southern European tradition in France, and indeed an alternative design might well have been deemed socially *un*acceptable in that country because it would have undermined the teacher's authority. On the other hand, many people in e.g. Denmark where Scandinavian attitudes are more prevalent, would view the current design of LYRE as socially unacceptable because it limits the students' potential for independent discovery.[9]

L I N G U I S T I C   D I F F E R E N C E S   A N D   S I M I L A R I T I E S

The linguistic realm focuses on the language requirements of a target user and how they affect reading dynamics. Writing for translation is very much a part of this international variable.

Some factors you need to consider include:

- **The target language.** This helps you understand fundamental differences between the source and target language.

- **Official national languages.** This helps to determine whether translation is necessary.

- **Text orientation.** This can help assess page layout.

- **Writing style.** This will help you assess the effectiveness of the source-information products.

The Target Language

David Victor, author of *International Business Communication*, discusses the influence of language on a person, concluding that the "tools for expressing oneself exist in one's language and . . . direct the way in which the speakers of that language analyze and understand the world around them."[10] He cites several examples of this, one of which is the language of the Eskimo people, called Inuit. Inuit has no specific word for *snow*, "although it has dozens of words for *types* of snow for which most European and Asian languages have no equivalent."[11] Victor continues, giving examples of words from various languages that cannot be easily translated into other languages because of their cultural significance.

Understanding a bit about the language of a target country can help you develop a sensitivity to writing in your own language. For example, if your native language is English, knowing about other languages can help you avoid using hidden plurals and noun strings, since they present translatability problems. Chapter 9 offers an extensive list of many other translatability problems for technical communicators who write in English.

The pronoun *you* when translated to Japanese provides an interesting example of how languages differ and how translators play an important role in the success of an information product. Choosing the correct pronoun in Japanese makes more of a statement than you might imagine. The famous Japanese linguist, Haruhiko Kindaichi, illustrates this fact, "It is characteristic of Japanese that from. . . brief expressions, one is able to guess that the speakers are a man and a woman, what their approximate ages are, and even what the relationship between the two is."[12]

Some good resources for researching the target language, aside from talking to your translators, include language tapes, introductory books on learning the target language, and linguistic efforts at describing the target language. Of the latter, *The Japanese Language* by Haruhiko Kindaichi is an excellent and interesting example of linguistic efforts at describing language.

Official National Languages

In some countries, there are official languages and those "tolerated by information users."[13] IBM provides an interesting table in its *National Language Support Reference* manual that lists official languages and non-official languages by country.

In Belgium, for example, the official languages are Belgian Dutch, Belgian French, and German. In India, the official languages are Hindi and English. Singapore's official languages are Chinese, Malay, Tamil, and English.

Being aware of the official languages in a country is important for legal reasons if you writing information for safety labels, for example. Knowing the official languages of a target country can also help you minimize the number of target languages into which your information products are translated.

Text Directionality

Text directionality is the direction and orientation of text on a page and within a book, for example. In English, people define the beginning and end of a book as being from left to right. Their eyes begin reading in the upper-left corner of a page and proceed in a zig zag to the lower-right corner of the page before moving to the next page.

English text directionality is not universal. Text printed in Arabic and Hebrew, for example, does not have the same text directionality as text printed in English. Arabic texts are read from the right to left. Their eyes begin reading the upper-right corner of a page and proceed to zig zag to the lower-left corner of the page before moving to the next page.

There are other examples of text directionality. Some forms of Japanese, particularly that used for marketing purposes, are read from top to bottom in columns that are read from right to left since the characters (ideographs) are printed in vertical lines.

Text directionality may detract from the effect of page layout and page design, particularly if the page was designed based on cultural expectations of the source country. Document and possibly diagram the reading dynamics of the target country and consider it when designing your information products. This topic is discussed in more detail in Chapter 6.

Writing Style

Writing styles vary from country to country. Many English-to-French translators describe American documentation as very repetitive, for example. Good English-to-French translators will delete the repetition in the American documentation to assume a more appropriate writing style for the French audience.

Be aware of the writing styles that prevail in other countries as compared to the writing style in your own country. Document your observations in the International Variables worksheet. If you are performing radical localization on an information product, you should instruct the translator to emulate the writing style of the target country as closely as possible.

TECHNOLOGICAL DIFFERENCES AND SIMILARITIES

The technological realm focuses on whether the target users have the technology that is required to use your company's product effectively.

Aldus Corporation experienced this. "Because Aldus's products are more valuable to customers (and more marketable) when used in conjunction with other existing software, hardware, and publishing processes, they cannot be localized in another country until suitable complementary technology is identified."[14]

Sometimes Aldus helps create new industry to support its products, while at other times, it adapts its products to accommodate the technology in the target country.

If your company's products rely on technology (for example, software like Microsoft Windows, hardware like a PostScript-compatible laser printer, or a reliable telephone connection), you need to know if that technology is compatible with that in the source country. If the technology on which your company's products rely is different, it will affect the information products.

First, identify the technology on which your company's product depends. Have the international team review this list. Then, research and document what compatible technology exists in the target country. You may want to investigate further into the reliability of the technology in the target country, too. For example, telephone service is not reliable in many countries in Eastern Europe—in Poland it is not unusual for the telephone system to be down for many hours. If your company's product relies on telephone technology and it is exported to Poland, you should consider adding special sections in the localized technical communication products about handling telephone disconnections and down time.

CHOOSING A MODEL OF CULTURE

This chapter reviews four popular models of culture that have been created by cultural anthropologists and international business consultants. Each model of culture identifies additional international variables that look below the surface and focus on the unconscious level of culture. Culture is learned and not inherited. These models offer ways to analyze people's cultural contexts.

- Use these models of culture to collect data for radical localization.

- Use these models to gain insight into the information needs and behavioral tendencies of users.

- Use these models of culture when performing multinational task analyses.

Each model is authored by a particular individual who has written extensively on his model. This section, then, merely summarizes the works of each author and points you to his relevant and original works.

It is interesting to note that the authors developed these models of culture as a result of questionnaires, surveys, extensive interviews, focus groups, and years of experience and observation. It is quite possible that by using the same methodologies, your international team can develop a model of culture that is particularly

TABLE 4.2: **The Focus of the Four Models of Culture**

AUTHOR	FOCUS OF MODEL OF CULTURE
Edward T. Hall	Determining what releases the right response rather than sends the right message.
David A. Victor	Determining the aspects of culture most likely to affect communication in a specifically business setting.
Geert Hofstede	Determining the patterns of thinking, feeling, and acting that form a culture's mental programming.
Fons Trompenaars	Determining the way in which a group of people solves problems.

well suited to your business arena and target audiences. Hofstede's model, for example, developed from an initial multinational study he did of IBM Corporation. He offers some useful ideas that explain how to develop your own model of culture in "Appendix: Reading Mental Programs," in *Cultures and Organizations: Software of the Mind* (New York: McGraw-Hill, 1991).

These models of culture offer you a place to begin. Note, too, that there are other models of culture that this book does not cover. Review the literature of cross-cultural communication for other models.

Table 4.2 provides a comparison of what data each model attempts to collect.

EDWARD T. HALL

Edward T. Hall is a highly respected anthropologist and cross-cultural communication consultant. His model of culture is based on years of observation and extensive interviewing throughout the world. To Hall, culture is a program for behavior. Effective cross-cultural communication "has more to do with releasing the right response than with sending the 'right' messages."[15]

Speed of Messages

Hall talks about the message velocity continuum, which refers to the speed with which people decode and act on messages. Some cultures are more comfortable with fast messages in many instances, while other cultures are more comfortable with slow messages.

Examples of slow messages include:

- Deep relationships
- Works of art
- Television documentaries

- Poetry
- Books

Examples of fast messages include:

- Headlines
- Cartoons
- Television commercials
- Manners
- Propaganda

Context

Hall articulated the idea of *contexting* in his book *Beyond Culture*. Contexting offers technical communicators a way of assessing the amount and kind of detail they should include in an information product for maximum effectiveness. Contexting is of particular interest to trainers and professionals who work on a one-on-one basis with users. Hall defines two kinds of contexting, *high context* and *low context*. Here is his definition of both:

> High context or low context refers to the amount of information that is in a given communication as a function of the context in which it occurs. A highly contexted communication is one in which most of the meaning is in the context while very little is in the transmitted message. A low context communication is similar to interacting with a computer—if the information is not explicitly stated, and the program followed religiously, the meaning is distorted. In the Western world, the law is low context, in comparison with daily transactions of an informal nature. People who know each other over a long period of years will tend to use high context communication.[16]

Hall offers several examples of problems that arise when people of low context communicate with people of high-context cultures. His favorite examples seem to be of Americans interacting with the Japanese; America is a low-context culture, and Japan is a high-context culture. Hall describes the legal systems of both countries. In America, we remove the context of the crime and rely on the plain, hard facts to decide a case. In Japan, they reenact the crime publicly, deliberately making its context literal for all to see, not the least of whom is the criminal.

Hall created a Context Square, which consists of context, information, and meaning to illustrate communication. The Context Square, shown in the background of Figure 4.3 uses two right triangles and a rectangle to show the relationship among context, information, and meaning. "[A]s context is lost, information must be added if the meaning is to remain constant. There can be no meaning without both information and context."[17]

Hall's writings are taken a bit further in David Victor's LESCANT model, explained next. Victor, though, provides an interesting diagram of high- and low-context cultures, which is superimposed on Hall's Context Square in Figure 4.3. Victor diagrams the context ranking of ten cultures on a continuum. First in the continuum for high-context cultures is Japan, where information is implicitly stated. Last in the low-context cultures are the Swiss-Germans, for whom information must be stated explicitly. The French and the British fall in the middle of the continuum.[18]

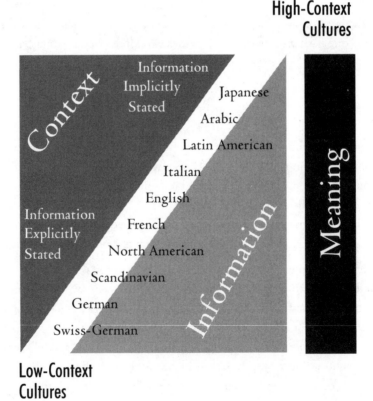

FIGURE 4.3: **Hall's Context Square and Victor's diagram of the context ranking of cultures (author's interpretation).**

Space

All cultures have different senses of space, or *invisible boundaries*. Hall qualifies these invisible boundaries in the following ways:

- **Territoriality.** This cultural trait includes "ownership" and extends to communicate power. The layout of the floors in an office building in Japan, for example, is very different from that in the U.S. In Japan, it is often difficult to identify who has power and authority based on the layout of a floor or even of a building. In the U.S., those with power typically have the largest and most lavish offices, which are often located on the top floors of a building.

- **Personal space.** Cultures have different expectations of personal space and therefore have unspoken and unconscious rules about when personal space is violated. Hall cites an example of how in northern Europe you do not touch others, and even brushing the overcoat sleeve of another in passing is enough to warrant an apology.

- **Multisensory space.** Invisible boundaries extend to all the five senses. Cultures have unconscious rules about what is too loud and intrusive, for example. In low-context cultures, like Germany, a loud conversation is perceived as infringing on another's private space. In high-context cultures, as in Italy, loud conversations are expected to take place and are not perceived as infringing on invisible boundaries.

- **Unconscious reactions to spatial differences.** The distance you keep when having a conversation can influence the response the person has to you and your conversation. For example, if you have a conversation with someone from a culture where maintaining a close physical distance during conversation is expected, and yet you converse at a greater distance than this, you send an unconscious and negative message to the other person.

Time

Time is an important and complex international variable in Hall's model of culture, and it features in the other three models of culture as well.

In its simplest form, time, as an international variable in Hall's model of culture, is of two types, *polychronic time* and *monochronic time*.

- **Polychronic time (P-time)** is characterized as simultaneous and concurrent. *Many-things-at-once* is the phrase Hall uses to define polychronic time.

- **Monochronic time (M-time)** is characterized as being sequential and linear. *One-thing-at-a-time* is the phrase Hall uses to define monochronic time.

TABLE 4.3: **Monochronic and Polychronic People**[19]

MONOCHRONIC PEOPLE	POLYCHRONIC PEOPLE
■ do one thing at a time	■ do many things at once
■ concentrate on the job	■ are highly distractible and subject to interruptions
■ view time commitments as critical	■ view time commitments as objectives
■ are low context and need information	■ are high context and already have information
■ are committed to the job	■ are committed to people and human relationships
■ adhere religiously to plans	■ change plans often and easily
■ emphasize promptness	■ base promptness on the importance of and significance of the relationship
■ are accustomed to short-term relationships	■ have a strong tendency to build lifetime relationships

Hall applies these definitions to cultures and speaks of polychronic cultures and monochronic cultures. Table 4.3 identifies the characteristics of both.

Examples of monochronic people include Northern European cultures. Examples of polychronic people include Middle Eastern, Latin American, and Mediterranean cultures. (Notice the geography at work here; warmer climates tend to be polychronic, while colder or erratic climates tend to be monochronic. Victor discusses this when explaining his environment international variable.)

Successful communication with these cultures is often attributed to a respect for their concept of time. Note that cultures are not exclusively polychronic or monochronic. The Japanese, for example, are polychronic in their dealings with other people, but monochronic in their approach to official business dealings. The relationship with a client and a rigid schedule for accomplishing goals are closely entwined.

Hall also talks of past- and future-oriented cultures. For example, he frequently speaks of Germans as very past oriented, and that their information needs are closely tied to this. "German time and German consciousness are steeped in the past. When they explain something, they often find it necessary to lay a proper foundation and as a result are apt to go back to Charlemagne."[20]

He notes an odd contrast to the Japanese, whose culture is also "steeped in history," but because of the high-context nature of their culture, they tend to plan far ahead into the future due to the value they place on long-term business.

Information Flow

Information flow is defined as the measure of "how long it takes for a message intended to produce an action to travel from one part of an organization to another and for that message to release the desired response."[21]

Hall states that in high-context cultures, which value relationships and information more than schedules, the information flow tends to be very fast and free. Knowing the right people is highly valued. In low-context cultures, where everything tends to be compartmentalized and where bureaucracies flourish, the information flow tends to be slow. Following procedure is highly valued.

Action Chains

An action chain is a sequence of events that lead to the accomplishment of a goal. Action chains are central to technical communication. Tasks, procedures, methods for performance, are all examples of action chains. "There are important rules governing the structure, though not the content, of action chains. . . . All planning must take into account the elaborate hierarchy of action chains."[22] Action chains should be considered when we do task analyses, for example.

DAVID A. VICTOR

David A. Victor's LESCANT model provides yet another view of culture and offers a rich array of variables that you can explore when performing an international user analysis. Victor's work is based primarily on extensive academic research, and thus pulls together a large collection of independent research and findings from throughout the world. Therefore, the following information provides merely an outline of his model.

A central theme in Victor's work is that cultural differences and similarities are essential to and inseparable from effective international business communication. His LESCANT model identifies the international variables where cultural differences and similarities are manifest. The following summarizes his logic:

> First, as global demands for products grow and international trade barriers decrease, the need of business people to communicate with their counterparts from other cultures increases. At the same time, as pressures for global conformity in such areas as consumer preference mount with the expanded volume of world trade, cultural differences will intensify as a defensive mechanism. Since the area over which people have the most individual control is their manner of communication, business communication in an integrated world economy will reflect an increase in cross-cultural differences in direct proportion to the decrease in other international barriers.[23]

LESCANT is an acronym based on the English words Language, Environment and technology, Social organization, Contexting, Authority conception, Nonverbal behavior, and Temporal conception, each of which is an international variable that is briefly described here:

Language
There is some interesting discussion about degrees of fluency, accents, and regional dialects and how they affect business communication. Also, Victor offers commentary on English as the international language of business.

Environment and Technology
A fascinating chapter about how larger issues like geography, population, concepts of physical space, and perceptions of technology affect business communication. Victor offers the radical example of Switzerland, where mountain ranges have contributed to the development of very distinct cultures within the same country.

Social Organization
Explores educational, economic, social, political, and religious systems as they affect business communication.

Contexting
Expands on Hall's model of contexting. Victor includes the research of Martin Rosch and Kay Segler, who ranked cultures using Hall's context square. This is illustrated in Figure 4.3.

Authority Conception
Discusses power, authority, and leadership, how they are perceived differently in cultures, and how this perception affects business communication.

Nonverbal Behavior
This is a broad category for many types of nonverbal behavior. This chapter is particularly relevant for technical communication products that use video, television, or multimedia.

Temporal Conception
In a word, time. Victor explores various perspectives of time and how they can affect business communication, particularly with respect to scheduling.

GEERT HOFSTEDE
Geert Hofstede founded and managed the personnel research department of IBM Europe from 1965 to 1971. While at IBM, he developed a multinational survey

that "dealt mainly with the employees' personal *values* related to the work situation. . . ."[24] The results of this survey greatly influenced the development of his model of culture, and led him to develop or refer to other multinational surveys that validated these initial findings. It is interesting to note the scope of the IBM survey, since it may be something that you want to pursue in your own company.

> The database was unusually extensive, covering employees in 72 national subsidiaries, 38 occupations, 20 languages, and at two points in time: around 1968 and around 1972. Altogether, there were more than 116,000 questionnaires with over 100 standardized questions each.[25]

Of equal importance is being familiar with Hofstede's definition of *culture*.

> Every person carries within him or herself patterns of thinking, feeling, and potential acting which were learned throughout their lifetime. . . . Using the analogy of the way in which computers are programmed, [Hofstede calls] such patterns of thinking, feeling, and acting *mental programs*, or . . . '*software of the mind*' . . . Mental programs vary as much as the social environments in which they were acquired. . . . Culture is always a collective phenomenon, because it is at least partly shared with people who live or lived within the same social environment, which is where it is learned. It is the *collective programming of the mind which distinguishes the members of one group or category of people from another.*[26]

The following international variables identify differences in mental programming.

Power Distance

Power distance measures how subordinates (employees, staff members) respond to power and authority (leaders, managers), which Hofstede summarizes as how subordinates value (respond to and perceive) inequality.

He created an index to measure this in his IBM surveys. What he found was that **high-power distances** tend to exist in Latin American countries, France, Spain, and in Asia and Africa. In these countries, subordinates tend to be afraid of their bosses, bosses tend not to confer with their subordinates, and bosses tend to be paternalistic or autocratic.

Low-power distance countries include the U.S., Great Britain, much of the rest of Europe (Sweden, Germany, Norway, the Netherlands, Denmark), New Zealand, and Israel. In these countries, subordinates are more likely to challenge bosses and bosses tend to use a consultative management style.

Collectivism versus Individualism

These polar values measure the ties among individuals in a society.

- In **individualistic cultures**, people are expected to look out for themselves. There is little social cohesion. Examples of countries that value individualism include U.S., France, Germany, South Africa, and Canada. Some values include personal time, freedom, and challenge.

- In **collectivist cultures**, individuals develop strong personal and protective ties and are also expected to provide unquestioning loyalty to the group during their lifetimes and sometimes beyond. Examples of countries that value collectivism include Japan, Costa Rica, Mexico, Korea, and Greece. Some values include training, physical conditions, and use of skills.

Femininity versus Masculinity

Hofstede's IBM survey found men's work goals were markedly different from women's work goals, and that these differences could be expressed on a masculine pole and a feminine pole. Table 4.4 summarizes some of these findings.

Examples of countries where the feminine index is more valued include Sweden, Israel, Spain, Korea, France, Denmark, Finland, and Indonesia. Examples where the masculine index is more valued are U.S., Japan, Mexico, Great Britain, Hong Kong, Italy, Germany, and New Zealand.

Uncertainty Avoidance

This international variable focuses on "the extent to which people feel threatened by uncertain or unknown situations." It is an attempt to plot on a continuum people's response to unknown situations. Hofstede characterizes uncertainty avoidance as "what is different, is dangerous." Uncertainty avoidance is measured using the units *strong* and *weak*.

TABLE 4.4: **Masculine and Feminine Work Goals Index**

MASCULINE INDEX	FEMININE INDEX
▪ have a high opportunity for earnings	▪ have a good working relationship with your direct supervisor
▪ get the recognition you deserve when you do a good job	▪ work with people who cooperate well with one another
▪ have an opportunity for advancement to a higher-level job	▪ live in an area desirable to you and your family
▪ have challenging work to do to derive a sense of accomplishment	▪ have the security that you will be able to work for your company as long as you want to

Strong uncertainty avoidance indicates that a culture tends to perceive unknown situations as threatening and people, therefore, tend to avoid these situations. Here are some of the characteristics that Hofstede lists for cultures that measure high on the uncertainty avoidance scale.[27]

- Uncertainty is a continuous threat that must be fought.

- Familiar risks are accepted, but ambiguous situations and unfamiliar risks are feared.

- What is different is dangerous.

- Students are comfortable in structured learning situations and concerned with the right answers.

- Teachers are expected to have all the answers.

- Precision comes naturally.

- Deviant ideas and behavior are suppressed.

- Innovation is resisted.

- Security and esteem or belongingness are motivating factors.

Examples of countries where this is so include Latin American countries, Japan, and South Korea.

Weak uncertainty avoidance indicates that a culture is less threatened by unknown situations. Here are some of the characteristics that Hofstede lists for cultures that measure low on the uncertainty avoidance scale:[28]

- Uncertainty is a normal feature of life.

- People feel comfortable with ambiguous situations and unfamiliar risks.

- What is different is a matter for curiosity.

- Students are comfortable with open-ended learning situations and concerned with good discussions.

- Teachers may say "I don't know."

- Precision has to be learned.

- Achievement and esteem or belongingness are motivating factors.

- Deviant and innovative ideas are tolerated.

Examples of countries where this is so include: the Netherlands, U.S., Singapore, Hong Kong, and Great Britain.

Long-Term versus Short-Term

This international variable came about after Hofstede performed his IBM surveys. It is the result of a long process of weeding out what he discovered to be cultural bias inherent in the original surveys; that is, the IBM surveys had a Western bias. The surveys did not consider non-Western values, particularly those of China and relating to the teaching of Confucius. An index measuring cultures' long-term versus short-term orientation toward life resulted.

The values for **long-term orientation** (concerned about the future) are:

- Persistence and perseverance

- Respect for a hierarchy of the status of relationships

- Thrift

- Having a sense of shame

Examples of countries that have a long-term orientation toward life include China, Hong Kong, Taiwan, Japan, and India.

The values for **short-term orientation** (concerned with the past and the present) are:

- Sense of security and stability

- Protecting your reputation

- Respect for tradition

- Reciprocation of greetings, favors, and gifts

Examples of countries that have a short-term orientation toward life include: Pakistan, the Philippines, Canada, Great Britain, Germany, Australia, and the U.S.

F O N S   T R O M P E N A A R S

Fons Trompenaars studied under Hofstede, so it is no wonder that there are artifacts from Hofstede's model in Trompenaars's seven dimensions of corporate culture, although their models are quite different. Trompenaars, like Hofstede, has quantified his model with data from an extensive multinational survey, the results of which are in *Riding the Waves of Culture: Understanding Cultural Diversity* (London; Nicholas Brealey, 1993). This survey posed 16 questions across 30 companies and 50 countries. The respondents were 15,000 managers in operations, sales, and marketing (75 percent) and general administrative staff (25 percent). The result is the Trompenaars Data Bank.

Trompenaars defines culture as the way in which a group of people solves problems.[29] He groups the problems into three headings, and then identifies seven dimensions of culture (value orientations) that typify the solutions that cultures apply when they solve these problems. They are:

1. Problems that arise from our relationships with other people:

   - Universalism *versus* particularism

   - Individualism *versus* collectivism

   - Neutral or emotional

   - Specific *versus* diffuse

   - Achievement *versus* ascription

2. Problems that come from the passage of time:

   - Attitudes to time

3. Problems that relate to the environment:

   - Attitudes to the environment

Universalism versus Particularism

Universalists are rules based. Rules define morality, ethics, or what is good and right. In a serious situation involving another person (what is becoming commonly referred to as an *ethical dilemma*), universalists tend to apply these rules regardless of their relationship with the other person. Examples of countries where universalism is the value orientation include Canada, U.S., Sweden, Great Britain, and the Netherlands.

Particularists are relationship based. In a serious situation involving another person, particularists base their solution to the problem on the relationship that they have with the other person and break the rules if necessary. Countries where particularism is the value orientation include South Korea, Russia, China, France, Japan, and Hong Kong.

Individualism versus Collectivism

Individualism and collectivism relate to self-perception: Do people perceive themselves primarily as individuals or as members of a group? This value-orientation pair also relates to a sense of responsibility. Trompenaars adds the following management problem: "Is it more important to focus [as a manager] on individuals so that they can contribute to the collective as and if they wish, or is it more important to consider the collective first since that is shared by many individuals?"[30] Thus, this dimension measures three facets of value orientation.

Examples of individualist countries valuing individual freedom include Canada, U.S., Norway, Spain, and Hong Kong. Countries where individual freedom is valued less include France, Greece, Kuwait, and South Korea.

Examples of countries where people prefer to work independently include Sweden, U.S., Czechoslovakia, and Switzerland. Examples of countries where people prefer to be members of a team: France, Italy, Japan, and Singapore.

Examples of countries that make the individual accountable for problems include Russia, Poland, Denmark, and Switzerland. Examples of countries in which individuals tend to share blame with others include Singapore, Japan, Great Britain, and the Philippines. The U.S. tends to fall at the middle of the scale.

Neutral versus Emotional

This value-orientation pair measures the range of emotions that people express when dealing with others in a business context.

Examples of countries where it is acceptable to express emotion when a conflict arises with another in a business situation include Italy, France, and U.S. Examples of countries where expressing emotion is discouraged when a conflict involves others in a business setting include Japan, Great Britain, and Norway.

Specific versus Diffuse

A *specific value orientation* is one where public and private life, and public and private personal spaces are compartmentalized. It measures the range of involvement that people have with others in their lives. In specific-oriented cultures (U.S., Australia, Great Britain, the Netherlands, and Sweden), there is a clear division of business relationships and private relationships with others. A good business relationship is often kept separate from a good friendship.

In *diffuse cultures,* there is very little differentiation between a public and private life, and business relationships are expected to be of a personal nature. Hence the diffusion of public and private boundaries, spaces, and relationships. Countries that value diffuse relationships include China, Singapore, Japan, Mexico, and France.

It is interesting to note that Trompenaars recorded regional differences as well. For example, in the U.S., people on the west coast have a greater tendency to express sympathy or outrage at specific issues than do people on the east coast, who tend to respond judgementally (approve or disapprove) to specific issues.

Achievement versus Ascription

This value orientation measures how status is accorded. In achievement-oriented cultures, status is accorded based on individual achievements. Examples of countries where this is the case include Norway, U.S., Canada, and Great Britain. In ascription-oriented cultures, status is accorded based on birth, kinship, gender, age, your connections, and your educational record; examples of countries include Russia, Japan, Spain, France, China, and Belgium.

Attitudes to Time

This international variable is similar to that of Hall's definition of M-time and P-time. It concerns a culture's attitude toward the past, the present, and the future, and the relationship of each to the others.

Trompenaars cites a methodology introduced by Tom Cottle, called the *Circles Test* which was used to measure a culture's perception of the relationship among the past, present, and future. Here are the instructions that were given to participants:

> Think of the past, present and future as being in the shape of circles. Please draw three circles on the space available, representing past, present, and future. Arrange these circles in any way you want that best shows how you feel about the relationship of the past, present and future. When you have finished, label each circle to show which one is past, which one is present and which one the future.[31]

In some cultures, time as a linear sequence of discrete events leads to some point in the future or some future goal. Examples of countries that demonstrated a sequential relationship of the past, present, and future in the Circles Test include U.S., and South Korea.

Other cultures think of time as "moving in a circle, the past and present together with future possibilities."[32] Examples of countries where the past, present, and future are integrated in the Circles Test include France, Belgium, and Venezuela. In some instances, as in Russia, Italy, and the Netherlands, the Circles Test indicated that there is little to no relationship among the past, the present, and the future.

Attitudes to the Environment

This value orientation measures people's attitudes toward their ability to control the environment and nature.

Countries in which people believe it is worth trying to control nature include Brazil, Portugal, and China. Countries who have the opposite inclination include Japan, Singapore, and Switzerland.

ANALYZING THE COMPETITION

Knowing about the competition in the target country can provide ideas on how to create effective international technical communication. Here are three questions you need to investigate regarding competition in the target country.

IS THERE COMPETITION IN THE TARGET COUNTRY?

Aldus Corporation asked this question about ten years ago. Aldus wanted to be first to market with its desktop-publishing software, hoping to gain a competitive advantage by building its business internationally as well as nationally in the U.S. Aldus had no competition, anywhere, for its products. The price it paid, though, was in having to find and help develop companies that could supply technology complementary to its products, like laser printers, computers, and operating systems. The development time for a localized version of an Aldus product was typically about one year. This effort paid off, since Aldus still maintains an aggressive and strong position in many countries.

Currently, however, Aldus is having to re-engineer many of its localized products. Ten years ago there were few if any tools for localization, so Aldus created them itself. Now there are many more tools available, making it easier for companies to localize their products. For instance, if your company develops software that runs on a Sun SparcStation, Apple Macintosh, or Microsoft Windows platform, it has access to international versions of each platform, plus many publications and consulting services developed specifically to help with localization.

So, while it may seem that no competition is a good thing, it brings with it costly choices.

IS THE COMPETITION LOCAL TO THE TARGET COUNTRY?

If there is competition in the target country, you need to research whether the companies are local to the target country. This makes a great difference in countries where national loyalty is great, as in Japan and many countries in Europe. Here are some questions that can guide your research.

- How long has the company been in business?
- What is the trend of customer loyalty in the target country? If very loyal, you need to research the appeal of the competition, which you might be able to use to your advantage.

- Analyze the competition's product marketing. Details are everything in marketing, so analyze all the details. What are they appealing to? What colors and design do they use? Why? What is the tone and writing style?

- Obtain information products from the competition from the sales staff. Analyze the style and layout. Are there many graphics? What is the style of the graphics? Did the competition hire professional technical communicators to create its information products, or did its engineering staff create them? Can you get any sense of how customers respond to the information products?

- Attend trade fairs to see how the competion's products are being marketed.

- Collect reviews of the competition's products in the target country. Have members of the international team who work in the target country provide you with translations of the reviews. How can you use information in the reviews to your advantage?

Is the Competition Non-Local?

You may find that the competition in the target country is the same competition in the source country. Does the competition compete with your company in other countries? Is it successful there too? Why?

Analyze marketing, advertising, and technical communication material for a sense of their message and how they project themselves. What sense of audience is there? How can this information help you in your international user analysis?

Identifying International Resources

Because there are so many things to consider when creating international technical communication, you can greatly simplify matters by knowing whom to contact for specific information. Knowing who your international resources are can also expedite the whole process of creating international technical communication. International resources can help you understand:

- The business interest in and economic concerns regarding the localization of a product for a particular target country

- The needs and expectations of users in the target country

- If and how each international resource can help you throughout the information development cycle for international technical communication

There are four categories of international resources:

1. Corporate international resources

2. Third-party international resources

3. National and local resources

4. Customers

Your company's strategy for doing business in the target country often determines the relationship of these international resources to you and to the information development cycle. In general, the first two categories of international resources form the international team, while the latter two categories form additional resources that can supply general and specific information about the target country, the target market, and the users in the target country.

COMMUNICATING WITH INTERNATIONAL RESOURCES

Your international resources may not be from the source country. These individuals may not be able to communicate in your language well or at all. Here are some suggestions for communicating with them, especially when they are from other countries.[33]

Building Relationships

Letitia Baldrige, who has served as a social secretary to the U.S. embassies in Paris and Rome and as the Chief of Staff to the late First Lady Jacqueline Kennedy, writes: "Whether you're dealing with someone from another country on his turf or yours, the same principle applies: If one of you makes an obvious effort to be accommodating, sympathetic, and kind, business will transpire, deals will be made, and profits and goals will be realized."[34] For the most part, this is true. Consider a few more principles:

- People's concept of time varies from country to country. Americans, for example, tend to want everything done yesterday or sooner. Arabs tend to want to build relationships first and do business later; the Japanese are like this, too. There are obvious conflicts here, which you need to consider when building relationships with your international contacts.

- People's loyalty to their companies varies from country to country. In the U.S., people change jobs and companies frequently, which means that you might be dealing with different people from year to year if you do business with the United States. In Switzerland and Japan, though, people stay with their companies for years and sometimes for life.

■ People's concept of relationships with business colleagues varies from country to country. In America, people tend to prefer an informal relationship during business hours and after business hours. In other countries, as in Switzerland, relationships often remain very formal, professional, and distant during business hours and after; informal relationships among business colleagues are rare.

Telephone Conversations

Always remember differences in time zones. International technical communication requires that you be flexible with your schedule. Many international technical communicators rearrange their schedules around international telephone calls; sometimes they go to work early, and sometimes they stay at work late to have telephone conversations with people several time zones away. In the U.S., some companies reimburse employees for telephone charges incurred when they have called customers or international contacts from their homes to accommodate time zone differences.

In some countries, it is expected that you exchange home telephone numbers. In Japan, the home telephone number is printed on every business card. In the U.S., this practice is often considered an intrusion of privacy. You need to consider conflicts like this when communicating with your international contacts.

You also need to consider the International Date Line when scheduling any and all telephone calls and deadlines across the Pacific Ocean. Holidays differ from country to country, too. Little to no business is done in Europe during the months of July and August, for example, as most employees go on vacation for some weeks. If you do business with Germany and Australia, you need to be aware that companies in both countries have liberal vacation policies. It is not unusual to have a German or Australian contact who will be on holiday for six weeks.

Call your contact and arrange a time for a more lengthy telephone discussion about your project. After the telephone call, write a list of the topics you want to talk about with your international contact. Fax or send (by regular or electronic mail) these topics to your international contact so that he or she can be prepared for your telephone discussion. On that day, choose a room that is quiet and offers no distractions. A speaker phone allows you to spread out your notes and related papers.

Speak slowly. Listen carefully. Enunciate. Pause frequently because of the time lag inherent in telecommunications.

Avoid using slang and jargon that is particular to your country or your industry. Avoid any humor that might not be understood or that could be conceived as culturally offensive. After the telephone discussion, write up a summary of the conversation and fax or send (by regular or electronic mail) it to your international contact. This allows your contact to review your understanding of the conversation and clarify any misunderstandings.

Written Correspondence

It is advisable to research how formal business letters are addressed and written to individuals in the target country. Your letter may lose its effect if it is not written in the business style of the target country.

In general, formality is the preferred method for doing business, even after you have developed a working relationship with someone over the course of several years. Perhaps the only country that may deviate from this is the U.S., where formality dissolves into informality quickly, and where formality is sometimes misunderstood.

Always use corporate stationery, unless the correspondence is intended to be more personal. Avoid slang and jargon. Apply the information provided in Chapter 9, "Writing Issues."

Meetings

Understand the business etiquette of meetings in the target country. If you are hosting the meeting in the source country, consider the expectations of the international contacts. Depending on the title and position your visitors have in their respective companies, they may expect certain seating arrangements. If you are hosting the meeting and colleagues from your country are also attending, you may want to educate your colleagues about the cultural context of your visitors.

Provide all attendees with a written agenda of the meeting in advance. This gives your visitors an opportunity to prepare material for the meeting.

Give consideration to where people sit. Research protocol in the target country. The United Nations, for example, has an Office of Protocol that has specific criteria for where people sit at particular events. Seating arrangements may have more significance than you realize. You might also consider providing a seating plan that allows attendees to identify people by where they sit.

Provide name tags with text large enough to be clearly visible from three meters (about 10 feet). You can alternatively use placards. Go out of your way to make introductions. It may help your visitors if you can provide them with a list of the individuals who will be attending the meeting. The list should include titles, addresses, and possibly some information about the individual's role in the project.

Jakob Nielsen made an interesting observation about names in the preface to his book *Designing User Interfaces for International Users.* Nielsen suggested that you should always spell out a person's entire name and abbreviate none of it. The reason, he notes, is because in countries like Denmark, many people share the same family name; "The three most popular names (Jensen, Nielsen, and Hansen) account for approximately 25% of the Danes."[35] If you address a letter or fax to J. Nielsen in any organization in Denmark, your letter might get routed to many different J. Nielsens. He adds that the French make this mistake in their traditional form of formal address. The French almost always abbreviate *Monsieur* as "M."; if they communicate with someone in Denmark and address a letter to "M. Nielsen," the letter will get routed to any person whose first name begins with "M" and whose last name is Nielsen.

Roger E. Axtell, author of *Do's and Taboos Around the World,* comments that forms of address differ around the world. Axtell advises that you should always ask the individual how he or she wants to be addressed.

Also, in some countries, it is common for the visitor to bring a small gift to the host or hostess, while in others, it is proper for you to give your visitor a small gift. Often an inexpensive gift that is unique to your part of the world will be an instant success. Do some research on what kinds of gifts are culturally acceptable in the target country. For instance, liquor may not be culturally acceptable in parts of the Middle East, where liquor is prohibited by the Islamic religion.

Keep a Daily Diary or Journal

In his preface to the first edition of his book, Roger Axtell, an American, describes one evening in the mid-1960s when he suddenly realized that cultural expectations can make as well as break business deals. About an evening in the company of seven Arab brothers who were very important business clients, Axtell writes: "Two thoughts prevailed. First, avoid any social blunders in this most important moment. Second, get back to the hotel room and make notes on proper behavior and this extraordinary evening." Axtell recognized that a diary of notes describing effective communication, proper behavior, and similar cultural phenomena could help him succeed in international business.

Keeping a diary can help you learn how to work well with your international resources. Write down the times and dates of telephone conversations, and summarize what was said. Always document what you promised and what your international resource promised, to avoid misunderstandings. Write down when you send letters, faxes, and electronic mail, and when you receive it; summarize each message sent and received. Also write down phrases and behaviors that seem different from your own, since they may have more significance than you may realize. Research these differences at a later date.

Write down people's birthdays, color preferences, favorite foods, and favorite music. Write down the names of their spouses and children. Write down how they hold their eating utensils, how they answer the telephone, and how they introduce you to other people. Write down anything about these international resources that provides you with cultural clues for how to interact with them effectively. This data can be invaluable if your international resources have cultural expectations that are different from your own.

Identifying Members of the International Team

Your contacts form an international team of which you are a member by default. The more representative the international team and the more effort you put into building relationships with its members, the better your chances are for creating world-class information products. An international team consists of corporate international resources and third-party resources. A representative international team for a software product might include localization engineers, human factors and usability engineers, international technical communicators and editors, international marketing specialists, distributors, international sales people, technical and customer support personnel, trainers, translators, and printers who can produce written material in the target language. It is important that you identify all the members of the international team and that you keep the list up to date for each project, or, more generally, for each target country.

These professionals may be physically located in the target countries. Having access to resources in each of the target countries is an invaluable asset and one that can improve the quality of the localization effort substantially. Make sure that your list of international resources includes the names and contact information for people in each of the target countries to which your company is exporting.

Figure 4.4 provides an example of the kind of information you should gather and keep current. In Figure 4.4, the source country is Great Britain. The target country is the U.S. Note that the contact information for the international

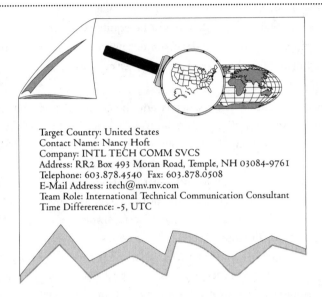

Target Country: United States
Contact Name: Nancy Hoft
Company: INTL TECH COMM SVCS
Address: RR2 Box 493 Moran Road, Temple, NH 03084-9761
Telephone: 603.878.4540 Fax: 603.878.0508
E-Mail Address: itech@mv.mv.com
Team Role: International Technical Communication Consultant
Time Differerence: -5, UTC

FIGURE 4.4: **A sample database entry of an international resource.**

resource includes the contact's mailing address, electronic mail address, and telephone and fax numbers. The time difference between the source country and the target country is denoted by the number of hours and preceded by a minus sign. You could also consider denoting the time difference using Universal Time, coordinated (UTC), which measures time differences from the Greenwich meridian.

Beyond knowing who the members of the international team are, you need to know how they can help you during the international technical communication development cycle. The sections that follow offer many ideas for the ways in which the members of the international team can help you. Re-diagram your international technical communication development cycle for each target country, identifying the team members and their roles.

CORPORATE INTERNATIONAL RESOURCES

Your primary international resources are individuals in your own company. The size of your company and its organization determine the extent of these resources. Companies that have been doing international business for a while already have many corporate international resources in place. Companies that are new to international business might have limited corporate international resources; in this case, third-party international resources become the primary resources for information.

Some companies open offices in one or more target countries. These offices might be for sales staff only, or they might be equipped for full-scale operation of a manufacturing or research and development process. You should understand how your company has organized itself in other countries.

Business Needs

When researching business needs, determine the countries to which your company currently exports and the countries to which it wants to export in the future. Focus the economic half of your equation on creating effective international technical communication on the business needs of your company at all times. Look at these resources for information about your company's international commitments and goals: annual reports, letters to shareholders, white papers, the employee package that is provided to employees on their first day at your company, company newsletters and magazines, press releases about the company, memos from the human resources department and from upper-management personnel, and scripts for speeches given by upper-management personnel. Make a list of the employees mentioned with respect to international subjects in any of these sources and contact these people to find out more about what they do.

If your company has an electronic bulletin board or conferencing system, read public notices posted by management and human resources, sales, and marketing departments about your company's involvement in international trade. Make appointments to interview your management about corporate goals. Interview upper management personnel, sales managers, and marketing managers about company goals and on the future plans of the company.

Interview the engineering and research and development managers who are involved in the internationalization effort. Understand the technical issues that they have to address when localizing products for the target country.

Talk with peers who have visited the target countries on business. Read their trip reports.

Find out if your company has in-house corporate lawyers who are active in the international issues, or if it has hired an outside law firm. If you have in-house lawyers, then their time has already been paid for and you may be able to interview them without adding to your company's legal bill. The lawyers can help you with international copyright, trademark, truth in advertising, and legal and patent issues that may affect your project. While legal issues are discussed in more detail later in this chapter, they are a major concern of many high-technology companies. Countries do not offer the same degree of protection against intellectual-property infringement.

Another source that is often overlooked is the finance department. They can tell you a lot about business trends and monetary concerns in the international arena as they relate to your company and its products. They can also tell you about fluctuations in exchange rates, which is helpful information if you have to provide budget data.

The shipping department must deal with many export regulations. They might be able to advise you on any packaging requirements for your project. They can also help you factor shipping time into any schedules you create. International shipping can take a long time because of customs delays.

User Needs

When researching user needs, talk to the field service people in your company for information as to what features in your company's products users in other countries find troublesome. Other corporate resources for similar information include help desk personnel, technical support personnel, public relations personnel, and trainers, particularly if any of these people have been involved in the installation, support, or training of your company's product in another country. Look over logs of technical support calls to see what complaints and areas of confusion users from other countries have regarding your company's products.

If your company has an electronic mail or public bulletin board, you might consider posting a general notice asking for information about the target country. Your notice should encourage people who have traveled to, lived in, or who speak the language of the target country to respond. Then, initiate conversations with the respondents. You never know who may have studied in the target country, whose hobby is to read history books about the target country, or whose daughter is attending a university in the target country. Find out about customs, traditions, and any differences or similarities between the source country and the target country. Informal relationships like these can provide a rich and interesting assortment of information that may come in handy at some time in the future. You should be aware, however, of the potential for gathering inaccurate information from these resources.

Contact the human factors or usability group, if your company has one, and see if any of them subscribe to journals and magazines that might help you in your research.

If your company is large enough to have a corporate library, talk to the librarian and see if he or she can do a literature search for you. Most corporate libraries have agreements with other libraries that allow them to borrow books from each other, which would allow you to do most of your research on site. (See the section on National and Local International Resources later in this chapter for more information on libraries.)

Customer Needs

Customer needs can be different from user needs. Chauncey Wilson, a human factors specialist, notes that a customer may want all online documentation, for example, but the users may need a hard copy of a getting-started pamphlet.

Many of the people you contact when researching business needs can also help you assess customer needs. Marketing and sales people, for example, are highly skilled at identifying customer needs. The engineering staff may have had to meet with potential customers before beginning localization. Upper management is certain to have met with important potential customers in the target countries. And the finance department can tell you a lot about currencies and economic issues in other countries, which may affect some of the content of your technical communication products, examples that use currency signs.

Summary

Tables 4.5 and 4.6 summarize various corporate international resources that you can use when researching business needs and user needs.

TABLE 4.5: **Departments with Staff that Can Supply Helpful Information**

HELPFUL PEOPLE

Human resources

Training

Marketing

Sales

Engineering

Research & development

Legal

Finance

Shipping

Executive management

Field service

Technical support

TABLE 4.5: *Continued*

Customer service

Quality assurance

Corporate library

Public relations

TABLE 4.6: **Printed Matter That Can Supply Helpful Information**

HELPFUL PRINTED MATTER

Annual reports

Letters to stockholders

Human resources publications and employee materials

Trip reports

Corporate newsletters

Corporate magazines

Press releases

White papers

Letters to employees

Executive training materials

Scripts for speeches

Electronic mail messages

Help desk logs

Sales reports

Marketing material

Customer and field service notes

THIRD-PARTY INTERNATIONAL RESOURCES

Third parties with which your company has a legal agreement or arrangement are your secondary international resources. Third parties are valuable resources, because they are specialists. You need to understand your company's relationship with them, though, because they may charge your company for the time they spend answering your questions. While this may still be necessary, it suggests that you need to spend time formulating your questions to minimize the time that third-party contacts spend with you. Some examples of third-party resources that charge your company for the time they spend on your project are legal firms and consultants. Note that you may need to get permission from the account representative to the third party before approaching the third party.

This section does not group third-party resources by business needs and user needs, since most of these resources can offer significant insight to both sides of the effective international technical communication equation. Instead, this section draws attention to the resources themselves. Note that most if not all of these resources will be members of the international team.

International Distribution Channels

How does your company export its products to the target country? The answer to this question can provide a potentially rich assortment of international resources. While the specifics vary from country to country and from year to year, companies around the world tend to export their products using one of these two international distribution channels: exporting through intermediaries or direct exporting. The difference between the two channels is control. When your company exports its products through an intermediary, it relinquishes control over how its products are exported and sold in the target country. It is up to the intermediary to do all exporting and selling. Direct exporting gives your company more control over how the product is exported.

Exporting through Intermediaries. In companies that choose to export through an intermediary, the intermediary typically manages the localization process, which includes translating and localizing the technical communication products, and performing all of the product training, among other tasks. This channel is popular with companies that are new to exporting, and that do not have the resources, financial or otherwise, to do the internationalization themselves.

An example of an intermediary for U.S. companies is described in a document entitled "The EMC—Your Export Department," published by the U.S. Government Printing Office. An export management company (EMC) "provides a multitude of services, including market research, appointing overseas distributors or commission representatives, exhibiting a client's products at international trade shows, and handling financing, advertising, shipping, and documentation. All the U.S. manufacturer has to do is fill the order."[36] An EMC, then, allows the U.S. company to relinquish all control of export responsibilities. Small U.S. companies that are new to exporting use EMCs.

When intermediaries manage the internationalization process, they may contact you for files containing the product documentation and graphics. They may also have their translators contact you for clarification of concepts, terms, or procedures in the product documentation. Your communication with the intermediary, then, may be reduced to a very occasional telephone call, letter, or fax.

In international business, seemingly minor and insignificant relationships can suddenly become very important ones. You may actually get involved in internationalization after your company has exported through an intermediary for years and then decides that it is ready to export directly to the target country. If this is the case, the intermediary can provide some vital information about your audience in the target country. If you established a professional rapport with the intermediary during your occasional exchanges, you have a better chance of getting more information about your expanded, now international, audience.

Exporting Directly. In the previous exporting example, the company hires an EMC, which then hires foreign distributors. When exporting directly, the company hires foreign distributors or distributes its own products. This export method, then, is one that the company has more control over.

A company that exports directly can do so in a variety of ways.

- It can create a subsidiary in the target country.

- It can form a legal relationship with a company that already exists in the target country; the partner might do product reselling, or be a value-added reseller (VAR). A VAR might offer product training, technical support, or technical communication services, for example.

- Your company may have relationships with many direct exporting channels.

Whatever the relationship or service they provide, the direct exporting channels are certain to be excellent resources for your international user analysis.

Direct exporting channels are often based in the target country. It is likely that they deal directly with customers, and that they are familiar with the customers' needs and cultural expectations.

Translation Companies
Businesses either hire translation companies or they hire translators on a freelance or full-time basis. (The latter is discussed under "Consultants.") The translation company might be located in the source country, in the target country, or in a country to which your company does not currently export.

The translation company and the technical-communication department must work together closely for the project to go smoothly. The translation company can educate you about the nuances of language and many of the cultural concerns you need to factor into your information products. The company can also help you discover tools and techniques for enabling and globalizing, and help you write and design your information products with translation in mind. Translation companies can offer you a wealth of expertise on the process for creating international technical communication, the information product's design and translatability, and on the needs and cultural expectations of your target audience.

Some translation companies have expanded their services to go beyond translation. Some offer localization services that can deliver turnkey software systems. Others offer publishing and production services for printed matter. You must be aware of what services they do offer and for which services your firm has hired them. For example, if the translation company does not offer typesetting in the target language, you may have to find a printer that does typeset in that language.

(Chapter 8 offers information on choosing and working with translators.)

Internationalization Companies

Because more and more companies are exporting, a market for new companies that specialize in internationalization is growing. Many internationalization companies tend to specialize in software.

These companies often internationalize and localize everything, from the product itself to the information products. This means that you will have about as much involvement in the international process as you would if your company exports through intermediaries. However, an internationalization company can teach you how to create information products with internationalization and localization in mind. Since they are familiar with the information products your department produces, they can offer specific advice and, even better, specific solutions.

Consultants

There are a number of consultants who might be involved in the project who can contribute to your international-user analysis. Cross-cultural communication consultants who specialize in the target country can offer detailed information about the target country and, possibly, your target audience. Engineers and other technical consultants are excellent sources of information on how the product will be localized and why it will be adapted that way.

If your company hires an international consultant to manage the entire internationalization project, learn from the consultant about how to create an effective management strategy for international technical communication.

As the arena of internationalization grows, and as more companies realize that they need more effective and efficient international technical communication, they may hire consultants who specialize in international technical communication. These consultants can help you create an internationalization strategy, educate technical communicators about internationalization, and analyze existing information for cultural bias and localization.

A variety of other consultants might be involved: freelance translators, graphic designers, international marketing professionals, usability consultants, and trainers. Your job is to identify these people and to find out what their specialties are. Once you know this, you need to interview them for your international-user analysis.

Printing Companies

If your company is having information products translated, it needs to have access to a company that can typeset or publish the printed material in the target language. If the translation firm does not offer this service, it may refer you to one or more printers in the source country or in another country. Your other international resources may be able to recommend printers to investigate, too. The printer can tell you about what happens to the page design when the translated text is used.

The printer can also tell you about software products that make easier file transfer from the software that the translation company or translator uses to that used by the printer. File format compatibility, then, is an important consideration.

You may find that it is less expensive to use a printer located outside your country. When doing a cost analysis, though, factor in hidden costs and logistics (see Chapter 3). For example, if you have manuals written in America printed in Singapore, how will you get the translated American manual to Singapore, how will you proof the galleys, and how will you ship the printed manuals to the necessary distribution sites?

User Groups

If your company produces a product that has a user group, attend user-group meetings to meet members and learn of their concerns. You might even consider being one of the speakers at the user-group meeting to get feedback from your target audience.

Contact the officers of the user group and engage them in your research. Consult any printed material produced by the user group. Talk to members of the user group who live and work in other countries. See if you can get users from other countries to test drafts of the translated information products or be technical reviewers of the translated printed matter.

Legal Firms and Legal Advisors

Third-party legal firms and legal advisors are critical international resources for your company. Consequently, they are important international contacts for you. Many companies hire legal firms in each of the target countries to which they export. Before contacting one of the lawyers, either in the source country or the target country, you should consider that their time will be expensive ($100-$300 USD per hour is an average range for lawyers in the U.S.). It may be more prudent to have a manager or even an executive gather the information you need from the lawyers.

When doing international business, companies need to consider the laws of the source country, the target country, international law, and any regional or economic agreements and cartels (the Organization of Petroleum Exporting Companies (OPEC), for example) that exist. This tangle of legal issues can create problems for the technical-communication department, which publishes information about warranties and copyright and trademark protection.

Legal issues can plague internationalization efforts. Piracy abounds in many countries and costs companies exporting to those countries huge sums of money. The International Intellectual Property Alliance, a Washington, D.C., lobbying group, estimates that in 1992, piracy in Asia cost U.S. companies at least $2 billion.[37]

There are many more laws throughout the world now (post-1992) that protect trademarks, trade secrets, copyrights, patents, which makes exporting more attractive to companies. However, as Steven Weinberg, a Phoenix attorney and executive editor of a newsletter called the *Trademark Reporter* states, "It's one thing to have a law on the books. It's another thing to have cultural values and views change in order to accommodate, particularly, the interests of people who are from outside the country or region."[38]

International law, laws of the source country and of the target country, and regional agreements can greatly affect if and how your company does business in a target country. Warranties, disclaimers, copyright notices, and many other legally binding entries in technical manuals, on packaging, and in online displays can vary from country to country, depending on how your company's attorneys have structured your company's launch into the target country with respect to various laws and practices.

It is possible that the translators will need to translate different legal texts for various country versions. If the target users cannot read the legal text because it is written in a language that they cannot understand, how binding can a legal agreement be, especially when the agreement is implied? Apple Computer Corporation had an interesting attempt to accommodate the language barrier. It printed a book that contained multiple warranties printed in the language of each country to which it exported.

You also need to find out if there are trademarks that should not be translated, whether they are the trademarks of your company or another company. In the latter case, you may need to consult the other company's legal advisors to verify trademark information for its international distribution.

If the trademarks are to be translated, they should be thoroughly researched before an attorney registers them in other countries. David Ricks, author of *Blunders in International Business*, devotes an entire chapter to providing examples of companies that did and did not translate the names of their products, and the disasters that resulted from their decision.[39] The Coca-Cola Company, for example, wanted to sell its soda in China. The company wanted to have the name of the soda in Chinese, but the Chinese pronunciation had to sound like the English "Coca-Cola." A translator fulfilled this request, but the translated Chinese characters meant "a wax-flattened mare" or "bite the wax tadpole." In another example, Ricks tells of a company that marketed its product, called Grab Bucket in English, to Germany. The company did not want to have the name of its product translated. But, *grab* in German is interpreted to mean "grave" and *bucket* is pronounced like the German word for "bouquet."

Standardization and Certification Bodies

Standardization and certification bodies are excellent resources on a country-by-country basis. Companies around the world struggle to conform with established standards that are not global. Companies also try to have their products certified by established certification bodies in target countries to show consumers in those countries that their products are of high quality. When researching international resources, then, you must inevitably contact standardization and certification bodies to learn more about expectations that consumers and the government have of products in a specific country. (See Appendix C for the names and addresses of some standardization bodies.)

Standardization bodies establish standards that attempt to ensure the safety and health of people who use the product sold in their respective countries. They also draft guidelines that companies should follow if they want to export their products to that country. Because there are so many standards, and because these standards can be government sponsored, industry sponsored, and company sponsored, it is important that you consider the advice Bill Tuthill gives in the *Solaris International Developer's Guide*: ". . . standards are a business tool and should be used for business reasons."[40]

There are two kinds of standards: *de facto* and *de jure*. De facto standards come about through common use, indicating a wide acceptance. De jure standards are created by committees and are legislated. Some standards might be mandatory in some countries, while others serve as guidelines. Your company may decide to localize its products by following de facto standards or by de jure standards, or both. As Tuthill states, it is a business decision.

Standards vary around the world. This is one of the issues the European Union is currently struggling with. Germany, for example, has very strict standards for products as compared to other member states in the European Union. In an effort to support the goal of borderless trade within the European Union, standards have been created to harmonize the different standards within the European Union.

If you want to learn more about various standards, contact any number of standardization bodies. There is a standards organization in almost every country in the world. Contact the standards organization in your country for information on standards in your own and in other countries.

Certification bodies exist in many countries to test products for compliance with national and, in some cases, multinational standards of safety, health, and quality, among other categories of compliance. Examples of some certification bodies include Underwriter's Laboratories (UL) in the U.S., Technischer Ueberwachungsverein e.V. (TUV) in Germany, and the Japanese Standards Association (JSA) in Japan. Certification bodies apply a *mark* to the product if it has satisfactorily passed various tests. Some of the marks applied by these certification bodies are: **UL** by Underwriters' Laboratories for a variety of product testing, **GS** (*geprüfte Sicherheit*, for mechanical products), and **VDE** (*Verband Deutscher Elektrotechnischer*, for electrical components) by TUV, and **T** (for all electrical appliances and components) and **S** (for a limited number of products that need to comply with safety regulations, like bicycle helmets) by JSA.

The European Union deserves some attention here, since it has created a multinational mark that attempts to harmonize the broad range of health, safety, and quality standards, among others, that exist in its member countries. The mark is the **CE** mark, which is meant to supersede all other marks required by member states in the European Union.

The CE mark is illustrative of the confusion involved in getting a product certified for sale in another country. For example, in a paper written for the U.S. Department of Commerce's International Trade Administration, Christian Failmezger, the German desk intern, describes the confusion American companies experience when investigating the possibility of doing business in Germany. He calls attention to the confusion in Europe about what regulations take precedence—the European Union's or those of the target country (Germany)? Since the European Union is still formulating many of the standards, it has stated that companies must comply with established European Union standards. When the European Union standards fail to cover an area, then the regulations of the target country take precedence.

Certification bodies can supply you with information about standards that your company's products must or should comply with. They can also tell you about why various standards are in place, which can sometimes explain some cultural expectations of the target users.

Summary

Table 4.7 summarizes the third-party resources that can assist you in researching international variables and improving the processes for creating effective international technical communication.

TABLE 4.7: **A Summary of Possible Third-Party International Resources**

THIRD-PARTY RESOURCES

International distribution channels

- Intermediary distribution channels
- Direct exporting channels

Translation firms

Internationalization firms

Consultants

- Cross-cultural communication consultants
- International business consultants

Continued

TABLE 4.7: **A Summary of Possible Third-Party International Resources** *Continued*

- International technical communication consultants
- International engineering consultants
- International marketing consultants
- Human factors and usability consultants
- Freelance translators
- Trainers
- Graphic designers

Printers

Shipping companies

Legal firms

Standardization and certification bodies

INTERNATIONAL, NATIONAL, AND LOCAL RESOURCES

There are myriad international, national, and local resources that can provide you with information on the business needs and user needs that influence your international technical communication efforts. Appendix C provides descriptions and names and addresses of various international, national, and local resources. Table 4.8 provides a summary of these resources.

TABLE 4.8: **A Summary of Possible International, National, and Local Resources**

INTERNATIONAL, NATIONAL, AND LOCAL RESOURCES

International organizations

Consulates and embassies

Government offices

Chambers of commerce

Professional and trade associations

Trade shows

Universities and colleges

Ethnic and social groups

Libraries

Airlines and travel agencies

Electronic communication

Miscellaneous media

CUSTOMERS AS INTERNATIONAL RESOURCES

The ultimate resource for creating effective international technical communication is the customer. Customers in the target country can provide many clues as to what features in a product make sense to them, what features are missing, how effective the information products are, and if the translation and localization of an information product was effective.

Chapter 13 offers ideas for gathering information from customers to ensure the quality of an information product.

SYNTHESIZING THE DATA

Once you collect data about the international variables, you need to synthesize it for the specific purpose of internationalizing and localizing your information products.

For instance, you might notice that most of the users in the target country are highly educated and that their second language is the source language. You might discuss with the international team the option of not having information products translated into the target language. Instead, you might suggest that the information product be edited only slightly to reflect minor differences like date formats and units of measurement. This could save your company a substantial amount of money and still accommodate the needs of your users.

Figure 4.5 uses the Iceberg Model to map the international variables presented in this chapter. The international variables are not exhaustive, nor are they necessarily applicable to your situation. Add and delete international variables to create your own model of culture. Note that the placement of the international variables in Figure 4.5 is relative. Some of the international variables could be both above and below the water line, depending on your perspective.

One exercise that you can perform is to map the results of your international-user analysis on the Iceberg Model to determine whether general localization or radical localization will be more meaningful for a target audience. Balance these finding with the business case for exporting to the target country.

Another interesting exercise that you can perform is to pin the completed International Variables worksheets to a wall to form a storyboard. Invite the technical communicators in your department and other members of the international team to participate in focus groups that discuss these findings. Share your knowledge.

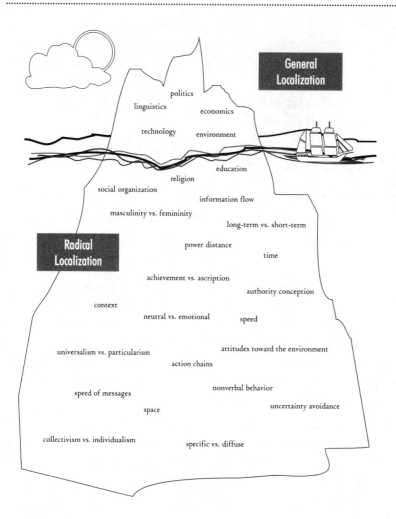

FIGURE 4.5: **The mapping of international variables on the Iceberg Model.**

You can also work with human factors and usability engineers to develop surveys and questionnaires that either test the validity of your findings, or that can be used to gather data to apply to the International Variables worksheets for the target countries.

Here are some questions to answer when synthesizing the data in the International Variables worksheets. Remember that creating effective international technical communication balances economy (business needs) with cultural understanding (user needs). Do not localize for the sake of localizing. Localize when it makes business sense to do so.

- What degree of localization is necessary? Do you need to address only superficial cultural differences, or, for business reasons, is it more prudent to address deeper cultural differences like learning styles? If radical localization is required, how can you redesign the information to facilitate these sweeping changes?

- Do any global data exist? Could they qualify as information for reuse?

- What should be translated and what should not be translated?

- Based on the cultural information that you gathered about the target countries, does the source information product contain culturally biased information? Chapter 5 discusses cultural bias in detail.

- How can the source information be modified to accommodate the cultural differences with the target countries? Look at examples, graphics, and text. Will it all make sense to users in the target countries?

END NOTES

1 The Iceberg Model is a cornerstone of intercultural communication training. Here are two of the sources in which it is described, although this list is not complete by any means: Sylvia Odenwald, *Global Training*, Business One Irwin, Illinois, 1993, p. 47; from a handout by Heather Robinson and Jeanne Parrent, "Cross-Cultural Communication," presented at the *Seminar on International Technical Communication,* which was sponsored by the Society for Technical Communication and held in Seattle, Washington, March 2, 1992.

2 From notes taken at a presentation by Jeremy Butler at *Global Opportunities*, a two-day seminar sponsored by the Washington Software Association, Monday, April 8, 1991, Seattle, Washington.

3 "EC Product Standards Under the Internal Market Program," p. 10, issued by the U.S. Department of Commerce, International Trade Administration, on February 10, 1993.

4 Ibid., p. 11.

5 Ricks, *Blunders in International Business*, Blackwell Publishers, Cambridge, Massachusetts, 1993, p. 3.

6 Here are some resources to get you started. Roger E. Axtell, *Do's and Taboos Around the World*, 3rd Ed., John Wiley & Sons, Inc., New York, 1993. Lennie Copeland and Lewis Griggs, *Going International: How to Make Friends and Deal Effectively in the Global Marketplace*, Penguin Books, New York, 1985. Diana Rowland, *Japanese Business Etiquette: A Practical Guide to Success with the Japanese*, Warner Books, 1985. Edward T. Hall and Mildred Reed Hall, *Understanding Cultural Differences: Germans, French, and Americans,* Intercultural Press, Yarmouth, Maine, 1990.

[7] *Adult Literacy in America*, Irwin S. Kirsch, Ann Jungeblut, Lynn Jenkins, and Andrew Kolstad, U.S. Government Printing Office [GPO stock number 065-000-00588-3], September 1993, Washington, D.C., p. xiv.

[8] Hall and Hall, pp. 99–102.

[9] Jacob Nielsen, "Usability Testing of International Interfaces," *Designing User Interfaces for International Use, Elsevier*, New York, 1990, p. 39.

[10] David A. Victor, *International Business Communication*, Harper Collins Publishers, New York, 1992, p. 20.

[11] Ibid.

[12] Haruhiko Kindaichi, *The Japanese Language*, trans. Umeyo Hirano, Charles E. Tuttle Company, Rutland, Vermont, 1990, p. 73.

[13] IBM, *National Language Support Reference Manual*, Vol. 2, 3rd Ed., May 1992, p. 7-1.

[14] Nancy Hoft, "Preparing for the Inevitable: Localizing Computer Documentation," *SIG-DOC '91 Proceedings*, p. 37.

[15] Hall and Hall, p. 4.

[16] Edward T. Hall, *The Dance of Life*, Anchor Books, New York, N.Y., 1983, p. 229.

[17] Ibid., p. 61.

[18] Victor, p. 143.

[19] Hall and Hall, p. 15.

[20] Ibid., p. 35.

[21] Ibid., p. 22.

[22] Ibid., p. 25.

[23] Victor, p. 143.

[24] Geert Hofstede, *Cultures and Organizations: Software of the Mind*, McGraw-Hill, New York, 1991, p. 251.

25 Ibid.

26 Ibid., pp. 4-5.

27 Ibid., p. 125.

28 Ibid.

29 Fons Trompenaars, *Riding the Waves of Culture: Understanding Cultural Diversity in Business*, Nicholas Brealey, London, 1993, p. 6.

30 Ibid., p. 9.

31 Ibid., p. 113. The original text: Tom Cottle, "The Circles Test; an investigation of perception of temporal relatedness and dominance," *Journal of Projective Techniques and Personality Assessments*, No. 31, 1967, pp. 58-71.

32 Ibid., p. 10.

33 There are many sources for this kind of information. In the United States, some sources include: *Letitia Baldrige's New Complete Guide to Executive Manners* (Rawson Associates: New York, 1993), Diana Rowland's *Japanese Business Etiquette* (Warner Books, Inc.: New York, 1985), *Dos and Taboos Around the World* (R.E. Axtell, Ed., John Wiley & Sons: New York, 1987), and several publications offered through Intercultural Press, Inc., of Yarmouth, Maine, to name only a few. There are literally hundreds of books about these and related subjects written in English. Go to your library or look in any bookstore.

34 Baldridge, p. 229.

35 Jakob Nielsen, writing in the preface to *Designing User Interfaces for International Users*.

36 "The EMC—Your Export Department," U.S. Government Printing Office, 1980—311-065/195.

37 "Asian Trademark Litigation Continues," Junda Woo and Richard Borsuk, *Wall Street Journal,* February 16, 1994.

38 Ibid.

39 Ricks, pp. 32–44.

40 Bill Tuthill, *Solaris International Developer's Guide*, Prentice-Hall, Englewood Cliffs, New Jersey, 1993, p. 122.

5

CULTURAL BIAS HINDERS THE GOALS OF

INTERNATIONAL TECHNICAL COMMUNICATION.

LEARN HOW TO IDENTIFY IT. UNDERSTAND YOUR

OWN CULTURAL CONTEXT WELL. PERFORM

CULTURAL EDITS ROUTINELY.

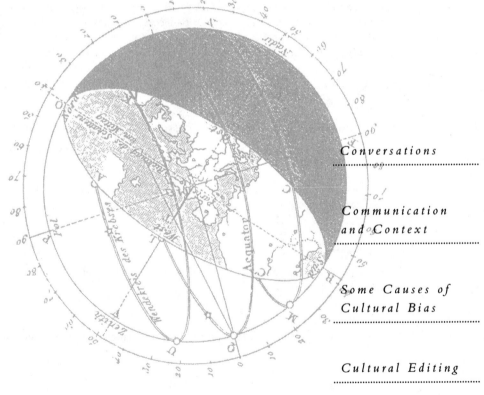

The founder of the European Community, Jean Monnet, once declared, "If I were again facing the challenge to integrate Europe, I would probably start with culture." Culture is the context in which things happen. . . .[1]

IDENTIFYING CULTURAL BIAS 5

Over the past five years, I have had many conversations with international managers, technical-communication managers, and technical communicators around the world about their approaches to international technical communication. I noticed patterns in these conversations. These patterns led to this chapter.

CONVERSATIONS

The question I posed to these people is this: "Do you do anything different to your technical communication when it must be used by people from another country, and if so, do you feel your approach was successful?"

CONVERSATION ONE:
TRANSLATION IS ALL WE NEED TO DO

One manager explained to me that his company did indeed do something different. They translated the documentation from the source language into the target language. That is all. I asked if they edited the source language before they had the translation done. No, he explained, there was no need to take the time to edit the source material. Both source- and target-language documentation described the same product. Why should they be any different? Their product was used the same way all over the world.

In this example, the manager equated translation with localization. To him, the only difference between a user in Tokyo and a user in Bonn was language. I'm sure that if you asked the user in Tokyo and the user in Bonn if they were of the same mind and persuasion, they would respond with an emphatic "No!" Japanese and German cultures are very different. Aside from geography, the most visible difference between the two cultures is, of course, language. However, cross-cultural communication specialists concur that "90 percent of all communication is conveyed by means other than language, in a culture's nonverbal messages. These messages are taken for granted and are transmitted more or less unconsciously."[2]

In international technical communication, we find verbal messages infused with cultural meaning, conveyed in graphics, color, writing style, and examples. By only translating information from one language to another, the manager communicated only a portion of the information. We can only guess at how that information was understood, and we can only guess at the quality of the translation.

The manager also missed an opportunity at saving money on translation. By editing the technical writing, he could have identified several pages of text and graphics that were irrelevant outside the source country. This information was thus translated unnecessarily. References to the Federal Communications Commission (FCC), for example, have relevance in the U.S., but absolutely no relevance in Europe, Asia, or in any other country. What does a reader in Japan or Germany, for example, do with information about the FCC?

CONVERSATION TWO: GOOD TECHNICAL WRITING IS UNIVERSALLY UNDERSTOOD

One technical writer stated that she wrote quality, award-winning technical material. "As long as I adhere to the principles of technical writing, my writing can be understood by anyone in the world. Technical writing is universal." I asked if she had performed an international-user analysis to confirm whether the information needs of the users in the target country were being met. She said "no" and explained that her job was to explain technical information. Technical information is neutral, she added, and is understood by everyone.

In a bold essay, Lorraine Parker of AT&T writes, "Because their writing is technical, writers of documentation believe it is accessible to all technologically literate readers of English. This is a misconception."[3] Parker offers the example of a Chinese woman who is a telecommunications traffic engineer, reads and writes English fluently, and is at AT&T attending a telecommunications traffic engineering course in the U.S. "She would see a chart illustrating seasonal variations of call patterns for Orlando, Florida, but she may not understand its significance. To a U.S. national, high usage in this vacation area during U.S. winter months is implicitly understood. To the Chinese engineer, it is not—or at least, not necessarily."

Like the manager in the previous example, the writers to whom Parker refers make a cultural assumption. In the former conversation, the manager assumed that language was the only barrier between cultures that he needed to overcome. The cultural assumption in this example is that technology is so universal that it automatically renders technical writing clear, understandable, and effective.

CONVERSATION THREE: WE DO NOT NEED TO TRANSLATE OR LOCALIZE ANYTHING

A manager told me simply that people were buying the source product in other countries. There was obviously no need to change anything. I asked if he had received any complaints from users that the source documentation was not translated. "I really don't know. Our distributors handle all that," he said. I asked if the users in other countries were satisfied with a product that had not been localized. He repeated, "our distributors handle all that."

While distributors have a financial investment in seeing that products sell well, they are not necessarily automatic experts in a user's information needs. Distributors are primarily salespeople. They are not technical communicators.

This manager's nonchalance disturbed me. He was not concerned about what happened to the documentation once it left his country. What kind of a message does this attitude send to a user in another country? How would you respond if you were a target user of this product?

Unlike in the other two conversations, this manager admitted that he did not know anything about the users of his company's product in other countries. Unfortunately, he lost a tremendous opportunity to further his cultural knowledge, which could increase the number of international sales and satisfied customers in the end. Had this manager spent some time querying his international distributors, he would have learned how to improve his product and the technical documentation so that both addressed a broader range of user needs. Considering that many successful companies reap over half of their revenue from international sales, this manager made a disappointing decision in ignoring his international buyers.

C O N C L U S I O N S

These conversations exemplify attitudes of cultural bias and demonstrate poor business decisions. In all three cases, it is doubtful that either the user needs or the business needs are being met. The overriding attitude in these cases is, "What I am doing and what I have been doing is good enough." Clearly this attitude is one of mediocrity and not one that puts the user and quality processes first.

If you are succeeding on domestic soil, whether you are a project manager, vice president, or technical writer, you cannot assume that you will automatically succeed in the international arena. Many international-management books attest to this.[4] The same is true for technical communication. Your domestic technical communication is not necessarily transferable to the international arena. To assume as much is to demonstrate cultural bias.

C O M M U N I C A T I O N   A N D   C O N T E X T

Our *cultural context* is a mosaic of values, behaviors, and beliefs that we learn during the course of our lives. Everything we communicate through our speech, behavior, dress, and writing reflects our cultural context. "It is the concrete, observable things like language, food or dress. Culture comes in layers, like an onion. To understand it you have to unpeel it layer by layer."[5]

We introduce cultural bias in international technical communication when we emphasize, consciously or subconsciously, our cultural context.

Cross-cultural communication takes place when people from different cultural contexts need to communicate. International technical communication is a cross-cultural communication vehicle, since it conveys information to people from different cultural contexts.

An important step in minimizing cultural bias in our international technical communication so that we can communicate cross-culturally is to understand our own cultural contexts first. This is not easy. After all, how objective can we really be? But to recognize that how we perform a task, think out a problem, and expect information to be presented is to discover that the most *basic* things we do every day are the products of cultural influence.

Most of our technical communication is based on cultural influences. To date, there are no international standards for international technical communication. The standards that affect international technical communication are often a combination of corporate technical communication standards manuals and very loosely applied industry standards (medical writing standards, software writing standards, government writing standards, etc.), most of which originate in the U.S.[6] All of these standards reflect the cultural context of their creators, and it is often not obvious whether the creators factored in cultural differences when they created the standards. International technical communication that adheres to standards which do not take into account cultural differences, most likely reflect the cultural context within which the standards were created.

Like the technical writer who assumed that technology was universal and the manager who assumed that translation alone was sufficient, we all probably assume, unless we are trained in international technical communication, that the way that we present technical information makes sense to everyone in the world. But this is not necessarily so.

Dr. Jan Ulijn at Eindhoven University of Technology in the Netherlands has conducted some revealing research on culture and technical writing. His research strongly suggests that the cultural context of technical information influences a reader's response to writing. In a recent experiment, Ulijn had 242 French and Dutch participants put the table of contents of a user's manual for a coffee maker in an order that seemed to make sense to them. The seven parts of the table of contents, translated into English, were:

1. Introduction

2. Structure of equipment

3. Technical data

4. Operation

5. Maintenance

6. Troubleshooting

7. Appendix: Service

Both the French and the Dutch subjects agreed on the placement of the Introduction, Structure of Equipment, and the Appendix. However, they disagreed on the placement of remaining parts of the manual. "In sum, the Dutch would prefer more the operation: *What do I have to do to make it work?* The French would stress both operation and technical details: *Why does it work that way?*"[7]

Ulijn's research indicates that we do not all think the same way. We order and filter information to fit our cultural context. When creating international technical communication for people with different cultural contexts, we need to re-examine how we present information.

Cross-cultural communication specialists analyze people's cultural contexts by studying their:

- Responses to messages
- Programs for behavior
- Problem-solving methodologies

The sections that follow will discuss these concepts in greater detail.

RESPONSE TO MESSAGES

Edward T. Hall and Mildred Reed Hall, noted cultural anthropologists, write, "Cultural communications are deeper and more complex than spoken or written messages. *The essence of effective cross-cultural communication has more to do with releasing the right responses than with sending the 'right' messages.*"[8]

As we see in Ulijn's research, the 242 participants had different responses to the order in which the same information in a user's manual was presented. Re-ordering the information engaged the reader's interest and attention more.

In order to release the right response in your readers, you need to understand the context that would most likely cause such a response. This is persuasion. This is communication. International technical communication must be flexible enough to accommodate different communication styles simply because this is what an international audience demands. International competition makes it too easy for your audience to turn to another source for its information, a source that accommodates your audience's cultural context in every aspect of the communication process in a better way.

MENTAL PROGRAMMING, PROGRAMS FOR BEHAVIOR

Geert Hofstede, author of *Cultures and Organizations: Software of the Mind*, defines culture as "patterns of thinking, feeling, and acting *mental programs*, or, as the subtitle goes, *software of the mind*."[9]

Edward T. Hall defines culture this way:

Because culture is experienced personally, very few individuals see it for what it is—*a program for behavior*. Members of a common culture not only share information, they share methods of coding, storing, and retrieving that information. These methods vary from culture to culture. Knowing what kind of information people from other cultures require is one key to effective international communication.[10]

In a paper review research on reading and its effect on document design, Jan H. Spyridakis and Michael J. Wenger note research on cultural influence and reading comprehension. The research they cite seems to confirm that of Hofstede and Hall. They conclude:

> Many researchers have noted the profound influence that cultural schemata can exert on a reader's comprehension. Steffensen, Joag-Dev, and Anderson compared the performance of readers from different countries (India, U.S.) and found a significant interaction of nationality and content, with each cultural group performing best (recalling more idea units and reading more quickly) with a passage from its own culture [M.S. Steffenson, C. Joag-Dev, and R.C. Anderson, "A Cross-cultural Perspective on Reading Comprehension," *Reading Research Quarterly 15,* no. 1 (1979):10–29]. When reading passages based on other cultures, each cultural group made more errors in elaborating idea units and constructed inappropriate schemata based on content schemata from its own culture.[11]

If we create international technical communication that assumes a specific program for behavior, and if our audience's program for behavior is different from the one we assume, we run the risk of poor communication, or worse, eliciting a response other than the one intended.

We find an example of cultural assumptions and technical communication in a paper by Mohsen Mirshafiei, Assistant Professor of English and Comparative Literatures at California State University. He noticed that his technical writing students, many of whom were from countries other than the U.S., had a difficult time presenting technical information in a clear, straightforward manner. "For example, my Middle Eastern students were using circular instead of linear structures to communicate technical and scientific information. My Japanese students write in a vague manner which was difficult to understand."[12] He offers an example of a letter of recommendation from Iran that he received on behalf of a student, Afshin. From this letter, which is written in a style that is markedly different from a typical American recommendation, Mirshafiei concludes that culture has a distinct influence on how facts (technical information) are presented in technical writing.[13]

While he provides some rich evidence to support the existence of different communication styles, Mirshafiei makes the cultural assumption throughout his paper
that the American writing style (clear, direct, straightforward) is how these
students should be presenting technical information. However, there is no
evidence to support this cultural assumption, unless Mirshafiei further assumes
that his students will write to an exclusively American audience. Mirshafiei does
not take his research a step further to ask the question, "Do these cultural
differences in writing style contribute to or detract from reading comprehension
in the target cultures, respectively?" In this case, would Afshin be able to communicate technical information more effectively with Iranian readers if he wrote in
his culturally learned communication style than if he wrote using an American
communication style? Mirshafiei implies as much, but does not provide supporting evidence.

PROBLEM-SOLVING METHODOLOGY

"Every culture distinguishes itself from others by the specific solutions it chooses
to certain problems."[14]

As we saw in the LYRE example in Chapter 4, the design of the LYRE software,
which let students analyze poetry, relied on cultural assumptions of problem solving that were inaccurate for some Scandinavian students. Students were taught to
solve a particular problem—analyze a poem—in a certain way. The software prohibited students from analyzing poetry independently. The students had to
choose from a set of predetermined responses to questions about the poems. In
France this was culturally acceptable, since the teacher would remain the ultimate
authority on how to interpret the poem. This design was culturally unacceptable
in Scandinavian countries, since students in those countries were encouraged to
interpret the poems on their own.[15]

We can infer from this example that French students were taught to consult an
authority on a subject to solve a problem. The Scandinavian students were taught
to create their own solutions to a problem. The two problem-solving methodologies are different. International technical communication (and, of course, the
product that it describes) that teaches users how to perform a particular task needs
to consider how people in a target country approach new tasks if it is to communicate successfully.

SOME CAUSES OF CULTURAL BIAS

There are many causes of cultural bias. Here are four that you will need to
understand to communicate successfully.

TECHNOLOGY IS NOT A UNIVERSAL LANGUAGE

Technology is not understood in the same way around the world, nor is it necessarily used for the same reasons around the world. Technical communicators need to seek more culturally accurate ways of explaining technology to people in target countries. It is already difficult for people to learn how to use technology. Let us not make it more difficult for them by introducing culturally bound examples and communication styles.

SENIORITY IN A COMPANY REDUCES CROSS-CULTURAL SENSITIVITY

Lorraine Parker, who wrote of cultural bias in technical writing at AT&T, comments: "If you have more than five years with AT&T, you will have to examine your documentation for 'self-explanatory' allusions which are anything but self-explanatory to the new employee—especially the local country national."[16]

If we restrict our environment, we limit our range of influence and reflect a set of values, behaviors, and beliefs more predictably. However, we also restrict the breadth of our values, behaviors, and beliefs—a body of knowledge—which may cause us to introduce cultural bias into our technical communication.

In Parker's example, technical writers who had been at AT&T for more than five years had, in her opinion, restricted their corporate environment. They assumed that AT&T employees worldwide shared the same corporate values, behaviors, and beliefs as AT&T employees in the U.S., where AT&T's corporate headquarters are located. The technical manuals, which were written by U.S.-based AT&T technical writers, were consequently unsuccessful when exported.

LARGE COUNTRIES WITH LARGE DOMESTIC MARKETS ENCOURAGE ETHNOCENTRISM

David Victor, a professor of business at Eastern Michigan University, describes cultural bias as more common in companies based in countries large enough to support a domestic market. "The large domestic markets of these nations and the resulting freedom to adopt ethnocentric principles to their overall strategy make truly international leadership unlikely. No necessity exists to force supranational cooperation, and thus tendencies become the norm even among the most multinational Japanese or U.S. enterprises."[17]

Ulijn, a native of the Netherlands and an associate professor in Technology and Communication in the Psychology and Language section at Eindhoven University of Technology, confirms this observation, "In the Netherlands, you cannot work for more than 5 years without constant interaction outside the country."[18] This is because of the small size of the country, the size of its domestic market, and its proximity to other countries.

INCREASING GLOBAL COOPERATION ALSO INCREASES PAROCHIALISM

Commenting on how Europeans seemed to be responding to the European Union, Marcio Moreira, the chief creative officer of the international division of McCann Erickson Advertising Agency, wrote in 1990, "The British have never been more British, the French never more French, the Italians never more Italian. As the idea of a unified Europe comes to fruition, the various nationalities' sense of cultural identity becomes heightened and people just retrench."[19]

It is easy to speculate that this heightened awareness of cultural identity will only increase over the next several years, as many parts of the world cultivate their economic alliances. If such a situation holds true, then technical communicators need to be even more aware of their readers' cultural contexts. Implied in the quotation by Moreira is the notion that anything "new" or "different" is threatening. Technology falls into both categories, especially when it is used in the economic climate causing the stress. At the very least, technical writers need to empathize with changes in Europe and in other parts of the world where economic situations are slowly adapting to these radical changes. Information products that have been localized for these specific areas may indeed be well received.

CULTURAL EDITING

There are no cultural bias checkers, like there are spelling checkers and grammar checkers. And how could there be unless we stereotyped every culture in the world? Identifying cultural bias in your information products, then, is a necessary but subjective process.

There is very little information available about cultural bias in information products. This whole arena is new and still developing. Maybe, two to five years from now, we will have tools or processes to perform cultural edits with more certainty.

There are known categories of information to start with against which you can check your international technical communication for cultural bias. These categories have been developed over the past five to seven years by the computer software industry. The software industry identified these categories out of a need to internationalize software products efficiently, effectively, and affordably.

Following these categories, I provide a procedure for honing your sensitivity to cultural bias. The object of the procedure is to make you aware of your cultural context and how it can influence your international technical communication.

CATEGORIES FOR CULTURAL EDITING

The following is a list of categories that can be culturally bound. This list is not complete, but it does provide a place to begin. Editing for cultural content is different from editing for translation, so some categories you might expect to see are not listed here, but are covered in Chapter 9.

You do not need to remove information in these categories from your international technical communication. Rather, you need to ask yourself: Does information in this category absolutely have to be in this product to convey the information I need to convey? Research the answer to this question.

If the information does not need to be in the product, remove it. If the information does need to be in the product, start compiling a list of all the cultural variations in that category that are relevant to the countries to which your company is exporting. Discover ways to accommodate many cultural contexts through better internationalization and localization processes.

- Dates and date formats
- Currency and currency formats
- Number formatting
- Accounting practices
- List separators
- Sorting and collating orders
- Time, time zones, and time formats
- Units of measurement
- Symbols (in English, some symbols are / and &)
- Telephone numbers
- Addresses and address formats

- Date formats

- Historic events

- Acronyms and abbreviations (including ones in Latin)

- Forms of address and titles

- Geographic references

- Technology (electrical outlets, computer keyboards, printer page size capabilities)

- Legal information (warranties, copyrights, patents, trademarks, health- and safety-related information)

- Page sizes

- Binding methods

- Illustrations of people

- Hand gestures

- Clothing

- Many everyday items (refrigerators, trash cans, post office boxes)

- Architecture

- Popular culture

- The role of women in the workplace

- The relationship of men and women in the workplace

- Management practices

- Languages

- Text directionality

- Humor

- Colors

- Communication styles

- Learning styles (the relationship of the instructor and the students)

HONING CULTURAL SENSITIVITY

The following steps focus on finding artifacts of *your* cultural context in information products (a user's guide, training manual, illustration, user interface design, or online help system). Learning more about your own cultural context can make you more aware of your cultural identity and biases.

1. Complete the international variables worksheet, presented in Chapter 4, for your country. Consider both superficial international variables and those that probe beneath the surface.

2. Create your cultural profile based on the information you collected from the international variables worksheet. Ask yourself these questions:

   ▪ How do you respond to different situations?

   ▪ How do you behave in different situations?

   ▪ How do you solve problems?

3. Identify all the occurrences in your information product that suggest your cultural context, using the categories for cultural editing, the international variables worksheet, and your cultural profile.

4. Consider ways that you can adapt your international technical communication to accommodate many cultural differences. For example, you could show all units of measurement in inches and in their metric equivalents. You could redesign the training modules to accommodate different learning and teaching styles.

5. Update your corporate technical communication style guide to reflect what you have learned about your cultural context.

SOME CURES FOR CULTURAL BIAS

Any information product that reflects a particular cultural context is a *localized variant*. A localized variant is very effective if its audience has a similar or compatible cultural context to that of the communicator. A localized variant is inappropriate and possibly disastrous if the cultural context of the audience is different from that of the communicator. As stated earlier, effective international technical communication balances cultural understanding and economy. How much money do you spend and what is the trade-off? Therefore, creating a localized variant makes sense only if it makes good business sense.

International technical communication needs to accommodate many cultural contexts—simultaneously. If it does so, it becomes an internationalized product and not a localized variant. A localized variant builds from an internationalized product, as explained in Chapter 2.

I think it is especially difficult for technical communicators whose native language is English to learn that an information product in English is only a variant. English is spoken in so many parts of the world, and it is often the language of choice for many international business meetings. Its ubiquitousness has made it too easy for native English speakers to assume that information products written in English must be the internationalized product itself. Microsoft has even created an acronym to address this bias toward English, *EJAL*, "English is just another language."[20] Also, English around the world differs greatly. Loreto Todd and Ian Hancock filled a 520-page book with as many of the nuances of English as they could collect. They have entries, for example, on American English, British English, Canadian English, Australian English, New Zealand English, Indian English, and so on.[21] Aside from the nuances of language, the cultural context of native English-speaking people is vastly different.

Some additional ways to make your international technical communication less dependent on your cultural context are explained here. I have also provided some exercises you can try to continue to hone your cultural sensitivity.

U N D E R S T A N D Y O U R C U L T U R A L C O N T E X T — W H E R E A R E Y O U C O M I N G F R O M ?

Glenn Fisher, a U.S. Foreign Service officer for twenty-two years, and currently a professor-diplomat at the Monterey Institute of International Studies, put it best:

> Looking for contrasts in the information bases that contribute to your and your counterpart's mindsets should be routine. . . . One takes the content of the local press and media seriously and analyzes it carefully (and does the same with one's own press and media). . . . The objective is to be able to diagnose mindsets in terms of the information bases that help explain them.[22]

Fisher recommends that we study and analyze current events and trends (popular culture) to learn more about ourselves and other cultural contexts. This is very good advice, and it is certainly easy to do.

One exercise you can do is to follow one international news story and go to the library and compare how the press in different countries covered the same story. Monitor and collect the stories over time. Analyze the style, content, and facts presented in the stories. The three questions to ask when analyzing and comparing the stories in different countries are:

1. What are the cultural contexts that caused people to respond to a particular situation?

2. How do people behave in different situations?

3. How do people solve problems?

Another exercise is to look at the contexting square in Chapter 4. Identify a country on the contexting diagonal that seems as far from your country as possible. Use this country as a point for comparison. Research the audience in that country to discover where your communication style might pose some problems. For example, Switzerland and Japan are at exactly opposite ends of the diagonal. The cultural contexts of the Swiss and the Japanese are at the highest degree of difference. Studying the cultural context of one country makes the other more visible.

EMBRACE DIVERSITY—ADJUST YOUR ATTITUDE

There are many frustrations and incompatibilities that arise when communicating to a multicultural audience. Simply accept this. If your attitude toward these differences is in any way negative, you risk introducing cultural bias in your communication. View the experience as a way of learning how to do things differently, or expanding your cultural IQ. This can only improve your ability to communicate technical information to a multicultural audience. You may find that another approach to a problem is a better one. Embrace this slogan: **Think globally, act locally**.

SEEK MULTICULTURAL EXPERIENCES—BROADEN YOUR HORIZONS

Travel. Read about other countries and other cultures. Learn another language. Entertain people who are visiting from other countries. Host an international student. Attend lectures on other countries that are given by people from other countries. Eat at an ethnic restaurant. Join a chamber of commerce from another country. Join an ethnic social group to participate in traditions from other countries. Correspond with people from other countries.

All of these experiences expose you to different ideas, different ways of thinking, different values. This sort of exposure develops your international attitude and makes you a better international communicator.

SOLICIT FEEDBACK—
COMMUNICATE WITH TARGET USERS

Always ask for feedback. Find out how users in other countries responded to your international technical communication. If possible, communicate with them in person, by telephone, by fax, modem, or mail. Have them help you understand where your cultural contexts differ and where in your international technical communication you failed to consider their approach to problems.

Stephen Rhinesmith, a former U.S. ambassador, also offers this advice to international managers. "Ask a colleague from another culture to give you semiannual feedback on how your management actions are seen from his or her cultural perspective."[23] Consider doing this monthly, since the economic landscape changes rapidly.

As a technical communicator, consider using one of the professional organizations, like the Society for Technical Communication (STC) or the International Council for Technical Communication (INTECOM), to find a colleague in another country. Exchange samples of international technical communication with this person and focus on providing each other with cultural feedback. Ask your colleague to identify parts of your international technical communication that are unclear, or that seem culturally biased. Explore with your colleague other ways of presenting the same information. Use these observations to improve your international technical communication.

END NOTES

[1] Fons Trompenaars, *Riding the Waves of Culture: Understanding Cultural Diversity in Business*, Nicholas Brealey Publishing, London, 1993, p. 8.

[2] Edward T. Hall and Mildred Reed Hall, *Understanding Cultural Differences*, Intercultural Press, Yarmouth, Maine, 1990, p. xiv.

[3] Lorraine Parker, "Documentation for the Global Market: Some Useful Guidelines," *The Proceedings of the Third Annual AT&T Customer Documentation Symposium*, October 1990.

[4] Here are some sources, but note that this list is not complete. Philip R. Harris and Robert T. Moran, *Managing Cultural Differences*, 3rd Ed., Gulf Publishing Company, Houston, 1991. Glen Fisher, *Mindsets: The Role of Culture and Perception in International Relations*, Intercultural Press, Yarmouth, Maine, 1988. Stephen H. Rhinesmith, *A Manager's Guide to Globalization*, Business One, Irwin, Homewood, Illinois, 1993. Daniel Burstein, *Euroquake*, Simon & Schuster, New York, 1991. Collin Randlesome, William Brierly, Kevin Bruton, Colin Gordon, and Peter King, *Business Cultures in Europe*, Butterworth-Heinemann, Boston, Massachusetts, 1991. David A. Ricks, *Blunders in International Business*, Blackwell Publishers, Cambridge, Massachusetts, 1993. Gary P. Ferraro, *The Cultural Dimension of International Business*, 2nd Ed., Prentice-Hall, Englewood Cliffs, New Jersey, 1994.

5 Trompenaars, p. 6.

6 There is currently much work being done in Germany and in Japan regarding standards for technical communication. Whether these standards apply to technical communication for domestic use or for international use is a question I cannot answer. These countries can develop technical communication standards that educate the rest of the world on how to communicate technical information to people in their countries and optimize comprehension and effectiveness.

7 Jan Ulijn, "Is Cultural Rewriting of American Technical Documents Needed for the European Market: Some Experimental Evidence from French and Dutch Technical Documents," *International Dimensions of Technical Communication*, Society for Technical Communication, 1995.

8 Hall and Hall, p. 4.

9 Geert Hofstede, p. 4.

10 Hall and Hall, p. xiv.

11 Jan H. Spyridakis and Michael J. Wenger, "Writing for Human Performance: Relating Reading Research to Document Design," *Technical Communication*, 39, no. 2 (1992) 210.

12 Moshen Mirshafiei, "Culture as an Element in Teaching Technical Writing," *1992 Proceedings*, Society for Technical Communication, p. 557.

13 Mirshafiei, p. 558.

14 Trompenaars, p. 8.

15 Jakob Nielsen, *Designing User Interfaces for International Use*, Elsevier, New York, 1990, p. 39.

16 Parker, p. 2.

17 David Victor, *International Business Communication*, Harper Collins, New York, 1992, p. 57.

18 Correspondence with Dr. Jan Ulijn, August 1, 1994.

19 M. Moreira, "As the World Turns," *Advertising Age*, April, 2, 1990, p. 17.

20 Ulrich Henes, "Building a Case for (and against) Localization: How Symantec, Apple, Lotus and Microsoft Decide When to Localize," *Software Publisher*, July/August 1994, p. 33.

21 Ian Hancock and Loreto Todd, *International English Usage*, New York University Press, New York, 1987.

22 Fisher, p. 175.

23 Rhinesmith, p. 218.

6

GOOD DESIGN TRADITIONALLY ENHANCES READABILITY. NEW DESIGNS ARE NEEDED TO CONSIDER THE EFFECTS OF TRANSLATION AND LOCALIZATION.

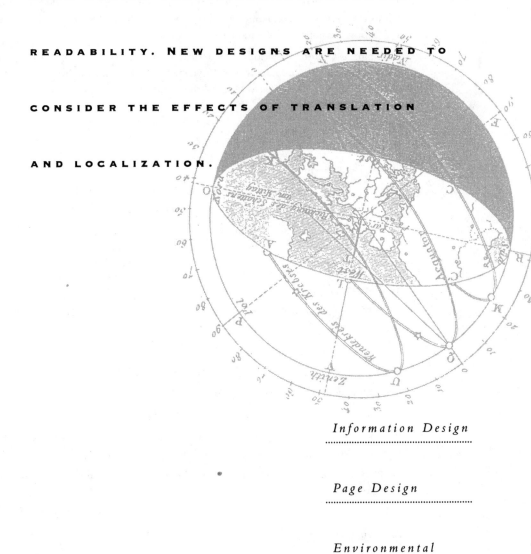

Information Design

....

Page Design

....

Environmental Concerns

....

DESIGN ISSUES

6

There are some general design issues that you should consider at the beginning of an international technical communication project. The word *design* is used in its broadest sense here. These design issues can affect graphics, text, online information, and multimedia, and your entire approach to an international technical-communication project. Considering these design issues before beginning an international technical-communication project ensures a smoother and more efficient project-development cycle.

The design issues discussed in this chapter include:

- Information design   ■ Page design   ■ Environmental concerns

INFORMATION DESIGN

A design for international technical communication, whether it is printed or available online, should meet these criteria:

- A design must allow for easy and minimal localization and minimal translation.

- A design must minimize redundancy, which adds to the cost of translation.

- A design must be flexible, accommodating, and, in the end, more cost effective.

- A design must be sensitive to the cultural expectations of a target audience.

- A design must maximize usability.

A review of some of the more popular information designs since the mid-1980s reveals the flaws in most designs concerning international technical

communication. The truth is that no one design to date offers a solution
that addresses all the complex design requirements for international technical
communication.

MODULAR PUBLICATIONS

In the mid-1980s, the concept of modular design in technical publications was
introduced most successfully by Edmond Weiss, in his book *How to Write a Usable
User Manual*. In this book, Weiss defines a modular publication as "a series of
small, cohesive chunks of technical communication of predictable size, content,
and appearance. Once the design—the exact sequence—of the modules is frozen,
it becomes possible to treat the one, large, complicated manual as a set of many,
small, nearly independent manuals."[1]

Many technical publications departments that I worked in as an independent
technical writing consultant during that time tried to apply Weiss's suggestions.
They all failed for a few reasons. Weiss's suggestions required that they repeat
information for the sake of keeping these modules independent. Readers hated
this repetition, so most technical publications departments replaced the repetition
with endless cross-references. Readers hated this, too, since they had to flip
through the same or, worse, many books to complete a task. So, while the idea of
modularity made much sense as a writing technique, no company that I worked
with was able to make it work for users.

TASK-ORIENTED PUBLICATIONS

Then, in the late 1980s and early 1990s, the modular manual was replaced by the
task-oriented manual. This approach remains very popular in many software
companies in the U.S. However, is it the best design with respect to ease of localization and the need for minimal translation?

A task-oriented manual identifies most if not all of the tasks that someone can
perform by using a product. Marcia Sweezey, an internationalization consultant,
notes that when task-oriented manuals were first introduced, tasks were often
defined in terms of the product (How to Delete a File) and not in terms of the
tasks users were trying to perform (Cleaning Up the Office).[2]

Many readers, in the U.S. at least, tend to like the task-oriented design when it
describes user tasks and not product tasks, because it is oriented toward productivity, and immediate gratification. The product becomes a productivity tool, one
that does not need to be understood as much as it needs to be used to accomplish
some task. Most chapter headings are task oriented. The chapter contents are

really procedures that offer step-by-step instructions on how to perform the specific task. There are many variations on the task-oriented manual, but, for the most part, this description is essentially the norm.

The task-oriented manual has some flaws with respect to ease of localization and the need for minimal translation. For one, performing a task can require using many features in a software product. What if one or more features are customized or even removed from a localized variant of the product that will be exported to one or more target countries? One or more tasks may need to be rewritten to accommodate these changes. This means that one or more versions of the manual need to be maintained.

Another flaw in task-oriented manuals is that they are designed with the impatient American user in mind. These manuals assume that the user wants to open the book to task 3, for example, and finish it as soon as possible. The users may never read instructions for task 4 or 5. This approach is based on a cultural assumption and may not work in other countries. Users from other countries may want to learn all about a product, from its design philosophy to its most intimate technical details. Clearly a user's information needs and how task-oriented manuals address them should be more carefully examined.

And finally, task-oriented manuals repeat information, although not as much as modular manuals do. Users are told how to fill in the same dialog boxes, for example, since some dialog boxes are used repeatedly within the same software product. While some repetition is necessary, and even desirable in some cases, it does add to the word count on which translation is based.

THE ALPHABETIC REFERENCE MANUAL

This design is a favorite among engineers and other very technical users in the U.S. This design usually provides dense technical details organized under a single heading, like a command name, all of which is then organized alphabetically. The way that these manuals are used is analogous to the way that encyclopedias and dictionaries are used. This design assumes a sophisticated level of understanding of the product and that the manual is used only as reference material or for significant technical information that cannot be derived from using the product.

It is very common for companies to decide against having very technical information translated. The assumption is, at least in the U.S., that very technical people read English. There is no need to translate. The concern here is that while this may be true today, will it be true tomorrow?

This design is also often applied to information for a less technical audience. Word-Perfect continues to organize its user manual alphabetically, for example.

The problem with organizing information alphabetically is that when it is translated, key words are different and begin with a different letter. You have to reorder everything. This means that every language variant of the manual would need to be reorganized. The Spanish version and the French version would be different from the German and the Dutch versions. This presents obvious cost and maintenance issues.

Minimalist Publications

The latest trend is toward minimalist manuals, an idea based on the writings of John Carroll.[3] The design principle of minimalism is analogous to that of Mies van der Rohe, an architect, whose famous quotation is "less is more." Reduce the content of the manual to its minimum, allowing users to learn on their own and to apply their own learning styles. Introductory information, summaries, thorough procedures, and a thorough discussion of all tasks are elements that minimalism discourages.

There is no discussion in minimalist writing about a multicultural audience. Learning style is a cultural issue. Minimalism requires much usability testing and a thorough user analysis. It is very possible that usability testing and a thorough user analysis performed for many target countries will yield contradictory results. In this case, how do you determine what information to exclude and what information to include?

This design is very good for reducing the amount of information in a book, and therefore reducing the amount of words that need to be translated. There are two problems with this method, though. Translators might have a more difficult time with a book like this because they rely often on this explanatory information to provide better, more accurate translations. Minimalism would also require more than one version if it was expected to handle different user needs and learning styles. Sweezey notes, "Minimalist documents only work when the rest of the product (software, for example) is designed such that it is intuitive."[4]

Commercial How-to Books

There is another current trend that needs some serious attention. There is currently a high-volume business in selling how-to books for the high-technology market, mostly relating to software for the personal computer. Almost every major book publisher in the world is active in this market. In the U.S., for

Modularity

example, the *Dummies* series is enormously popular (*DOS for Dummies, Word for Dummies, 1-2-3 for Dummies, Internet for Dummies*, and so on). There are hundreds of books aimed at a more computer-literate audience, too. Books on UNIX, programming in C, and so on, which are not textbooks but are written for practicing professionals, are numerous.

On a trip through Europe and Asia, Sweezey found that users were using these how-to books more often than they were using the manuals provided with the products. This is also true in the U.S. Why?

It would seem that these books address a need for varying levels of information that is audience specific and culturally targeted. The popularity of these books seems to suggest that the manuals provided by software manufacturers, for example, do not satisfy the information needs of many users, which is the contention of the minimalists.

Since these books are written independently of the corporate environment, they pose no overhead or additional expenses to a company. They are an attractive alternative to solving the often contradictory needs of many target users, domestic and international. These how-to books produced by independent writers seem to meet users' needs for content, cost, and size.

However, these books usually offer the approach of one author, and often assume a very particular level of technical knowledge. These books are also hardly exhaustive and sometimes not even comprehensive. They reflect the knowledge and technical skills of the writer. Also, clearly, the company that manufactures the product has little or no control over what the author of the book says about the product.

Also, for as many products that these how-to books describe, there are as many and probably more products that they do not. Would this type of book be appropriate for all products?

ONE COMPANY'S INFORMATION DESIGNS

In the Digital book *Developing International User Information*, the authors introduce a new meaning to the idea of modular publications. "[M]odularity means the separation of information into discrete entities, or modules. Using modular user information, translators can rearrange and translate information as necessary, without having to extensively restructure and rewrite the original user information set."[5] The authors go on to describe three modular designs:

- **Modularity by audience.** This design involves creating separate manuals that address the needs of a specific audience. Some audience-specific manuals include installation guide, getting started guide, user's guide, quick reference guide, and programmer's reference manual. Some of this information is duplicated in online tutorials and help systems.

Advantages: The design allows you to segregate information that is to be translated from information that is not to be translated. For example, programmer's reference guides are not translated at Digital.

Disadvantages: There are many manuals. There is duplication of information between the printed information and the online information.

- **Modularity by task**. This design is the same as the task-oriented publications described previously. The design focuses on the tasks that users can perform to be productive using the system.

Advantages: This design focuses on productivity.

Disadvantages: Tasks span many product features, which may be replaced or customized for target countries. Tasks assume a particular learning style that may not be appropriate for a target audience. Tasks repeat information.

- **Modularity by function**. This design focuses on the functions of the product itself, like software functions or hardware features.

Advantages: This is a truly modular design and can be modified with more ease than any other design.

Disadvantages: This design does not teach users how to use the product in the context of their work; it only describes what the product is or what it contains.

ONLINE INFORMATION AND PRINTED INFORMATION

In addition to selecting an information design, you need to determine the relationship between online information and printed information. More and more companies are offering online information in addition to or instead of their printed information. Online help systems, tutorials, CD-ROMs that contain entire documentation sets, and multimedia presentations are all common online information products.

Repeating information in the online information products and the printed products may not be desirable, since this could add to the cost of translation.

Jon Lavine, a senior editor at Berlitz Translation Services, notes, "If there is an easy way to pick up and drop repeated information into information products in different media, it may not be so hard or add to the cost."[6] However, consider the effect of redundancy on the information needs of your users.

I discuss later in this chapter additional considerations like the user's physical environment and your choice of tools for creating online information that may also affect your design decision on the relationship between online and printed information.

A POSSIBLE SOLUTION: COORDINATED INFORMATION

Marcia Sweezey created an information design that may provide a solution to the problems that localization and translation introduce. The design is called *Coordinated Information Solution*.[7] Sweezey describes the design as offering a project management solution to the information design problems that occur in international technical communication. Figure 6.1 illustrates the Coordinated Information Solution as a 4-panel window.

FIGURE 6.1: **The elements of Sweezey's Coordinated Information Solution.**

The elements are:

- **User Interface.** This should strive to make the product accessible to users. It should include context-sensitive help.

- **Online Information.** The bulk of the information should be here, where it is integrated into the product. The content should depend on user needs (online tutorial), as should the media (multimedia presentation).

- **Training.** This should be designed to add value over and above printed and online information. Usually it is only a rehash of what is in the documentation, adding little value for customers. Customers should not have to create their own customized training to account for the redundancy in training and documentation.

- **Printed Documentation.** This should offer a getting-started guide, and that is all. There should be a minimal amount of printed documentation. Sweezey notes, "This is where you can save the most money in localization. By minimizing the amount of printed documentation, [Digital Equipment Corporation] reduced its localization budget by nearly 26 percent. Much of it was a result of eliminating paper (printing) and unnecessary redundancy (translation of redundancy, time spent looking for redundancy) and all the overhead associated that goes with tracking this overhead."

Some of the advantages that Sweezey's design offers include:

- All the elements share a terms glossary (product terms, conventions for documentation)

- Each element is designed for ease of localization.

- All elements share core information—invariant information that can be reused. This can include graphics, text blocks, and tables.

Sweezey adds that you can modify the elements of the design to include other information products, like marketing messages. The point of the design is to integrate information products to make localization and translation easy and affordable. By approaching information design from a project management perspective, Sweezey states, you can begin to address these problems. Chapter 14 introduces many ways to integrate information throughout a corporation.

PAGE DESIGN

The design of a single page or of a two-page spread has an important effect on the ease with which information can be translated and localized for target countries, and on its usability.

TEXT EXPANSION

Text expansion, also referred to as *translation spread*, is a phenomenon that can occur when text is translated from the source language into a target language. The translation may require more physical space on a page than the source text occupied. For example, when English text is translated into Spanish or German, its translation typically requires 30 percent more physical space on a page than the English text occupied.

In general, most translation companies recommend that you create a page and document design that can accommodate a 30 percent text expansion rate, which is a statistical average across all languages. (See Table 10.1 for text expansion percentages.) Jon Lavine, a senior translation editor at Berlitz Translation Services, adds, "Translations, in general, tend to be wordier than the source document because of the nuances that translators add to ensure meaning. Also, if English is the source language and Chinese is the target language, you often get shrinkage and not expansion."[8]

International Language Engineering (ILE) Corporation notes that individual words and phrases can sometimes require 200 percent text expansion because the character count doubles in the target language.[9] Headings, callouts for graphics, and the title of a manual, are examples of text that can double in length after translation. ILE adds:

> Documentation designed without considering text expansion is difficult to localize: graphics may require relocation, or even redesign—as may tables whose cells are nearly full in English. Page and section breaks that work well in your original may not work as well when migrated to other languages.[10]

Fonts in other languages may not correspond in type size to the type size of the target language. You should research the font choices you have in target languages when creating the page design; for example, if the source language uses a Roman alphabet (English, French, German), research the fonts and type sizes of Korean, Japanese, and Chinese, and those of Middle Eastern and Eastern European languages.

Some suggestions that can help you reserve space for text expansion follow.

- Choose a larger type size for the source language, if the source language tends to expand after translation. Use a smaller type size for the translation. John Deere's tractor documentation does this.[11] I conducted a small test of my own, too, which you might consider doing on your source documentation.[12] I filled a page with text in 10-point type. I used Times Roman for my font. I selected all of the text and changed it to 12-point type. The increase in the point size forced repagination. The first page remained full of text, but now there was a second page that had text on it. About one third of the second page was filled with text. This simple experiment provided me with a way to accommodate a 30 percent text expansion from English into a target language like German or Spanish.

  Consider doing this with headlines, too.

  The drawback to this suggestion is that the source document is longer, which may increase the production cost of the document, among other problems.

- Increase the width of the margins for the source document if the text expands after translation. Decrease the margin size for the translation. In another simple test I conducted, I set all four margins to one inch (2.54 cm). I filled the page with text. Then I doubled the width of the left and right margins. I did not increase the top or bottom margins, since these rarely change in size in documentation. Once again, the increase in the margin forced repagination. The first page was filled with text and about one third of the second page was filled with text. The increase in the margins allowed me to accommodate a 30 percent text expansion rate after translation from the English source text.

- More complex suggestions require a fairly sophisticated knowledge of typography and publishing, plus software that can support this complexity. Kerning, leading, and space between paragraphs are all parts of a page design that can be adapted to accommodate text expansion in target variants of the documentation.

Another very important consideration regarding text expansion is the tool you use to create the source text. Will it allow for some of these suggestions? See Chapter 12, "Tools Issues," for more information.

GRAPHICS AND TEXT

The page design should consider how graphics and text relate to one another, especially when text expansion occurs. Text expansion can force the repagination of a document. If your information product is a newsletter, a product-data sheet, or information for packaging, where space is at a premium, repagination can create some serious problems in the design if you have not left room for expansion. And if you use a software product that locks graphics onto a certain page and not to a certain part of the text, you can create problems that a translator may not catch, especially if you do not reference the graphic in text. Also, most translation companies that offer publishing services strive to have the translated document look exactly like the original, page breaks and all. Repagination is something that they look out for.

If you need to change any of the graphics, like screen shots of a localized variant, is this easy to do in your design? Like the information design, page design needs to be flexible. You do not want the translation company to have to re-create your page design manually. You should strive to make as much of your page design as automatic or as structured as possible to increase the ease with which it can be localized.

Aldus Corporation wanted to have graphics in its documentation be culturally specific for some of the target countries to which it was exported. This was a business decision. Aldus felt that its product, Aldus PageMaker, was a publishing tool that had to demonstrate its capabilities in the documentation that accompanied it. Aldus's product was also competing with more traditional publishing methods that were predominant in many target countries. Aldus felt that if it addressed cultural considerations in both its product and its documentation, it would be more successful in the target countries.

Aldus created a page design to accommodate its need to have different graphics for many of the target countries to which it exported some of its products. The page design used a two-page spread, as shown in Figure 6.2.

There are two flows in this design. The flow on the left-hand pages is reserved for graphics. The flow on the right-hand pages is reserved for text. Both flows were largely independent of the other. Thus, the page design was actually a skeleton for two separate flows of information. There are many software products that allow you to identify separate flows (sometimes called *streams*) and assign them to specific parts of your page design.[13]

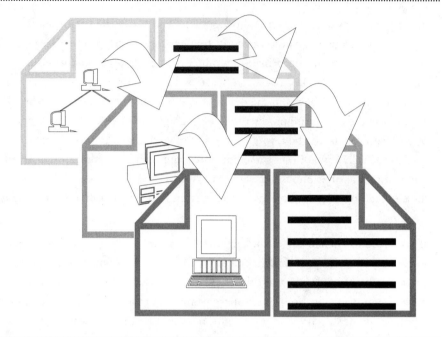

FIGURE 6.2: **Representation of a page design Aldus Corporation used to accommodate localized graphics in its documentation.**

For a localized variant of the Aldus PageMaker documentation, two files were imported into the document skeleton:

1. A file of graphics containing graphics that were specifically designed with the cultural context of the target users in mind.

2. A file of text that was translated into the target language and that was localized to reflect the cultural context of the target users. The text also reflected any engineering changes that were made to the localized variant of Aldus PageMaker.

The advantage of this page design is that it allowed Aldus to change graphics and text easily to accommodate the cultural context of the target users. It also allowed for text expansion with no impact on the page design.

The potential disadvantage of this page design is that it may cost more money to maintain separate documentation variants that are so localized.

Aldus Corporation did not go to these extremes for every target country. It did this only for target countries in which its product, Aldus PageMaker, was to be the first product of this kind to the target market and therefore would be competing with traditional publishing methods. In other words, Aldus used radical localization of graphics and text as a market-entry strategy.

Companies other than Aldus Corporation have different solutions to designing pages to accommodate graphics and text.

Some companies use a two-column grid like the one shown in Figure 6.3. The two-column grid allows for graphic and text independence, and for text expansion. A good example of how a two-column design is used for text and graphics is in William Horton's book *Illustrating Computer Documentation*.

Perhaps the most common page design for text and graphics is one where graphics are inserted in frames. The frame is anchored in the text so that when the text expands, forcing repagination, the frame is still associated with the text that refers to it. Some software products may not have this capability, but most do. If you have a choice of using a floating frame or an anchored frame, you should choose to use an anchored frame to allow for the repagination due to text expansion. See Figure 6.4 for an example.

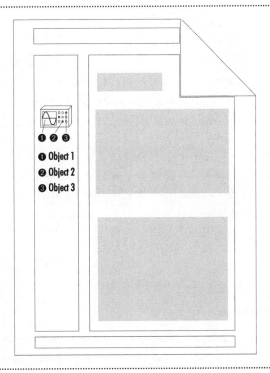

FIGURE 6.3: **A two-column grid design.**

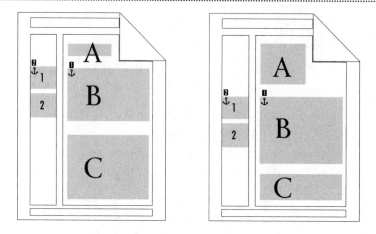

FIGURE 6.4: **An anchored frame containing a graphic image before and after text expansion.**

Similar to the idea of anchored frames is the idea of including a reference to the graphics file in the text. When the document file is processed, the processor physically inserts the content of the graphics file into the document exactly where specified. Markup languages like the Standardized General Markup Language (SGML) allow this method of inserting graphics in text. Text expansion is not affected. However, you have to make sure that the translation company has access to the graphics files and tools. The translation company must be able to use the pathnames specified in the file references you include in a marked-up document.

T E X T   D I R E C T I O N A L I T Y

The directionality of text on a page and in a document can change depending on the language. Text directionality is the direction in which text is written both on a page and in a book or even printed on a computer screen. There are three possibilities for text directionality:

1. Left to right

2. Right to left

3. Vertical columns

These text directionalities are often combined in some languages, especially when the text contains numbers or words borrowed from other languages.

The text directionality in English is illustrated in Figure 6.5. This text directionality is used in many languages, and is referred to in international software engineering circles as *LTR*, which means left to right.

However, technical information that is written in Hebrew and Arabic, for example, does not use the same text directionality. Hebrew and Arabic, for example, use the text directionality shown in Figure 6.6. These languages are commonly referred to as *bidi*, which means bi-directional, in international software engineering circles. This is because the text directionality for Hebrew and Arabic words is right to left, but text usually contains words from other languages, like English, as well as numbers that are read from left to right. In this sense, computer software must support both text directionalities.[14]

If you are localizing technical information for some target countries, be aware that most ideographic writing systems formally recognize a vertical text directionality, as in Japanese, Chinese, and Korean. "Japanese schoolchildren start out writing vertically. But when they learn mathematics, they also learn to write horizontally, so literate Japanese are comfortable reading both ways. Japanese symbols are designed so that handwriting is most efficiently done in a vertical line."[15] In some page designs, vertical text orientation can be considered a design advantage. Figure 6.7 illustrates the vertical text directionality in Japanese that is used in marketing and journalism.

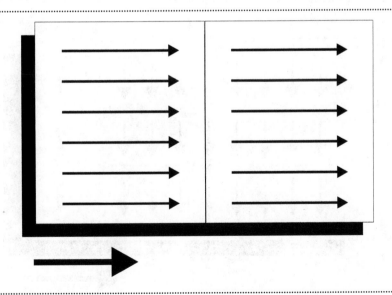

FIGURE 6.5: **Text directionality on a page and in a document in English.**

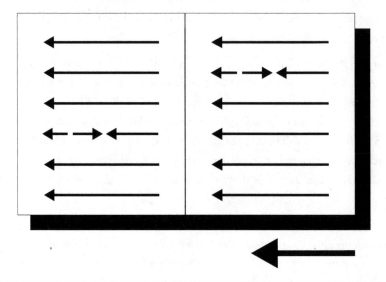

FIGURE 6.6: **Text directionality on a page and in a document in Hebrew and Arabic.**
When creating a page design or a screen design, consider the text directionality of other languages and whether your design is flexible enough to support this difference. If you are localizing the page design or screen design for a target country, consider reviewing the technical information produced by companies that are native to the target country for design ideas.

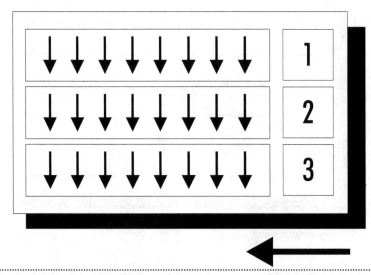

FIGURE 6.7: **Vertical text directionality used in Japanese marketing literature and journalism.**

PAGE SIZE

North Americans use one set of paper-size standards. Many other countries throughout the world use the paper sizes specified by the International Organization for Standardization (ISO).

There are two ISO paper standards, referred to as A4 and A5. The A4 paper size is based on the German Industry Standard (DIN standard) 66008. (Japan has adopted the A4 and A5 paper sizes, although it does have different standards for the B series that specifies the sizes of folders).[16]

Table 6.1 identifies the differences between these standard paper sizes in millimeters and in inches.

You need to be aware of page sizes when creating a page design. Information that is photocopied, transmitted with a fax machine, or printed on a printer needs to have sufficient margins to accommodate these paper sizes, otherwise information will be lost.[17]

FORMATTING

Most software products that format text use some means of global coding to make formatting faster. Global coding goes by many names: styles, tags, codes, elements, and components. Most software products also allow you to change the format at a local level, like changing the indentation of a single paragraph, italicizing a word, or changing the font of a phrase.

For text that is translated, formatting styles can pose a problem. If you have asked your translators to preserve the formatting in the source document, you need to consider the following guidelines when designing the formatting codes:

- **Limit the number of formatting styles.** Fifty or even 100 formatting codes for a single document make it very difficult for writers, let alone translators, to use your design. Style information is also carried around with the

TABLE 6.1: Paper-Size Standards for North America and the International Standards Organization (ISO)

	MILLIMETERS	INCHES
North America	216 x 279	8.5 x 11
	178 x 229	7 x 9
ISO	210 x 297 (A4)	8.25 x 11.66
	148 x 210 (A5)	5.875 x 8.5

document (in a template or catalog, for example) and can degrade system performance because of the size of the document file and the complexity of its content. (This is often noticeable when you scroll through a document; the computer can take a long time to redraw the screen, which makes working with the file frustrating.)

- **Restrict the use of local formatting styles.** Local formatting might highlight a particular word, which may become a phrase or even an entire sentence in a target language. If you want the translators to preserve this formatting, they will need to be aware of your local formatting conventions. Standardize local formatting or at least use local formatting consistently throughout a file. Identify all local formatting in your notes to translators.

Much formatting is dependent on the tools you use to create text. See Chapter 12, "Tools Issues," for more information.

ENVIRONMENTAL CONCERNS

There are two categories of environmental concerns that can affect the design of international technical communication. One relates to the physical working environment of the user. The other relates to the choice of materials that demonstrate a concern for the environment at large.

CONCERN FOR THE USER'S PHYSICAL ENVIRONMENT

It is usual to consider a user's physical environment when designing products. This principle is just as important when designing international technical communication. Considering a user's physical environment is particularly important when designing the medium used to present the information. Here are some common media available for presenting international technical communication:

- The information can be online, as in an online help system.

- The information can be visual, as in a video.

- The information can be printed, as in a single manual or a set of manuals.

- The information can be auditory, visual, printed, and electronic, like a multimedia system on a CD-ROM.

If users have their own offices with ample physical space but share computer resources with other users, then perhaps online information and CD-ROM presentations are not advisable. You might consider offering information in printed manuals or in videos.

If users share office space but have their own computing resources, then online information, CD–ROM presentations, and possibly video are recommended. Manuals could be a poor choice because there might be no room to store them. In Japan, for example, physical space is at a premium. Media other than printed manuals are becoming more popular.

If users have access to ample physical space and their own computing resources, then you might consider their preferences for media.

JoAnn Hackos, author of *Managing Documentation Projects*, adds these considerations of the user's physical environment:

- Are there differences in some users' workplace behaviors that will affect their use of the product or process?

- Is the user's workplace behavior prescribed by a trade union or a professional association?[18]

GLOBAL CONCERN FOR THE ENVIRONMENT

A concern for the environment—our Earth—is thankfully not a fad, but a very serious worldwide issue. The packaging you use, the paper on which your text is printed, the glues used for binding pages, and the ink used for printing, among other things, need to be chosen with the Earth in mind. This is part of the responsibility of thinking globally.

There are other reasons for choosing your materials with care. In my town, for example, there is no trash pickup. I have to sort all my waste, drive it to the local recycling center, and put it in its proper recycling bin. The recycling center then sells the waste to companies that reuse it. This was also the situation I encountered in many countries throughout Europe. It's not just a "nice" thing to do or even a "responsible" thing to do; there is nowhere else to dispose of the waste.

The information you design is timely. It is quickly outdated and needs replacing in a very short period of time. The manuals, then, become outdated and need to be replaced or updated regularly. Many companies still do not have a paper-recycling program to support the short life cycle of technical information. You can help address the Earth's concerns by supporting recycling and by choosing ways of presenting technical information that minimize the use of non-biodegradable materials.

E N D   N O T E S

[1] Weiss (1985), p. 82.

[2] Marcia Sweezey, written correspondence, September 15, 1994.

[3] John M. Carroll, *The Nurnberg Funnel: Designing Minimalist Instruction for Practical Computer Skill,* The MIT Press, Cambridge, Massachusetts, 1990.

[4] Marcia Sweezey, written correspondence, September 15, 1994.

[5] *Digital Guide to Developing International User Information*, Digital Press, 1992, p. 24.

[6] Telephone interview with Jon Lavine, September 28, 1994.

[7] Based on telephone discussions with Marcia Sweezey, and notes she added to a draft of this chapter. Her design is included here with her permission. The illustration is my conceptualization of Sweezey's design.

[8] Telephone interview with Jon Lavine, September 28, 1994.

[9] *Accent on Internationalization: Guidelines for Software Internationalization*, International Language Engineering (ILE) Corporation, Boulder, Colorado, 1994, p. 31.

[10] Ibid., p. 23.

11 John Brockmann, *Writing Better Computer User Documentation: From Paper to Hypertext*, Version 2.0, John Wiley & Sons, 1990, p. 114–115.

12 Special thanks to Chauncey Wilson, a human factors specialist, who suggested this test.

13 This book is not intended to promote the use of a particular software product or tool over another.

14 *National Language Design Guide: Designing Enabled Products*, Volume 1, 2nd Ed., IBM Canada, National Language Technical Center, January 1991, pp. 8–1:8–8.

15 *Localization for Japan: For Macintosh Computers*, Apple Computer, Inc., 1992, p. 39.

16 *The National Language Design Guide*, Volume 2, and *Software Internationalization and Localization: An Introduction*, by Uren, Howard, and Perinotti, provide tables of ISO and North American paper sizes. Uren, Howard, and Perinotti's book also provides some Japanese page size standards. It is always recommended that you contact the standards organization of the target country to verify the page sizes that are actually supported in the target country.

17 *Digital Guide to Developing International User Information*, pp. 120–121.

18 JoAnn Hackos, *Managing Your Documentation Projects*, John Wiley & Sons, New York, 1994, pp. 578–579.

7

CREATE THE FOUNDATION FOR ECONOMICAL LOCALIZATION. IDENTIFY INFORMATION THAT CAN BE REUSED. RECYCLE.

CREATING CORE INFORMATION 7

In Chapter 2, I defined international technical communication as consisting of two general components: international variables and core information. In Chapter 4, I discussed how to collect information on a target user's cultural context using the international variables in the model of culture you selected. In this chapter, I will discuss how to create core information.

WHAT IS CORE INFORMATION?

In international technical communication, *core information* is invariant information that can be reused. You can think of core information as a shell, form, or mold that is filled in with the information from the international variables. This is the idea behind internationalization. It is the separation of form from function. You create an internationalized shell of a product that can be localized easily. This is the essence of a world-ready product. Figure 7.1 illustrates this concept.

Here are some characteristics of core information:

- Core information is a long-term investment. It is not suited for one-time, quick-turnaround projects; these defeat the purpose of using core information.

- Core information is that which remains the same throughout the information sources describing a related collection of functions, products, or processes.

- Core information is that which remains the same in all the information sources describing a single product or process.

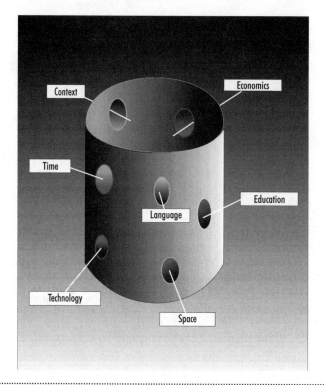

FIGURE 7.1: **Core information and international variables conceptualizing a world-ready product.**

- Core information is that which remains the same in all the information sources describing a single product or process that is used in different environments, like different computer operating systems, different hardware platforms, different departments, or different organizations.

- Core information should be a large chunk of information. A large chunk of information can be a chapter, a training module, one or more complete paragraphs, a graphic image, a table, a chart, a checklist, and so on. Core information is not a word or a phrase. This kind of information belongs in a glossary for translation (see Chapter 8 for information on glossaries for translation). Core information is never isolated from the larger part that gives it context; examples of non-core information include a sentence isolated from its paragraph, part of an illustration, or part of a table.

- Core information is recyclable information. If it does not change, and if it can be used in more than one information product, it is reusable information.

- Core information can be translated into another language. It is still core information if its translation remains unchanged and can be reused.

There is only one rule for using core information: DO NOT TOUCH! Core information is thoroughly edited and tested for usability, accuracy, style, cultural bias, and translatability before it can be used in information products. After core information is edited and tested, it cannot be modified. You can think of the do-not-touch rule as similar to a code freeze, which is when all software development stops. Core information can be modified only if it contains technically inaccurate information. Core information cannot be edited for style, grammar, or anything else. Core information, if created properly, is reusable. It stands the test of time and can be reused for major cross-platform projects.

OBJECTS AND CATEGORIES

A similar concept exists in software engineering in the development of objects when using object-oriented programming techniques. An object is a self-contained unit that interacts with other objects. Objects are assigned to classes. Many objects can be members of the same class. A class is a category that defines the types of objects it contains and how it should behave.[1]

Core information is very similar to objects and the way that they are used. Core information is also self-contained, like objects. Core information is categorized so that it is associated with related core information. Figure 7.2 illustrates the relationship of classes to objects and categories to core information.

EXAMPLES OF CORE INFORMATION

Any of the following can be core information. This list is not complete.

- product descriptions

- standard warning phrases

- functional description of a local-area network

- paragraph explaining how to select a menu item from a user interface

- illustration of a particular computer monitor

- information about the company for creating proposals

- icon from the graphical user interface

Classes and Their Objects

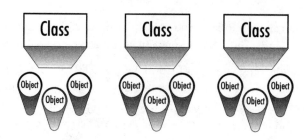

Categories and Core Information

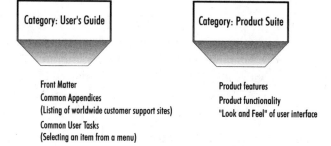

FIGURE 7.2: **Comparing classes of objects to categories of core information.**

- product warranties and licenses for France, Japan, and Germany
- forms for ordering parts
- online help text describing how to use the help facility
- video clip of a product installation
- table of character sets
- chapter on documentation conventions for user's guides
- audio clip providing directions to a training facility
- the corporate logo

BENEFITS OF USING CORE INFORMATION

I present the benefits of using core information here. As you will see, the benefits are significant. However, you should consider the disadvantages, presented later, before you embark on implementing the use of core information. Of equal weight are the benefits to using core information and the effort required to achieve those benefits.

CREATING CORE INFORMATION CAN SAVE MONEY

Digital Equipment Corporation found that 30 percent of the information in its hardware manuals qualified as recyclable information.[2] The following estimates the financial impact of this statement.

- The average number of pages in a hardware manual = 100.

- Thirty percent of 100 pages = 33.3 pages that contain recyclable information.

- Average cost of translating one page of text into one target language = $50 USD.

- Estimated savings by recognizing recyclable text per language per manual = $50 \times 33.3 = \$1665$ USD.

- If three hardware manuals contain the recyclable information and are translated into ten languages, **the potential savings are just under $50,000 USD.**

CREATING CORE INFORMATION CAN SAVE TIME

Reusing information in an information product saves time because the information is translated only once. The information is researched, articulated, edited, reviewed, and translated only once. The more core information, the less time, theoretically, it takes to complete an information product.

CREATING CORE INFORMATION SIGNIFICANTLY REDUCES THE NEED FOR RETRANSLATION

Retranslation is not economical. It adds to the time it takes to complete a project, and it costs money. If the core information is invariant, retranslation is unnecessary. Once you have core information translated into the target languages your company requires, you can store the translations in a database or something analogous for use in other information products.

CREATING CORE INFORMATION ENSURES CONSISTENT PRESENTATION OF INFORMATION AND CONSISTENT TRANSLATION

One of the complaints of users and of translators regarding international technical communication is that the same information is presented in many ways. There is some history behind this statement in the U.S. that is worth mentioning. In the U.S., all children and college students are required to learn the basic principles of expository writing. One of the suggestions that expository writing instructors offer to their students is that presenting the same idea in a different way makes expository writing more interesting to read.

While this suggestion is good advice for expository writing, it can create many problems in technical communication. A translator might think that a rephrasing of an idea is a new idea altogether. Some translators will telephone you and ask if the rephrased idea is a new idea or not. This takes time and can be very frustrating if rephrasing occurs frequently.

For the user, consistent presentation of information enhances readability. Most users typically do not read a technical manual from beginning to end, as they would expository writing. However, as Chauncey Wilson, a human factors specialist, mentions, users do tend to read tutorials and getting-started manuals from cover to cover.[3]

Core information, when reused, presents the same information in the same way. Its translation is also reused. Therefore, the core information and its translation should be consistent every time.

DISADVANTAGES OF USING CORE INFORMATION

Core information may seem like a perfect solution to the more visible problems of time and money that communicating to an international audience introduces. But using core information can introduce problems. Consider the impact of the disadvantages before choosing to implement core information about them. All the disadvantages listed here can be easily overcome if you plan for them and educate those who will use core information about them. Core information needs to be advertised throughout the corporation. People need to know that it exists, where they can find it, and how to use it.

CORE INFORMATION IS DIFFICULT TO MANAGE

Using core information requires some policing, making it a potential management problem.

1. Core information must be treated as a standard. It cannot be modified unless it is inaccurate. Verifying that the core information has been treated as a standard requires spot checking and an occasional audit of information products to verify conformance to the standard.

2. If core information must be changed, its translations will need to be updated. All information products and their translations that use the core information will need to be updated.

3. Using core information requires a system for tracking where it is used. You need to know where core information is located in each information product. Without a tracking system, updating the core information is tedious, time consuming, and far too manual a process to make using core information worth the effort.

4. Core information needs to be used wherever possible.

CORE INFORMATION IS MET WITH RESISTANCE

Most technical communicators like some degree of creative freedom when they develop international technical communication. Using core information restricts creative freedom, since the core information itself cannot be altered. The more core information there is, the more restrictive an international technical-communication project becomes. Chauncey Wilson notes that technical communication can focus on improving non-core information. There should be some rewards for using core information.[4]

It is also normal and possibly a professional habit of technical communicators to want to edit existing information to personalize it or to improve upon it. Because core information cannot be edited or changed in any way unless it is inaccurate, it creates a dilemma for those whose habits are to personalize or improve the presentation of technical information.

Using core information may also impede the design of a new information product. The style of communication in the core information may not be compatible with a new design idea. For situations like these, a decision-making body or authority must decide whether consistency is more important than usability or new information designs. Decisions like these can add to development time.

CORE INFORMATION IS A MAJOR INTEGRATION EFFORT

There are several ways in which core information needs to be integrated into your current international technical-communication process to make it work for you.

1. The use of core information needs to be integrated into the corporate standards for international technical communication. Doing so indicates a commitment to using core information and provides a uniform approach to using core information.

2. Core information must be supported by upper and middle management. Corporate standards are not sufficient.

3. All technical communicators need to be educated as to the existence of the core information, why it is important for them to use it, and how they should use it. Educating technical communicators through the corporate standards manual is not enough. Successful integration requires thorough training to secure each technical communicator's acceptance of this new process.

   - Consider offering a two- or three-hour training session to technical communicators. Consider offering the same class periodically to groups of new hires and to technical communicators who want retraining. Make sure everyone is trained and periodically reinforce the training information through paper or electronic memos to all technical communicators.

   - Consider training translators, even if they are not employees. They, too, need to understand how to use the core information successfully.

4. Core information and its translations need to be easily accessible to technical communicators and translators. There needs to be a database system that can provide technical communicators with core information quickly and easily. The system should be able to handle multimedia whether the core information is audio, video, or animation. The system also needs to have excellent search capabilities (fuzzy searching or indexing) so that the technical communicators can find the information with ease. It also must

be able to provide core information in a file format that is compatible with the international technical communication with which it is being integrated. See "Implementation" for more on this topic.

5. The style of the core information and its translations need to be compatible with the style used in all the information products created at your company. Ideally, this decision should be made by the editors at your company. If your company does not have an editor, do the best you can to make the core information stylistically generic. Consider that style is often culturally influenced. Try to make the core information as acceptable in as many cultures as possible.

AUDITING EXISTING INFORMATION FOR CORE INFORMATION

Here are some guidelines for creating core information and for creating business formulas (metrics) that measure its success.

GUIDELINES

1. Audit an existing information product. Core information should come from a stable, tested base, not from one that is unstable and under constant development, as it is in a new international technical project.

   Focus on only one small project at a time, since this kind of audit is time consuming and can generate a tremendous amount of data that you need to sort through and test. Narrowing your focus to smaller amounts of information gets you results more quickly and with more accuracy.

2. Isolate the core information from its context so that you can view it objectively, as a self-contained unit.

3. Test the core information. Core information *must* meet these criteria:

   - Core information must be free of cultural bias. See Chapter 5, "Identifying Cultural Bias," for ideas on how to test for cultural bias. Core information is translated into as many languages as your company requires. Therefore, it must be culturally generic. Both the source language version of the core information and its translations will be used over and over again.

   - Core information must be usable for users and technical communicators. Users have to understand the core information. Technical communicators need to integrate the core information into new international technical communication projects easily.

- Core information must be accurate, technically and grammatically. At the very least, core information should be written well.

4. Submit the core information for review to all the people who need to commit to it. Core information can work with strong and consistent support from management and the technical-communication staff.

   Include your translation team in the review, even if you contract out your translation. The core information needs to be reviewed for translatability.

   If you normally submit reviews to marketing, engineering, quality assurance, and other departments, submit the core information to them for review. Plan for a longer review cycle.

5. Meet with management. Meet with key people outside the technical-communication department. Meet with translators and many technical communicators. Review their comments with them to continue to solicit their commitment to using core information by involving them in the process.

6. Translate the approved core information into all of the languages your company requires.

7. Submit the translations for review by sending them to subject matter experts in the target countries. The subject matter experts should be native speakers of the language versions you send them.

8. Develop an integration plan for the core information. An integration plan focuses on people and processes. See "Integration" for ideas.

9. Develop an implementation plan for the core information. An implementation plan focuses on storing and retrieving the core information. See "Implementation" for ideas.

10. Educate everyone who will use or review the core information on the implementation and integration plans. Everyone needs to know how to use your processes and procedures.

11. Use the core information.

METRICS

Auditing existing information for core information provides a good opportunity to create business formulas, metrics, for measuring cost, savings, time, and a variety of other variables. It is often best to apply metrics on a project or product basis. In this way, you have the statistics for justifying your methods to management. As stated earlier, using core information can succeed only if there is a commitment to using it. Applying these methods to subsequent projects and products in the future will be easier, since you will have management support and experience.

Here are ideas for metrics that can help *quantify* the benefits of using core information.

- The percentage of information that is core information

- The percentage of information that is dependent on international variables

- The time spent auditing existing international technical communication for core information

- Time saved using core information

- Money saved using core information

INTEGRATION

Using core information successfully requires a comprehensive process that is well integrated into your current international technical-communication development cycle.

Some subprocesses might be ongoing ones, while others might be occasional or one-time-only subprocesses. Above all, design subprocesses that are realistic within the context of your company and technical-communication department. And the transition required to integrate your subprocesses should be a smooth and easy one, possibly requiring a year or two to integrate fully the processes for using core information and advertising and educating people on its existence. You will have a hard time getting people to commit to using core information if they find the processes for using it too time consuming or difficult.

Table 7.1 lists subprocesses that you should consider incorporating into the overall design of the process for using core information.

TABLE 7.1: **Subprocesses for Integrating Core Information into an International Technical-Communication Development Cycle**

SUBPROCESS	DESCRIPTION
Using core information	Technical communicators and translators need to have a subprocess to follow to use core information. This subprocess can be disseminated in the corporate standards manual for international technical communication and in training.
Spot checking or full-scale audit	This verifies that core information is being used and that it has not been modified in any way. Translations should also be checked to verify that the target language versions of core information have not been modified. Depending on the size of your department, the time available, and the level of commitment to using core information, you can perform only spot checking for conformance, or do a full-scale audit.
Reviews	This should accommodate the reviewing of new core information and its translations and the reviewing of international technical communication that use core information and their translations, respectively. Consider applying some kind of visual marking (a change in color, special brackets, change in font) to identify core information when it is used in international technical communication that is in development. This serves as a visual reminder to technical communicators, translators, and reviewers that core information cannot be changed. Remove the markings when the information product is ready for production.
Updating and removing core information	Core information can become inaccurate if the product that it describes changes dramatically or no longer suits the needs of your information products. Some subprocess needs to be established for reviewing the core information periodically and for retiring it when the core information is no longer useful. Along with this subprocess should be some sort of designated authority to make these decisions. If your technical-communication department is small enough, the whole department can participate in these decisions.

TABLE 7.1: *Continued*

SUBPROCESS	DESCRIPTION
Broadcasting	When you modify or remove core information, you need to make everyone—technical communicators, translators, and quality engineering—aware of your action. Establish a subprocess for broadcasting your actions to others in a timely and informative manner.
Tracking	Establish a subprocess for tracking where specific core information is used. This makes it easier to find core information when it has been modified or removed. It also provides a way of maintaining a variety of statistics on whether core information is being used and if so, how effectively. You can use these statistics to improve your subprocesses.
Training	All technical communicators need to be trained in all the subprocesses associated with using core information. Translators, whether they are internal, contract, or the employees of a translation company, need to know how to use core information as well. Everyone needs to understand the value of using core information. Training is a very effective way of soliciting commitment in the subprocesses you develop for using core information. Consider offering periodic continuing-education courses to further the commitment to using core information. Training should not be self-paced, individualized study. To harness commitment, you need contact with people. Also, training should not require much time. Plan a two- or three-hour course.
Roles and responsibilities	If your approach to using core information involves assigning roles and responsibilities, you will need to identify those roles and describe the responsibilities associated with them. Two roles might be core information auditors and core information trainers.

Continued

TABLE 7.1: **Subprocesses for Integrating Core Information into an International Technical-Communication Development Cycle** *Continued*

SUBPROCESS	DESCRIPTION
File or database organization	Develop a schema for organizing the core information. Figure 7.3 offers an example of a schema for training modules. The categories of core information are multilayered. The top layer labels everything as core information. The middle layer identifies the type of information (training modules about hardware devices, specifically printers). The bottom layer identifies the categories of core information about printers (illustrations, tasks, and exercises). Each item at the bottom layer is information that can be reused in other training modules. The tasks, for example, are basic to all printers. For all printers, you unpack the printer the same way every time. You add more paper the same way every time.

The schema (data structure) contributes to the usability of the core information, since it can speed up or hinder the retrieval of core information. |
| **Develop file naming conventions** | Develop a system for naming files containing core information. This makes core information easier to find. |
| **Define and keep metrics** | It is always a good idea to maintain metrics. They can help you convince others that using core information can significantly save money, reduce the need for retranslation, save time, and ensure consistency. Establish guidelines on how to maintain the metrics you have chosen to focus on. |
| **Integrate core information principles into a standards manual for international technical communication** | Find ways of integrating the subprocesses you create into the standards manual for international technical communication. The corporate standards should provide technical communicators with the following information:

■ A functional definition of core information

■ Reasons for using core information and statistics supporting its benefits

■ A well-articulated procedure for finding, using, updating, and resolving disputes regarding the use of core information and its translations |

TABLE 7.1: *Continued*

SUBPROCESS	DESCRIPTION
	▪ A procedure for how translators should use the translations of core information
	▪ Examples of the proper and improper use of core information
	▪ A procedure for tracking the use of core information and its translations
	▪ A procedure for adding and removing core information and its translations
	▪ An appendix of official core information that is updated regularly—if some core information is not printable, like audio and video, add a description of the core information instead

IMPLEMENTATION

Technology is currently sophisticated enough to implement the requirements of storing and retrieving core information. You need to research and evaluate the tools that you use currently to determine if they can manage core information. Here is a list of tool requirements and methods for achieving them that some companies have used successfully. Use this list as a guide when developing your implementation strategy and when you review tools for making that implementation strategy real. You may find that your current tools can do the job. Chapter 12 provides more information on tools.

TOOLS CRITERIA FOR IMPLEMENTING CORE INFORMATION

- **Storing core information.** What kind of core information do you need to store? Text? Graphics? Audio? Video?

- **Retrieving core information.** Can you import core information from the storage area into the tool you use to develop international technical communication? Are the file formats and the interfaces compatible? Are they compatible with the tools used for translation?

- **Portability.** If you work in a multiplatform environment, are your tools compatible across all platforms?

- **Multiple language support.** Do your tools allow you to store translated core information and retrieve it? Do they support multiple languages?

Core Information

Training Modules
Hardware
Printers

Core Illustrations	Core Tasks	Core Exercises
Printer 1	Unpacking the printer	Unpacking the printer
Printer 2	Powering on and off	Powering on and off
Printer 3	Printing a test page	Printing a test page
	Changing the paper tray	Changing the paper tray
	Adding paper	Adding paper

FIGURE 7.3: **An example of a schema for core information.**

- **Ease of learning and use.** Are your tools for managing core information easy to learn and use?

- **Tools need to be network compatible or allow for core information portability.** Can you access and share core information across a local-area or wide-area network? If not, can you download core information onto media that allow the core information to be transferred to another machine?

- **File contention.** What happens if two or more people try to access the same core information simultaneously? What sort of controls are there for managing this problem?

- **Write protection.** Can you make core information read-only to control its modification?

- **Searching.** Can you perform searches to find core information? How sophisticated are the tools' search capabilities?

- **File and database management.** Whether you use a file system or database system to implement your core information strategy, you need to be able to reorganize and rename core information as you develop a data structure that works best for your environment.

METHODS FOR
IMPLEMENTING CORE INFORMATION

- Floppy diskettes or another portable storage medium. This is the simplest method. It is best used in a very small company with one or two technical communicators, or when there is no local area network. To exchange core information, you copy it from a portable storage medium onto your computer's hard disk and integrate it from there.

- Files on a network. This is another fairly simple method. All core information should be stored in a central storage facility that all technical communicators can access. The technical communicators need to know only the file system's structure, the file-naming conventions, and how to import the files.

- Database with search and retrieval capabilities. There are two ways to implement this.

  1. You can use a database to supplement the previous method, "Files on a network." The database would not contain the core information. It would, instead, provide a better interface to information on how to find the core information. An analogy is a computerized library search product. You use the library search product to search against book titles, authors' names, and subject matter. Often, these products let you read abstracts of what is in each book. Most database products would be able to provide this functionality.

  2. Some databases let you store core information in its native file format and add the same capabilities as described in number one. These databases require sophisticated computing resources and can be expensive.

- **Macros.** Some software products allow you to define macros that insert text and graphics. The text and graphics can be stored within the software product or elsewhere in your computer system.

- **Templates.** This is a way of controlling and enforcing the use of core information. The template would contain the core information itself. The technical communicator works around the core information and within the structure supplied by the template.

- **Glossaries.** This method is identical to using macros, but requires a different software mechanism than a macro. Translation companies rely on glossaries. I recommend that you contact your translation company for ideas on implementation ideas for such a method.

O**THER** S**OURCES FOR** I**MPLEMENTATION** I**DEAS**

The software industry continues to find ingenious ways of creating core software products that can be localized with ease. I recommend that you read books about how to create internationalized software products for some clever ideas on how to implement core information. See Appendix C for information about such books.

END NOTES

[1] Derived from definitions of *object*, *object-oriented programming*, and *class* in the *Microsoft Press Computer Dictionary*, Microsoft Press, 1991.

[2] *Developing International User Information*, Digital Equipment Corporation, 1992, p. 30.

[3] Chauncey Wilson, from his comments on a draft of this chapter, August 6, 1994.

[4] Ibid.

8

FORGE HEALTHY PARTNERSHIPS WITH PEOPLE

WHO CAN MAKE YOUR INTERNATIONAL

TECHNICAL COMMUNICATION SUCCESSFUL:

TECHNICAL TRANSLATORS AND TRANSLATION

REVIEWERS. DISCOVER WAYS TO BUILD AND

STRENGTHEN THESE RELATIONSHIPS.

About the
Translation Industry
....

Deciding on a
Translation Strategy
....

Strategies and Tools
for Working Together
....

Wish Lists
....

Translation is one of the most visible expenses associated with international technical communication. The average cost of translating a technical manual from English into European languages is, in the U.S., about $50 USD per page, which does not consider modifications to graphics, desktop publishing, printing, or any additional services provided by a translation company.[1] This means that every 200 pages cost, on average, $10,000 USD per European language. The cost escalates for Asian languages like Chinese, Japanese, and Korean.

Obviously, it is in a company's best interest to consider carefully whether a document needs to be translated at all, or whether only parts of a set of documentation need to be translated. Before making these decisions based solely on cost, consider these three important factors:

- International and national standards can require translation of certain documents describing certain products. These standards vary according to industry. It is best to consult a proper authority, like a standards council in the target country, before deciding not to translate. (Appendix C provides contact information for many standards organizations.)

- Liability laws are changing around the world. It is possible that you render your company more liable if documentation is not translated into the native language of the users in the target country. Target users might misuse your product and be injured because they misunderstood documentation that was not translated. Liability risks can also be created by bad translations. Some countries may require translation; France requires translation and this may be true in your target countries.

- Market share is certainly at risk if a product is less accessible by a target user population. Most markets are vulnerable to fierce competition today. A decision not to translate documentation for export to a target country can create an opportunity for a competitor, especially a competitor located in the target country. Target users may prefer a product that is less sophisticated or powerful if it has been designed and explained with them in mind.

Most companies either translate everything or only selected parts of a documentation set. Digital Equipment Corporation, for example, has everything except the very technical documentation translated. Their reasoning is that very technical people in the target country read English well and are accustomed to reading trade journals and magazines in English. They also reason that most highly technical material contains many examples of software code and related content, which cannot be translated.

It is also important to remember that a decision not to translate today may not be an option tomorrow. *Plan for translation*, even if you decide not to translate today.

A B O U T T H E T R A N S L A T I O N I N D U S T R Y

The development of the translation industry in the U.S. and in Europe[2] over the past ten years has been a fascinating one. It has been similar to the development of the technical-communication profession. Dick Crum, a senior editor at Berlitz Translation Services, who has been in the translation industry since the 1970s, describes the translation industry as a reactive one instead of a proactive one. As businesses in the 1970s closed down their internal translation departments for economic reasons, they started calling upon translation companies to handle their translation needs. "The old attitude was 'Translation agencies know it all,' when in fact we did not know it all. We were naive about the needs of global businesses."[3]

Jon Lavine, also a senior editor at Berlitz Translation Services, adds that the growth and shift in the translation industry, at least in the U.S., has paralleled that of American high-technology companies. The technical-communication profession has done the same. He identifies three changes that have shifted the focus of the translation industry: increased volume, skills development, and the expansion of the translation industry.[4]

Twenty years ago, there was not as much need for U.S. companies to enter the global marketplace as there is today. Also, at that time, the personal computer market did not even exist. Jaap van der Meer of R. R. Donnelly, a very large translation company, comments on the translation industry twenty years ago. "Translators at that time were still working on typewriters or with

Dictaphones. . . . [W]e generated indexes [and] cut and pasted illustrations. . . . "[5] And we know that technical communicators did the same.

In the 1980s, the personal computer entered. The high-technology industry grew very rapidly. U.S. businesses sought to expand quickly and entered the global marketplace. This created an increase in the demand for translated documentation and to some degree, localized software programs. Van der Meer continues. "The first challenge in the early days of localization towards the translators was to work in rather primitive text editors with complicated coding. Special training was required because the skills were not readily available."[6]

In 1985, Edmond Weiss wrote in his preface to *How to Write a Usable User Manual*, "These are interesting times for user documentation. . . . It is emerging as a distinct profession, incorporating elements of computer science, training, graphic arts, and traditional principles of rhetoric and composition."[7]

The global marketplace expanded. There are more players, and they are from all over the world. U.S. high-technology companies now have to be export driven to stay in businesses. As more companies enter the market, competition increases. This increase in competition fuels the fast pace of the high-technology industry. The fast pace and increased demand has shifted the focus of translation companies. Van der Meer describes how translation companies responded. "Organizationally we faced the challenge of forming translation teams that were able to turn around the massive jobs in the couple of months that were given to complete the projects. Consistency of style and terminology were new requirements presented to translators, who were trained to work as 'creative' translators. New terminology was invented to name the new devices and features of the computers that entered our lives at the office." Weiss describes the new requirements of technical communicators in the mid-1980s:

> Interestingly, the fundamental requirements for good user documentation have not changed much over the years. Manuals must still be **available on time**. They must be as **complete and accurate** as review and testing can make them. They must be written in **correct language** and edited for **clarity and readability**.
>
> . . . What has changed, though, are the tolerances and standards. Today's users—even the expert technicians and engineers—have less and less patience with unreadable and inaccessible publications. The old joke—when all else fails, read the instructions—is no longer funny.[8]

In the mid-1990s, ten years later, translation volumes are still large, new skills are always necessary, and both the translation industry and the technical-communication profession continue to expand. One difference that sets us apart in the U.S. and in Europe is education. In Europe, translators are well trained and educated in technical translation, but this is not the case in the U.S. In the U.S., there are few education programs for technical translation, so most training comes on the job. In Europe, there is very little training available for technical communicators, and technical communicators learn on the job. The opposite is true in the U.S. There are technical communication degree programs all over the country. Technical communicators today are well trained and educated in this field.

But for as much history as they share, translators and technical communicators have not developed the relationship that they need to develop in order to work well and to work economically together. The remainder of this chapter explores ways to improve this relationship so that we both are able to meet our respective goals.

DECIDING ON A TRANSLATION STRATEGY

There are many strategies for having text translated. All the variations offer their own rewards and problems. None of the variations is guaranteed to work well every time.

In general, ask these questions **before** you decide on a translation strategy:

- What services are required?
- What is the scope of the project?
- What are the languages you need?
- What is the budget?
- Why are you translating?[9]

Once you determine the answers to these questions, you need to determine **who** should do the translation. The real issues in choosing who should do your translations are really ones of control, cost, quality, speed, and volume. When deciding how your company should approach translation, thoroughly consider the following questions.

- **Control.** To what degree does your company want to have control over various aspects of translation?

- **Cost.** How much money can your company afford to spend on translation?

- **Quality.** What degree of quality does your company want the translation to reach?

- **Time.** How quickly does your company want the turnaround of translations?

- **Volume.** How much text needs to be translated?

The answers lie in the reality of how business needs and user needs are balanced in your company. Every company is different and therefore every solution is different.

After you determine who should do your translation, use these questions to screen them:

- What is their experience in your industry and in the translation industry?

- What are their technical capabilities?

- What is the quality of their quality assurance program?

- What are the logistics for doing business with them?

- Can they supply you with references you can check?[10]

These are the most common solutions to the translation strategy problem.

HIRE A TRANSLATION COMPANY

This is the most common strategy for having text translated. There are large and small translation companies, multinational translation companies, translation companies that are industry specialists, translation companies in your city, and translation companies based exclusively in specific target countries. How do you choose the right one? Consider beginning with a visit to their offices.

- **Control.** You should consider the proximity of the translation company to your company. If the translation company is in a different time zone, you will need to consider its effect on telephone communication. How quickly will you be able to address coordination issues?

- **Cost.** You should send out a request for proposals to large and small translation companies, and those both near and far. Consider all the hidden costs of doing business with them. Is your company willing to pay to have the translation tested by two to three users in the target country to make sure that

the terminology and the style make sense to a native speaker of the
target language?

- **Quality.** What processes do you have in place to have the translations
  reviewed? What are your expectations of quality? Are your expectations
  realistic? Will you be able to supply in-country reviewers who are subject-
  matter experts to review the translated material? How major an account are
  you to the translation company, and is this a pro or a con?

- **Time.** Is there time for training the translators and for preparing your staff
  and the translators to work together? Is your company expecting simultaneous translation and, if so, into how many languages?

- **Volume.** How large is the volume of the job, and can the translation company handle it? In most cases, only large translation companies have the
  resources to handle large-volume jobs, although some mid-sized agencies
  might be just as capable.

H I R E F R E E L A N C E T R A N S L A T O R S

Some companies, like the Vancouver Division of Hewlett Packard in the state of
Washington, hire freelance translators to work side by side with their technical-
communication staff and development team. Don Barnett, Learning Products
Manager at Hewlett Packard, states that their division needed to release their
products worldwide simultaneously in the U.S., Canada, Mexico, the Far East, and
Europe. The translation effort usually involved seven to nine languages.

Barnett's use of freelance translators balanced his needs for control, cost, quality,
speed, and volume. No other approaches worked for him. Consider how he
applied this approach:

> Translators are considered country experts. Part of their job function is to
> comment on the appropriateness of the English language documentation. Is
> the artwork appropriate? Should callouts or labels be used given the expan-
> sion rates of some languages? Is an example translatable? Translators also get
> to test the documentation against the product it describes, because they have
> access to the equipment.... To expedite the localization process, the tech-
> nical writers finish a chapter and immediately give a copy to the translators
> and to their technical reviewers. Thus, translation and technical reviews
> occur simultaneously.[11]

Hiring freelance translators introduces the standard set of management issues. You must have someone internally who can manage freelance translators to help address their needs.

American Translators International (ATI), a California-based translation company, offers these suggestions for screening translators.

- Five years of full-time translation experience

- A good college or university education, preferably with graduate training in a professional field

- Ability to read the source language fluently, and to write their native language for publication purposes

- Frequent contact with their native language, to assure proper use of current terminology

- Computer equipment

- Appropriate technical dictionaries and up-to-date journals

- Specialization in a technical field (e.g., computers, semiconductors, telecommunications, manufacturing, medicine); Robert Bononno, a technical translator who teaches technical translation at New York University, qualifies this statement, noting that translators try to limit themselves to a range of disciplines within the field of technical translation[12]

- Ability to work quickly, under pressure, weekends, and evenings, at a reasonable wage[13]

HIRE FULL-TIME TRANSLATORS

Some companies, like IBM and AT&T, have their own translation departments. These translation departments have full-time translators who cater to the translation needs of several divisions and departments throughout their organizations. AT&T's Global Information Solutions, for example, translates 10 million words per year. While its staff of 10 translators can handle some of the translation volume, most of the work is sent outside to translation companies.[14]

Having full-time translators assumes that you have a sizable volume of work to keep them busy throughout the year. Most companies with large volumes combine using their in-house translators with sending their translations to outside vendors when volume gets to be too much to manage.

Full-time translators also require translation tools to do their jobs well. Most companies that have their own translation departments have invested heavily in buying off-the-shelf translation tools, or they have had proprietary tools built for them. IBM did this, for example, and now sells one of its internal tools to the commercial market.

The most frequent complaint of internal translation departments is project turn-around. Your job goes into a queue, and it is not addressed until its time has arrived. Obviously this presents scheduling challenges that may not be suitable to the project.

So, where you gain in quality (translators are privy to terminology, technology, and training), you lose control of speed and cost (overhead). You lose control of the translation process, too, since this falls under the jurisdiction of another division or department. Scheduling and quality and cost may become political issues that you may not want to address.

SEND ALL TEXT TO A DISTRIBUTOR IN ONE OF THE TARGET COUNTRIES

This is an approach that many small companies take as their first launch into the international arena. It is the easiest approach if your company is uncomfortable with all the changes international business introduces. In 1991, Traveling Software, a small company in the state of Washington, "sent the American version of the documentation and software to the [German] distributor, who then took on the full translation effort." Jonathan Scott, Traveling Software's Chief Operating Officer, adds, "Distributors have the most invested in your product...." [15]

Using your distributor, however, could risk quality. Many distributors have bilingual or multilingual staff members translate the documentation. These staff members are often not professional translators, nor are they writers. They are often salespeople, friends, relatives, or spouses. While they are very familiar with terminology in the target language, they are not professional writers. Distributors often do this to control their own costs. Also, if the volume of translation is large, it is most probable that a distributor will hire a translation company to do all or some of the translation. Most distributors do not have a large, full-time translation staff to handle such volume. Using your distributor also relinquishes almost all of your control over the process.

ATI offers these words of caution when using a distributor.

> . . . [L]egal issues can arise when a distributor received control over transla-
> tions. For example, if a distributor relationship ends, the distributor typically
> retains the copyright of the translation and its terminology. The computer
> company must then re-do the translation, which can mean sales delays and
> users who are displeased to see "new" terminology.[16]

INVEST IN MACHINE TRANSLATION

Machine translation (MT) systems are still not living up to their creators' promises,
and will require a great amount of artificial-intelligence capabilities before they
can handle the nuances of a language, whatever it happens to be. However, there
are some companies that need MT systems now and they are willing to invest in
the future of this technology.

Consider the situation of Caterpillar, Inc. Caterpillar's translation needs are enormous, and due to international standards that require translation, Caterpillar must
translate everything. Writing about Caterpillar's unique situation, Sharlene Gallup,
Manager of Translation and Production, states:

> In 1992, over 98,000 Engineering Change Notices (ECN's) were received
> resulting in the creation of approximately 800 pages of English information
> per day. Presently, over 1.5 million previously created pages of English infor-
> mation are supported. All of this means that an average of 110 tons of paper
> is shipped per month to Caterpillar dealers. And finally, the average
> Caterpillar dealer has approximately 250 linear feet of shelf space for product
> support literature.

> Since 50% of Caterpillar sales are exported, Caterpillar translates much of
> their technical literature into over 30 languages. More than 20 human trans-
> lators are used for the more common foreign languages. Moreover, outside
> suppliers, Caterpillar foreign language offices and dealers are also used, espe-
> cially for languages with low volume requirements. Even with this help,
> many needed translations are not done either because of lack of manpower
> or because costs are prohibitive. The translation rate for human translators is
> about one page per hour . . . . Generally the elapsed time from assignment to
> printing averages 6 weeks depending on workload. The cost per page is
> approximately $40.[17]

Out of an obvious need for a more economical and timely solution, Caterpillar created a proprietary version of controlled English. It has since hired the Carnegie Group to develop a machine translation system that will convert the controlled English into an intermediary form called *interlingua*. The system will then convert the interlingua version into the supported target languages. Gallup concludes, "Translation processing time is expected to be around 40 pages per hour.... The cost per page is expected to be under $5.00...."[18]

The system that the Carnegie Group is creating for Caterpillar is costing the company millions of U.S. dollars. However, considering their translation requirements and volume, this is a seemingly small price to pay for a long term investment in international business.

Obviously not every company can afford the time and money that it takes to invest in a mammoth machine translation system like the one developed by the Carnegie Group. Before committing to any machine translation system, consider its limitations:

- All MT systems to date require simplified language for input. Pre-editing is required.

- No MT system to date can handle all or even most of the linguistic complexities in any given language. There is limited language support to date.

- Most MT systems deliver output that should be reviewed by a professional translator for accuracy before it is used. Extensive post-editing is common today.

Disagreement Among Translators About Liberties

In the assortment of literature I consulted, there was great disagreement among translators as to how much poetic license, or *liberty*, they have to translate a document. Some translators felt that they had to translate literally, keeping very close to the English sentence structure. Other translators felt that they needed to translate for the essence of meaning. Still others went further and argued that they needed to translate for meaning and add culturally appropriate idioms where applicable.

There was even greater disagreement among translators about how they should treat mistakes in the source document. Translators were divided about how they should treat typographical, technical, and grammatical errors. Do they correct them or bring them to the attention of you, the client? Robert Bononno states that both methods are valid, and the one that is used simply depends on the translator's relationship with the client.

Of course these issues are entirely your decision, but you need to make your expectations very, very clear so that you minimize confusion among the translators who work on your project. Make sure you have a process that can address errors in the source document, too.

In general, most companies prefer that translators contact them about any errors. They also prefer that translators do not translate word for word, and that they aim for meaning, adding culturally appropriate idioms where applicable. Most companies pay to have their documentation sound to a target user as if it were written by a native language speaker in the target country.

OWNERSHIP

There have been many arguments over who owns what when a translation is finished. The glossary illustrates this point.

The glossary, which is discussed in more detail later in this chapter, is a collection of terms that are unique to your project industry and that are used throughout your documentation. Very few customers provide a glossary when they submit documentation for translation, but some do. Unless you specifically request to have your glossary translated as a project deliverable, you cannot expect to own the translated terminology once the project is finished. The translated terminology is often bundled in with hundreds of other terms in the same industry and stored in a computer database that the translation company has developed over many years to make translation a more expedient and accurate process. Translators are more than willing to translate terminology for you as a separate deliverable item, but you will be charged for that effort. It is often a wise investment, however.

Another area of ownership problems is translation memory. *Translation memory* is a fairly recent technology that looks for sentences that are identical or similar as a translator translates. Translation memory is often used in conjunction with a CAT tool. The translation memory tool constantly searches for identical matches and similar matches, allowing the translator to use the same translation over and over throughout one or more documents. This tool is quite efficient, and some companies feel that they have the right to own the collection of sentences that are the same and their translations. Again, unless you specifically include this as a deliverable in your contract and pay for it as a separate item, you should expect no such thing. Translation memory, like a glossary, is a business investment translation companies make to meet the demands of their customers.

STRATEGIES AND TOOLS FOR WORKING TOGETHER

There are no right or wrong ways to have your international technical communication translated. However, there are proven strategies that maximize control, cost, quality, and speed.

CLEAR WRITING

One of the more disturbing patterns I noticed throughout my research was the constant request to have writers write clearly. Well, most professional writers do write clearly, so I asked some technical translator colleagues why this request kept coming up, especially when the translators were receiving professionally written documentation.[19]

Jon Lavine, a senior translator at Berlitz Translation Services, offered this explanation. "Language is inherently ambiguous, and different languages are ambiguous in different ways. It is a permanent problem. It's a misnomer to say 'clear writing.' It does not mean that it is bad writing. It is more a way of saying 'write the English to make it less ambiguous.' "

Robert Bononno commented: "Translators can and do encounter [long sentences] all the time in their work and translate them accurately. The problem is not lengthy sentences, the problem is bad grammar and poor writing. I'm sure you've seen many examples of obscure or confusing technical texts in English. Many of these are difficult even for native speakers to understand. One of the things we need to bear in mind is that translators are perhaps the best critics of the source text because they read it so closely. The nature of their work forces them to examine the microstructure of the text, so they are acutely aware of any problems in sentence structure. If your writing is readable, it will be understood by the translator. We need to remain aware of the fact that much writing is inherently ambiguous and some writing is intentionally so (patents, for example, many legal texts). Translators are not simply required to 'deal' with this ambiguity, they must translate it somehow. And the target translation must be correct."

And finally Walter Popp, who is a technical translator and localization consultant based in France, stated: "The best translators are obviously those who write good copy in their own language. So far no disagreement. But in the course of my language career, I came to think that my concern for. . . .language makes me often a far better, attentive reader than your average American manual consumer. Good translators are very good linguists. . . .I would argue that writers are exposed to the same constraints as translators. Which means that you also have horizontal work sharing (different chapters written by different writers), insufficient information (the GUI has not been translated at the time you finish the User's Guide) and so on. . . .The problem with advanced vocabulary is not so much that we don't understand it, but that we can't translate it (because it is advanced, the word doesn't exist in our language. . . .) Very often the advanced vocabulary is unnecessary, it's just marketing. If a company decides to call its computer an electronic information enhancement device, the translator just might block, because what sounds sophisticated in the source just sounds ridiculous in the target language."

TRANSLATION COORDINATORS AND LOCALIZATION COORDINATORS

A translation coordinator who answers questions for the translation company is essential. Assign a person within your company to be the exclusive contact for questions from the translators. This person should be briefed on the importance of timely response to translators' questions and on the need to obtain thorough and accurate answers to their questions. If translators are unable to get answers to their questions quickly, you should expect a slip in the schedule. Clearly identify the responsibilities of the translation coordinator and the degree of authority that this person has to make decisions regarding the translation.

Always have a backup contact for the translators in the event that the translation coordinator is unavailable, out sick, or on vacation.

A good candidate for this position is a technical writer on the project itself. Most technical writers know the technical aspects of a product extremely well and are trained to research answers with efficiency and precision. They also know which engineers to contact to get the right answers quickly.

Digital Equipment Corporation has created two positions, translation coordinator and translation team leader, as described in Table 8.1.

Jill Monaco described some of her responsibilities as a localization coordinator for Hewlett-Packard's Learning Products Division in Colorado Springs, Colorado, in 1991.

Become an expert problem solver for localization problems. When solving the problems, understand the amount of time that you have. Some problems require long term searches for the best solution, for example, selecting a good database. Other problems, like a graphics file that locks up a translator's system, require immediate action. By recognizing the difference, and solving problems in a timely manner, you'll help localization projects run smoother. If you need help with a localization problem and aren't able to solve it, escalate your concerns to management. They might know of another solution or of another path to find the solution.[20]

GLOSSARIES

"The glossary is the most important document," states Peter Gelpi, operations manager for Aldus Corporation. Marcia Sweezey, an internationalization consultant, notes that, based on some work she did at Digital, a glossary can save up to 20 percent of the total cost of the information translation project.[21]

Many translation companies recommend that their clients provide them with source-language glossaries. A glossary is a translation tool. It often contains the translations of the following information into all target languages of interest to your company:

- Technical terms that are specific to your product, company, and industry

- Major verbs that are used in procedures

TABLE 8.1: **Job Responsibilities of a Translation Coordinator and a Translation Team Leader at Digital Equipment Corporation**[22]

TRANSLATION COORDINATOR	TRANSLATION TEAM LEADER
Liaison to corporate documentation group and translation team leader	Develops a translation strategy with translation coordinator, engineering project leader, and translation team
Negotiates file transfer dates	Publishes a formal localization plan
Supplies draft of user information, project plan, source files, and artwork to translation team leader	Reviews user information for locale-specific and culturally dependent content
Reviews user information for conformance to corporate standards and guidelines	Assembles the translation package and provides all necessary information and tools to the translation team
	Is focal point for questions from translators throughout the life of the project

- Sources to reference for industry-standard translations of technical terms

- Acronyms, initialisms, and abbreviations

- Words and phrases that must not be translated

The purpose of a glossary is to ensure consistent translation of the same terms throughout the life of a document, project, or product.

If your product runs on a platform like Microsoft Windows, an Apple Macintosh platform, or OS/2, for example, consider using the terminology that these vendors use. Your users will already be familiar with the terminology, and your translators can use the translated terms already introduced by those companies. Microsoft has recognized this need and published a book called *The GUI Guide: International Terminology for the Windows Interface* (European Edition, Microsoft Press, 1993).

Crum's *Translatability Seminar* provides a similar template for a pretranslation glossary entry, as shown in Table 8.2.

There are very few terminology-management database and computer-aided translation (CAT) tools that are commercially available if you want the glossary to be electronic. Before you purchase a glossary tool, make sure that it is compatible with the tools your translators use.

It is strongly recommended that you have the glossary be a separate deliverable and that you pay to own the translations of all terms into the target languages. In this way, you allow yourself the freedom of changing your translation strategy or translation company at some time in the future.

TABLE 8.2: **Template for Creating a Glossary for Translators**

TERM
Part of speech
Definition
Reference
Acceptable synonyms
Unacceptable synonyms
Target translations
French
German
Japanese

TRANSLATION KITS

If the translation company is translating help screens or error messages or building user interfaces or applications, you should supply the translators with all software required to rebuild them. Most software code is proprietary, so you will have to work with the engineering department to determine how the information that needs to be translated can be supplied and rebuilt separately from the main code. You will need to supply instructions for using the translation kit. Make sure that you determine early whether the translation company can successfully use the translation kit.

Robert Bononno adds, "Developers should supply the translator with a separate text file containing menus and help screens whenever possible. Documentation can, in many cases, be supplied in the original file format in the case of on-line documentation. As a rule translators do not want to be bothered working around formatting codes. This is extremely time consuming for the translator unless there is a way to automatically hide and protect codes in the application they are using to manipulate text. A separate ASCII file makes life much easier." [23]

The goal here is to make it easy for the translators to do their job. They should spend their time translating, not trying to figure out how to use the tools you supply them.

SUPPLEMENTAL MATERIAL

Just as technical communicators appreciate any supplemental material to learn more about a product, so do translators. If they are translating a hardware manual, provide them with a photograph or an illustration of the hardware, for example.

Another collection of information that Theodora Landgren, president of Bureau of Translation Services (BTS), Inc., recommends are the linguistic and formatting guidelines that are used by the technical communication department in both the source and in the target country, if these exist.

Here is a list of possible supplemental materials that can greatly assist a translator in understanding your documentation.

- Graphics
- Photographs
- Previous translations

- Memos and notes that you were given to write the documentation
- Copies of any presentations given in the target country about the product
- Promotional literature
- Style guide for source and target country, if possible
- Conventions in documentation, conventions in the target country
- Formatting conventions, file standards, and formats
- The product and hardware whenever possible
- Screen shots

CHECKLISTS

There is a lot to keep track of when you submit a project to a translation company, especially if your project is more complicated than just translating documentation. Use a checklist to help manage this process. Table 8.3 offers a sample checklist.

TRAINING

Many companies now invest in training translators, even if the translators work for a translation company. Traveling Software, for example, flew the German and French translators of its documentation, who were based in Europe, to its headquarters in the U.S. The translators were introduced to the Traveling Software staff members with whom they interacted on the telephone and through written correspondence. Translators were taught how to use the products properly. Traveling Software felt that investing in this training contributed to the high level of quality that their translations currently have.[24]

SCHEDULES

You need to establish realistic deadlines with the translation company. This may require more money, since tight deadlines may require more personnel. Simultaneous release of documentation in several languages will require careful coordination with the translation company. Work with the translation company to develop a schedule that makes sense. Also consider that every time a translator must stop and contact you for answers to questions can result in a schedule slip if the answer is not addressed promptly.

TABLE 8.3: **Example of an In-house Checklist for Translation Management**[25]

PROJECT	Provide a description of the project.
TECHNICAL COMMUNICATION TEAM	Provide the names of the people in the technical-communication department who are involved in the project, document their contact information, document their specific responsibilities.
SOURCE LANGUAGE	Identify the source language, if this can vary in your company.
TARGET LANGUAGES	Identify all the target languages into which this project will be translated.
NAME OF TRANSLATION COORDINATOR	Who is the point of contact in your company for any questions translators have about the project and source material?
NAME OF TRANSLATION COMPANY OR TRANSLATION COMPANIES	Provide the name of the company, relevant people to contact, and contact information; if you use different companies for certain target languages, identify all these and the target languages that they are responsible for.
TRANSLATION SCHEDULE	Identify very clearly what the deliverables are and the dates on which they are due. Expand these dates to include the full production cycle (printing and distribution, for example).
TOOLS AND FILE FORMATS	Identify the tools used to create the information you supply to the translation company. Keep track of diskettes and files. Identify file formats.
INFORMATION SUPPLIED TO TRANSLATION COMPANY	Keep a log of all information and supplemental materials that you supplied to the translation company. Keep a log of whether the entire project was submitted to the translation company at once, or what pieces of it were delivered and when. Keep track of what is returned.
TRANSLATION REVIEWERS	Identify who is reviewing the translations, when review copies were sent, and when they were returned. Identify what criteria were used to review the translation.
EDITS	Identify who incorporated edits suggested by in-country reviewers. Indicate whether edits were incorporated and who performed the spot check.
QUALITY ASSURANCE METHODS	Identify the steps taken to ensure the quality of the translation, and who performed them.

TOOLS

Many large companies do not have tools standards for creating international technical communication products. If you work with the same translation company every time, realize that the company must have the same tools that you have. Consider supplying these tools to the translation company. Consider developing corporate-wide tools standards to assist in the translation process.

Discuss with the translation company whether the tools you use for writing are compatible with those that the translators use. Most tools are, but you need to consider this aspect of the translation process. Translators need to preserve your document formatting and any automation you have incorporated in your document, like automatic numbering, index tags, and cross-references.

Translators need to know the platform your tools run on. Is it a Macintosh? Unix? DOS? Windows? OS/2? an AS400, or some other computer-operating environment?

Because most translators translate by typing over source text, they ideally want to receive pure text with no formatting. Since this is unlikely, it is preferable to use tools that allow a translator to view the codes instead of their application, which is what many WYSIWYG applications do. Translators can then avoid typing over formatting codes. The Standardized General Markup Language (SGML) is an international standard for document type definitions, for example, and is easy for translators to work with. (Chapter 12 discusses SGML in more detail.) More popular PC-based word processing products like Microsoft Word, for example, show you the result of formatting. You must save the document in Rich Text Format (RTF) to see the codes themselves. If you use Microsoft Word, for example, you should discuss with the translation company about what format they want the document in, its native Word format or RTF format. Consider that some formatting may be lost when the document is saved in another file format.

Also give some consideration to any graphics files and the file formats that can be used by the translation company. See Chapter 12 for more information on tools.

COMMUNICATION

Since time is always a consideration, make sure that your communications capabilities are compatible with those of the translation company. Or ask the translation company if they are willing to invest in communications capabilities as part of a long-term partnership. Consider:

- Electronic file-transfer capabilities

- Electronic mail for questions from translators, especially when they are in a different time zone

- Local-area and wide-area networks

- Conference-calling capabilities

- Video conferencing

Both you and the translation company need to take advantage of these tools, to make physical proximity at the translation company to your company unimportant.

REVIEWS

All translations should be reviewed by a subject-matter expert in the target country. The subject-matter expert plays an important role in assuring the quality of a translation and should be briefed accordingly. Jon Lavine of Berlitz Translation Services notes that *in-country reviewer* may be a new job title.

Subject-matter experts look for style, the appropriateness of cultural content, and the correct use of terminology. You should develop guidelines for subject-matter experts, since these people may not be writers or translators. Supply them with the source-language version, if they read the source language, so that they have something with which to compare the translation.

ATI offers this description of the reviewers they recommend:

"Competent foreign reviewers" of translations are people who have a native knowledge of the target language, as well as a good knowledge of the source language and the product. Like the translators, they must be skilled writers, and aware of software translation restrictions. Equal in importance to their linguistic competence, these reviewers must be willing to drop other projects in order to provide feedback quickly.[26]

Obviously it will be difficult to find people who meet these stringent recommendations. For this reason, most companies use the following people as in-country reviewers:

- Sales manager in the target country

- Manager or engineer in the subsidiary in the target country

- Distributor in the target country

- Freelance subject-matter expert in the target country

You should also be aware of the problems associated with using in-country reviewers, as ATI mentioned. In-country reviewers, especially if they are from a branch office in the target country, can use the translation review as a means of communicating their dissatisfaction with broader issues in your company. The in-country reviewer can also be wrong or demonstrate a real lack of technical knowledge about your product. And perhaps the biggest problem with in-country reviewers is their lack of sensitivity to the deadline for returning their comments on the translation. You need to find ways of addressing each of these issues and be an intermediary between the translators and the reviewers. You need to establish some criteria for deciding which review comments are relevant and which are not.

Legal content and licensing information also need reviewing. Identify people who are familiar with requirements in the target country and involve them in the review cycle.

QUALITY CONTROL

There are several ways of providing some degree of quality control in addition to usability testing, which is the subject of Chapter 13.

Even if you do not read the target language, you can still review a translated document for the accuracy of cross-references, table and figure numbers, index entries, and so on. Spot check the document.

Also, discuss with the translation company ways that they recommend for ensuring the quality of the translation. Many translation companies already employ target language editors, like your company might employ technical editors.

Jon Lavine of Berlitz Translation Services offers the following suggestions: [27]

- Consider submitting a typical chapter to the translators early to get initial feedback. Also have translators review the glossary early.

- Check the accuracy of the translation compared to the source language.

- Look at the style and idiomatic expressions. Check for the "look and feel" as it relates to the target country.

- Use acceptance criteria.

- Use some authority who is trusted by the person buying the translation.

W I S H   L I S T S

To facilitate effective international technical communication that balances business needs and user needs, technical communicators and translators need to work together very closely. There needs to be a marriage, in fact, between technical communication and translation. Without a close relationship, achieving this balance is doomed from the start. Theodora Landgren, president of BTS, Inc., adds, "We are an extension to your documentation department. Your selection criteria should include chemistry and a cooperative attitude. We allow our clients to play a part in selecting the project manager."[28]

Technical communicators and translators have a lot in common, as we have seen throughout this chapter. Our skills focus on our abilities to communicate technical information to a variety of audiences. We are experts in our native languages, in that we know how to use our native languages to communicate successfully. In a sense, we are translators of one language communicating with translators of another. We must thoroughly understand the products about which we communicate in order for us to be successful. We must meet tight deadlines that evolve around product availability. We need access to experts in the products about which we write. We need reliable technical information about these products.

What follows is a brief comparison of the most frequently mentioned needs of technical communicators and translators. It is important for each to understand the needs of the other to work effectively together.

N E E D S   O F
T E C H N I C A L   C O M M U N I C A T O R S

As technical communicators, we know all too well how difficult it is to write accurate and usable technical manuals when we do not have access to engineers and technical information. Not only is this true in the U.S., but it is also true throughout Europe and most probably throughout the world. In a 1992 survey issued to technical communicators throughout Europe that was conducted for the Commission of the European Communities (CEC), information gathering is rated the number-one problem of technical communicators throughout Europe. "[T]here is a clear majority of people who have severe to marked problems in connection with data collection. This is obviously one of the major headaches technical authors face. The answers correlate with the specific complaints uttered by several of those questioned (insufficient information flow, lack of feedback, lack of internal acceptance)."[29]

The Distributed Documenting Services (DIDOS) project summarized the main problems of technical communicators throughout Europe. Here are some of the problems listed in the DIDOS report:

- Information gathering

- Budgeting and cost containment

- Setting and meeting tight schedules

- Acquiring and keeping skilled personnel

- Planning and design

- Content management

- Taking account of product liability

- Compliance with directives and standards

- Language translation

- Training writers to write internationally

- Quality control

Needs of Translators

Consider, by comparison, the following items from a wish list developed from a survey of translation vendors:[30]

- Establishing more direct contact between translators and developers

- Setting deadlines that take into account time to perform quality-assurance testing

- Reviewing translations promptly

- Supplying all information up front and not in small doses throughout the project

- Providing better training on the product

- Consulting [translation] vendors before developing translation tools

- Using existing terminology for the product

- Providing more feedback on translation quality

- Controlling the quality of output that is supplied to translation vendors (disk versions and hard-copy correspondence)

- Using controlled source language

Consider carefully the wish list of technical communicators and that of the translation vendors. Clearly our needs overlap. We must seek ways of minimizing the needs we both face.

....

End Notes

[1] These figures are based on averages of 250 words per page at $0.30 USD a word, $75 USD a page, independent of graphics, desktop publishing, and additional value-added services.

[2] Jaap van der Meer of R. R. Donnelly, a large translation company, writes of this change throughout Europe in "Confusion in the Cost-Value Chain of Localization Services: A Modern History of the Translation Business," a paper presented to the Localization Industry Standards Association (LISA), August 24–26, 1994, Boston, Massachusetts.

[3] Telephone interview with Dick Crum, March 27, 1994.

[4] From several telephone interviews with Jon Lavine from August to October 1994.

[5] Van der Meer.

[6] Ibid.

[7] Edmund H. Weiss, *How to Write a Usable User Manual,* ISI Press, 1985, p. xi.

[8] Ibid., p. xii.

[9] Nancy Hoft and Marcia Sweezey, from handout offered at *Getting Started in Worldwise Technical Communication*, a seminar sponsored by the Northern New England Chapter of the Society for Technical Communication, Saturday, April 23, 1994.

[10] Ibid.

[11] Nancy Hoft, "Preparing for the Inevitable: Localizing Computer Documentation," *SIGDOC '91 Conference Proceedings*, Chicago, Illinois, October 10–12, 1991, p. 40.

[12] Correspondence with Robert Bononno, September 28, 1994.

[13] "Translating Computer Documentation and Software into Foreign Languages," a paper written and distributed by American Translators International, Inc (ATI)., Stanford, California, 1991, p. 2.

[14] Notes from a presentation by Alain Linden, Director of AT&T GIS, made at the LISA Forum, August 24–26, 1994, Boston, Massachusetts.

[15] Hoft, p. 41.

[16] ATI, p. 2.

[17] Sharlene Gallup, "Caterpillar Technical English and Automatic Machine Translation," *Proceedings*, Society for Technical Communication (1993), p. 421.

[18] Ibid., p. 424.

[19] Each response was either a quotation from a telephone interview (Lavine) or written comments on a draft of this chapter, all in September 1994.

[20] Jill Monaco, "Adventures in Localization: How to Adapt Your Product to Different Audiences," *Proceedings*, Society for Technical Communication (1991), p. RT–36.

[21] From correspondence with Marcia Sweezey, September 7, 1994.

[22] *Digital Guide to Developing International User Information*, Digital Press, 1992, pp. 18–19.

[23] From comments by Robert Bononno on a draft of this chapter, September 28, 1994.

[24] Hoft, p. 42.

[25] The content of this checklist was influenced by the *Validation Checklist for Translation* for COBE Laboratories, Inc., 1991.

[26] ATI, p. 3.

[27] Telephone interview with Jon Lavine, September 14, 1994.

[28] Telephone interview with Theodora Landgren, September 3, 1994.

[29] *Investigation of Technical Documentation Application Domains*, a deliverable to the CEC for the Distributed Documenting Services (DIDOS) Project, Project Number R2037, 31/07/92, p. 43.

[30] Derived from *Presentation Handouts*, "LISA Translation Vendors Survey," The LISA Forum, January 31–February 1, 1994, Runnymede, England.

9

LANGUAGE PROBLEMS FORM THE MAJORITY OF PROBLEMS IN INTERNATIONAL TECHNICAL COMMUNICATION. LANGUAGE PROBLEMS CAN BE GROUPED INTO TWO CATEGORIES: (1) PROBLEMS RELATED TO LANGUAGE STRUCTURE, AND (2) PROBLEMS RELATED TO THE EXPRESSION OF WRITTEN LANGUAGE USING DIFFERENT MEDIA.

WRITING ISSUES

International technical communication is particularly susceptible to the ambiguities and common problems of language, since either it will be translated into one or more languages or it will be read and used by non-native speakers of the source language. These ambiguities and common problems can manifest themselves in the overall cost and effectiveness of international technical communication. Language problems, when not properly addressed, have real and measurable consequences.

Language problems can have an effect on translation in the following ways:

- Translation can take longer, because translators might have to do more research to understand the source information.

- Translation can cost more, because some language problems might require major reorganization or substantial rewriting to correct.

- Translation quality can decrease, because the translation schedule might not allow time for translators to research or correct language problems in the target variants that are inherent in the source-information product.

Language problems can have an effect on non-native readers of the source language in the following ways when you do not translate:

- Non-native readers of the source language can become dissatisfied with a technical manual in the source language and project this dissatisfaction onto the product. These users might thus choose to use a competitor's product.

- Non-native readers of the source language can misunderstand information in a technical manual in the source language and misuse the product, which, in some cases, can lead to personal injury or property damage, depending on the type of product. In this case, there is the possibility that your company will be sued.

Companies have used a variety of tactics to minimize language problems that are introduced when they want to create world-ready information products. This chapter addresses common language problems and shares the solutions that many companies have adopted to address them. Common language problems that occur in English technical writing are provided as examples. It is possible that the problems that these examples identify will extend to languages other than English.

For the purposes of this book, language problems fall into two categories:

1. The structure of language: grammar, semantics, phonology, macrostructures

2. The media of language: graphology, graphic expression

THE STRUCTURE OF LANGUAGE

Languages differ in many ways. Language problems can occur at any point of contrast among languages, or they can be inherent and permanent problems in the source language alone. These problems become visible and are exacerbated when:

- Information is written and must be read in the absence of other sensory cues like sound and facial expressions.

- Written information is used as a tool for performance.

- Written information is translated into another language.

To appreciate the number of ways in which languages can differ, refer to Figure 9.1. Figure 9.1 offers a linguistic map of the structure of language as it is explained by linguists.[1]

Note that this map is not a thorough representation of language. Linguists might differ in their views on my choice of categories and their content. However, the purpose of this map is not to represent the science of language's complexity. The purpose of Figure 9.1 is to provide you with a place to begin thinking about each set of language problems as discriminating users of language (writers). Each set of language problems is used as a category throughout this chapter.

Here are some general comments on each category used to study the structure of language. Specific examples in English are offered later in this chapter.

GRAMMATICAL PROBLEMS

Information products about high technology, regardless of language, share some grammatical problems.

- New words are necessary to describe new technology. Each language has derivative properties that make the formation of new words easy or difficult.

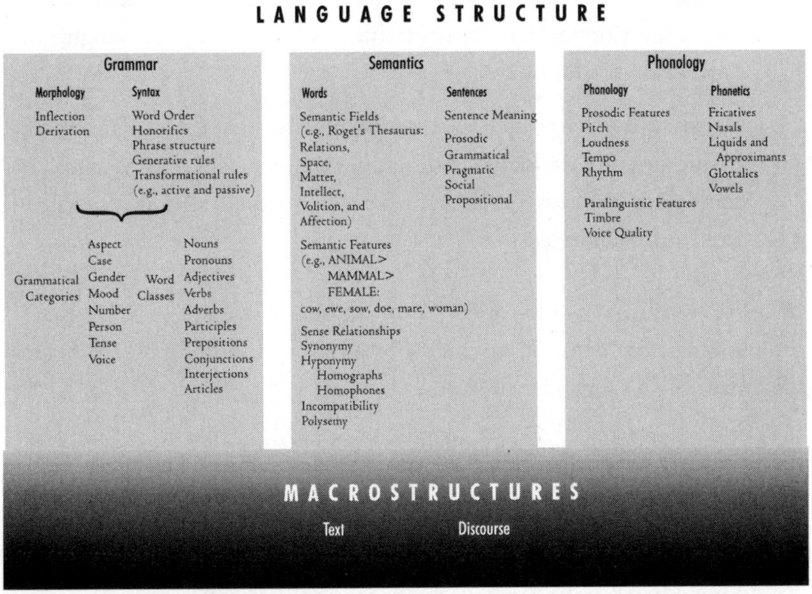

LANGUAGE STRUCTURE

Grammar			Semantics		Phonology	

Grammar

Morphology | Syntax

Inflection
Derivation

Word Order
Honorifics
Phrase structure
Generative rules
Transformational rules
(e.g., active and passive)

Grammatical Categories

Aspect
Case
Gender
Mood
Number
Person
Tense
Voice

Word Classes

Nouns
Pronouns
Adjectives
Verbs
Adverbs
Participles
Prepositions
Conjunctions
Interjections
Articles

Semantics

Words | Sentences

Semantic Fields
(e.g., Roget's Thesaurus:
Relations,
Space,
Matter,
Intellect,
Volition, and
Affection)

Semantic Features
(e.g., ANIMAL>
      MAMMAL>
         FEMALE:
cow, ewe, sow, doe, mare, woman)

Sense Relationships
Synonymy
Hyponymy
    Homographs
    Homophones
Incompatibility
Polysemy

Sentence Meaning

Prosodic
Grammatical
Pragmatic
Social
Propositional

Phonology

Phonology | Phonetics

Prosodic Features
Pitch
Loudness
Tempo
Rhythm

Paralinguistic Features
Timbre
Voice Quality

Fricatives
Nasals
Liquids and
   Approximants
Glottalics
Vowels

MACROSTRUCTURES

Text   Discourse

FIGURE 9.1: **A linguistic map of the structure of language.**

- The way that word classes change in aspect, case, gender, mood, number, person, tense, and voice vary. If the inflection of a word class is an important distinction in the source language, it may be lost in the target language if a similar inflection does not exist. If the inflection of a word class in the source language is inaccurate or ambiguous, its inflection in the target language may be inaccurate or ambiguous.

- Some languages have specific rules about how sentences can be formed, leaving little room for alternative constructions. Other languages are more flexible, allowing for a range of possible sentence constructions. Alternative constructions can have an effect on the meaning of the sentence and the number of ways in which it can be interpreted.

SEMANTIC PROBLEMS

The meaning of words and the meaning of combinations of words in sentences poses one of the most important problems in international technical communication.

- How languages and their native users deal with words and phrases from another language varies.

- The vocabulary of some languages is larger than in others. This can contribute to the wordiness or leanness of the translation.

- Words in the vocabulary of some languages can have limited shades of meaning, as opposed to words in the vocabulary of other languages that may have many shades of meaning.

- Words in one language can sound like words that exist in another language before they are translated. Sometimes the association of meaning before translation is positive, related, or helpful, at other times it is negative, unrelated, or detrimental.

PHONOLOGICAL PROBLEMS

Phonological problems do not factor into technical writing as demonstrably as grammatical and semantic problems.

- The sound and phonetic qualities of language as it is being read (silently or aloud) can sound native or foreign to a target reader. Translations of publishable quality are often successful because they not only convey the meaning of the source information, but they also sound natural to a target reader. Literal translations can sound as if they are translations to a target reader, even though they might convey the meaning of the source information well.

- Stylistic treatments of text in the source language that are phonological in nature (tempo, rhythm, and timbre) may not have an exact equivalent in the writing style of the target language. A literal translation may preserve the phonological effects, but they may be perceived as inappropriate or offensive in a target language. A skillful translator can create appropriate phonological effects for the target language.

MACROSTRUCTURES

Technical writing uses a variety of macrostructures to convey meaning depending on its purpose and intended audience.

- The structure of a user's guide can be different from that of a reference manual or a getting started guide.

- Macrostructures in information products that rely on grammatical constructions of the source language often require extensive reworking to account for differences in the grammatical constructions of the target languages.

- The macrostructure of an information product might be culturally meaningful in the source language but inappropriate or meaningless in the target language.

THE GRAPHICAL DEPICTION OF LANGUAGE: WRITING

Writing is a graphic medium of language. This is no surprise. All languages look different. However, describing the differences of the graphic symbols, called graphemes, and the characteristics of a written language that convey meaning is not so obvious. Graphic symbols and the characteristics of written languages differ considerably.

The problems associated with the graphical depiction of written language arise when:

- Information written in one language is translated and then written in another language.

- Written information is expressed in print, electronically, and sometimes in both media.

- Written information is graphically modified to convey meaning.

Figure 9.2 identifies the many ways that written languages differ.

Figure 9.2 is not complete, but it does offer sufficient detail for a discussion of how written languages differ in general, specifically, in print and electronically. Note that Figure 9.2 becomes very complex if we add the effects that multimedia has on the media of written language.

WRITING SYSTEMS

The writing systems of languages differ in many ways. There are two obvious differences, though: their *alphabets* and the *graphic symbols* that form their alphabets.

Some alphabets are large and contain thousands of characters. Korean, Chinese, and Japanese, for example, each have large alphabets. Korean has at least 2,000 characters, and Chinese nearly 50,000 characters (including many ancient characters) although only about 4,000 are in current use, and Japanese around 10,000 characters, although 2,000 characters constitute a basic level of literacy.

Other alphabets, like the Roman alphabet, are small. The Roman alphabet has 26 characters, but if you consider upper- and lowercase characters and characters with other diacritical marks you end up with about 200 characters. Most writing systems use alphabets that are similar in size to the Roman alphabet.

In some alphabets, the graphic symbols represent the sounds of speech. These are phonological writing systems.

In other alphabets, the graphic symbols are pictures of reality and/or pictures that represent ideas and concepts. These are non-phonological writing systems.

LANGUAGE MEDIA

| Speaking and Listening | Writing and Reading | Signing and Seeing |

Writing Systems

Phonological		Non-phonological	
Alphabetic (e.g., English, Cyrillic, Thai, Arabic)	Syllabic (e.g., Japanese kana)	Ideographic (concept) (e.g., Chinese, Japanese kanji, icons, signs)	Logographic (word) (e.g., mathematical symbols, scientific symbols)

Media and Expressions of Written Language

Handwritten	Written	Schematic	Pictorial
	Print	Electronic Media	Charts	Drawings
	Typography	Screen Resolution	Diagrams	Photographs
		Fonts		
		Character Sets		
		Input		
		Output		
		Physical Size (bytes)		

Examples of graphic contrasts that distinguish among writing systems and express meaning:

Alphabets
Spelling
Symbols
Capitalization
Spatial Organization (layout)
Punctuation
Abbreviations
  (e.g., acronyms, contractions)
Typographic variation
  (e.g., italic, bold, capitalization, color)

Text directionality
  (e.g., left-to-right, right-to-left, bidirectional, vertical)
Conventions
  (e.g., date formats, time formats, letter formats, address formats, currency formats, time formats, formats for units of measure)

FIGURE 9.2: **Writing systems, media for writing, and distinguishing characteristics of written language.**

Phonological Writing Systems

There are two kinds of phonological writing systems: *alphabetic* and *syllabic*. Phonological writing systems have small alphabets.

In alphabetic writing systems, the alphabet consists of graphic symbols that represent sounds. Writing systems that are alphabetic include English, Cyrillic, Thai, and Arabic.

The alphabets of syllabic writing systems consist of graphic symbols that represent syllables, usually a consonant-vowel pair. Japanese kana is an example of a syllabic writing system.

Phonological writing systems introduce problems in that their sound systems and the ways that these sounds can be pronounced can vary greatly. This leads to some interesting problems in the varieties of meaning just through sound and syllabic variation that are not easy to identify by alphabet alone. Often readers need to be familiar with the context of a word in order to "sound it out" and give it meaning. Another related problem is spelling. Some countries share a writing system and an alphabet, but for many possible reasons spell some words the same and others differently; for example, in the U.S., the spelling of *color* and in the U.K., the spelling of *colour*.

Non-Phonological Writing Systems

There are two kinds of non-phonological writing systems: ideographic and logographic. Non-phonological writing systems can have large alphabets.

In ideographic writing systems, graphic symbols called *ideographs* represent things, ideas, or concepts. Examples of ideographic writing systems include Chinese, Japanese kanji, icons, and signs.

In logographic writing systems, graphic symbols called *logograms* represent words. Many writing systems use logograms. Examples of logograms include mathematical and scientific symbols.

There is some disagreement as to whether Chinese and Japanese kanji are logographic writing systems or ideographic writing systems. Since most sources in high technology refer to Chinese and Japanese kanji as ideographic writing systems, I will follow suit.[2]

Some language problems that arise in non-phonological writing systems can include the similarity of graphic symbols in one alphabet to the graphic symbols in another alphabet and the amount of graphic symbols in the alphabet.

Graphic Contrasts of Writing Systems

Writing systems use a variety of conventions to express meaning graphically. These conventions often have meaning in one kind of writing system but no meaning in another. For example, capital letters have no significance in ideographic writing systems unless a word is borrowed from a writing system where capitalization has significance. Another problem among writing systems is the spelling of words. The juxtaposition of problems like these is the source of a variety of language problems that international technical communication must address.

THE MEDIA AND EXPRESSION OF WRITTEN LANGUAGE

Written language is the formal and permanent expression of a communication. Because of its special status, written language has associated with it distinguishing characteristics that are unique to each society, even if the society shares a writing system and a language with another society. These distinguishing characteristics can be elaborate or simple, and there are often many formal and informal rules associated with their proper use. The *Chicago Manual of Style*, for example, which is a classic reference for American writers, carefully identifies the distinguishing characteristics of bookmaking and its production and printing. The 14th edition is almost 200 pages longer than the 13th edition, mostly because of media changes and changes in conventions for different kinds of writing (academic, technical, and so on).

Information products make use of a variety of distinguishing characteristics that might be formally documented in a book like the *Chicago Manual of Style* or in a corporate style guide. These distinguishing characteristics can change depending on new research in readability, typography, human factors, usability, and so on. Sometimes the changes are the result of a change in a corporate look.

Perhaps the most significant changes to the distinguishing characteristics of written language are due to changes in technology (media). The change from printing to computerized printing, from paste-up to desktop publishing are examples of this. The shift from printed documents to online documents and even to multimedia presentations and talking books illustrate these changes even more. And with these shifts come changes in the expression of a written language, like the use of color. Color had not been used in most information products because it was cost prohibitive. Now color is an affordable option both on paper and online.

CONTROLLED LANGUAGES AND THEIR APPLICATIONS

In response to the variation of patterns in language structure and the variations in the media and expression of written language, some national governments, industries, and private companies have created modified versions of their native languages to facilitate successful communication for cultural and business reasons. These modifications to a language create what is commonly referred to as a *controlled language*. Controlled languages are sometimes referred to as simplified languages. The act of creating a controlled language is sometimes referred to as language planning.

A controlled language and its use typically offers the following features:[3]

- A limited, specialized vocabulary
- A dictionary defining the meaning and usage of all words in the vocabulary

- Simple writing rules and strict and rigorous punctuation rules that circumvent variant spellings and missing or misleading punctuation

- A review board or task force that periodically audits this sublanguage

Controlled languages are usually created for these reasons:

- To allow non-native speakers of a language to communicate

- To facilitate machine translation (MT)

Controlled languages, if they fail, tend to do so for the reasons provided here to explain why the British American Scientific International Commercial (BASIC) language developed by Charles Kay Ogden in 1930 failed:

> The system was strongly supported . . . by Churchill and Roosevelt, but there were also many criticisms. The simplification of the vocabulary is achieved at the expense of a more complex grammar and a greater reliance on idiomatic construction. The replacement forms are often unwieldy, involving lengthy circumlocutions. And although BASIC proved easy to learn to read, it proved very difficult to write in the language in such a way that meaning was clearly preserved.[4]

Controlled languages exist at four levels of society. Here are some examples.

- **National.** The most extensive effort at controlling language is seen in Chinese. Chinese language reform was necessary to provide a way for the people of China to be able to communicate at all. The eight main dialects of Chinese are to a large extent incompatible; the speaker of one dialect cannot be understood by the speaker of another dialect.

  Language planning for Chinese has met most of these goals:

    - To simplify the characters of classical written Chinese by reducing the number of strokes it takes to write a character

    - To provide a single means of spoken communication throughout the whole of China

    - To introduce a phonetic alphabet, which would eventually replace the Chinese characters in everyday use[5]

  We also see some degree of language control in France where l'Académie française concerns itself with terminology and other elements of French linguistics.

Canada has a similar body, the Terminology and Linguistic Services
Directorate of the Translation Bureau, but it does not have as much influence
or power as l'Académie française.

- **Industrial.** The aerospace industry created its own version of English,
  which it calls AECMA Simplified English. AECMA Simplified English is a
  joint effort of the Air Transport Association of America (ATA) and the
  Association européenne des constructeurs de matériel aérospatial (AECMA).
  This was created for the writing of maintenance and service manuals.

  The Standard Marine Navigation Vocabulary was created by the Inter-gov-
  ernmental Maritime Consultative Organisation (IMCO) to help navigators
  communicate with one another.[6]

- **Proprietary.** One of the most extensive uses of a proprietary controlled
  language is Caterpillar Technical English (also sometimes called Caterpillar
  Fundamental English) of the Caterpillar Tractor Company. Currently
  Caterpillar is working with the Carnegie Group to apply Caterpillar
  Technical English to machine translation (MT). At the time of this writing,
  the only language supported is English.

  Other companies that have created varying degrees of controlled languages
  include L. M. Ericsson, IBM Eastman Kodak, and Rank Xerox.[7]

- **Commercial.** The International Language for Service and Maintenance
  (ILSAM) and BASIC 800 are examples of commercially sold controlled languages. Both are derivatives of Caterpillar Technical English.[8]

  The remainder of this chapter identifies the common language problems that
  translators have identified in English technical writing.

EXAMPLES OF LANGUAGE STRUCTURE PROBLEMS IN ENGLISH TECHNICAL WRITING

Translators are very sensitive to the ambiguities of language. Here are examples of
the most common ambiguities that translators have found in English technical
writing.

GRAMMAR

Grammar relates to the structure of words, phrases, clauses, and sentences.

Invisible Plurals

Invisible plurals occur when you use a plural noun as an adjectival noun. We usually drop the plural ending from the noun and make it singular when we use it as

an adjective. When translating into French or Spanish, for example, a translator needs to know how to dissect your phrase and re-create it as a prepositional phrase. A translator needs to know whether the adjectival noun is singular or plural. Adjectives are not inflected and do not show whether they are singular or plural.

switch and jumper settings

This phrase can be translated in these ways:

1. the settings for one switch and one jumper

2. the settings for many switches and many jumpers

Rather than use a prepositional phrase, which can sound wordy to a native English reader, make sure that somewhere in the book you identify how many parallel and serial ports there are. Translators will rely on this information to add more meaning to the phrase to indicate whether the adjective is plural or singular. Additional examples of invisible plurals include: *console cabinet* and *instrument case*.

Modifier Strings

A modifier string is a series of adjectives that modify a noun. It is sometimes difficult to determine what words each adjective modifies, especially when you use a conjunction to join adjective phrases.

green plastic brackets and fasteners

This phrase can be interpreted in three ways:

1. Both the brackets and the fasteners are made of plastic. Both the brackets and the fasteners are green.

2. Only the brackets are made of plastic. Only the brackets are green.

3. Both the brackets and the fasteners are green, but only the brackets are made of plastic.

Some solutions include:

1. green plastic items: brackets and fasteners

2. brackets (green plastic) and fasteners

3. green plastic brackets and green metallic fasteners[9]

Dick Crum, a senior editor at Berlitz Translation Services, provides this modifier string, quoted from an unnamed publication and dubbed "the champion modifier string of 1970." (How would you parse it?)

The Commission was impressed by the Test Project command module reaction control system engine oxidizer vapor inhalation damage recovery results.

Elisa del Galdo, an independent consultant, suggests that you limit the number of adjectives to two or three, and that you use prepositions to clarify relationships. For example, *cable adapter number table* becomes *table of cable adapter numbers.*[10]

John Kohl, of SAS Institute, Inc., suggests that you hyphenate or bracket noun phrases either in the text, or on a translator's version of the text in the form of a translator's note. For example: *[file-sharing]-mode flags, terminal-interrupt handler.*[11]

Gerunds and Participles

A gerund is a verb form ending in *-ing* that is used as a noun; for example, *good writing comes from practice.* A participle is a verb form that is used as an adjective and ending in *-ing*; for example, *the chirping bird kept me awake.*

Gerunds and participles are *homographs*, since they are spelled the same but can be different parts of speech depending on their contexts. In some cases a homograph can be both a gerund and a participle, depending on how you interpret the sentence. Crum offers this example in his Translatability Seminar:

searching the database

Is *searching* functioning as a noun or as a verb in this phrase? As a chapter title, *searching* functions as a noun (gerund), since it identifies a task. As a message that is displayed on a monitor, *searching* functions as a verb, since it indicates that the system is performing a task. Crum suggests that you rewrite the phase to indicate as what part of speech the homograph should function. This makes it much easier for translators.

1. How to search the database

2. Database search in progress

Helping Verbs

Helping verbs, also called *modals*, *auxiliary verbs*, and *modal auxiliaries*, help the main verb express an action or make a statement. Helping verbs that introduce ambiguity include:

shall be, may be, may have, would have, would be, should have, should be, might have, might have been[12]

Helping verbs cause problems for translators, because they are not precise. Writers tend to use some of these helping verbs to be "polite."

TABLE 9.1: **Recommended Definitions of Common Helping Verbs**

HELPING VERB	MEANING
Can	Ability or capability
May	Possibility
Might	Lesser possibility
Should	Obligation

Harris and Moran, authors of *Managing Cultural Differences*, cite the ambiguity of the helping verb *should*: Does it mean "moral obligation, expectation, social obligation, or advice"?[13]

The *Digital Guide to Developing International User Information* offers the following example: *No initial value may be specified*. The intended meaning of this sentence is: Do not specify an initial value. There is a big difference between what was stated and what was intended. The *Digital Guide* suggests that you use the definitions provided in Table 9.1 for other troublesome helping verbs.[14]

Most formal versions of restricted English forbid the use of helping verbs.

Adverbs

The *Digital Guide to Developing International User Information* observes that the adverbs *when*, *where*, and *while* are often misused. These adverbs should be used to indicate time and place, but instead are used to mean "in contrast to" or "in comparison with."[15] However, Fowler states that a proper meaning of *while* can be "whereas" or "though," in addition to "during the time that."[16] All we can say in this case is that these adverbs can introduce ambiguity.

Conjunctions

As shown in the examples for modifier strings, a conjunction joins words and phrases, but does not always clarify the relationship between or among the words and phrases. Citing how conjunctions are handled in Caterpillar Technical English (CTE), a proprietary version of Controlled English, the Carnegie Group offers this example:

Non-CTE: *Replace and tighten the bushings.*

CTE: *Replace the bushings. Tighten the bushings.*[17]

Controlled English removes all the ambiguities by breaking the sentence into two sentences. Conjunctions, in this case, become almost commands for editors or writers that indicate how to break up a sentence into smaller chunks.

Relative Pronouns

Relative pronouns introduce subordinate clauses. Relative pronouns include: *who, whom, which, that,* and *whose.* Some sources note that the omission of the relative pronoun *that* creates ambiguity.

Fowler's Modern English Usage states that *that* is often dropped from sentences in writing, probably because it is dropped from sentences in speech. This tendency toward omission, it seems, has become almost idiomatic in English. Kohl offers numerous examples of places in sentences where *that* is often omitted. Kohl recommends that we make every effort to include *that* in our sentences wherever possible to enhance clarity. Some places in sentences where Kohl recommends we insert *that* include:

1. Past participles. *Practically none of the studies actually test the materials [that were] judged to be easier or harder.*

2. Present participles. *Another approach [that is] receiving attention is the use of Controlled English.*

3. Before noun-clause complements. *I cannot assume [that] you understand this sentence.*[18]

The Carnegie Group, in discussing Caterpillar Technical English (CTE), refers to the *that* omission as a reduced relative clause. They offer this example of how this sentence would be rewritten in CTE.

Non-CTE: *The valve actuated by the solenoid . . .*
CTE: *The valve that is actuated by the solenoid . . .*[19]

Bill Tuthill, author of the *Solaris International Developer's Guide,* draws attention to essential (restrictive) and nonessential (non-restrictive) clauses. Tuthill recommends that we be aware of using one kind of clause over another, since each kind of clause offers its own meaning to a sentence.[20] *Warriner's English Grammar and Composition* defines a nonessential clause as "a subordinate clause that is not essential to the meaning of a the sentence but merely adds an idea to the sentence."[21] Here are some examples:

Essential clause: *Note the ready light that is on the front panel.*
Nonessential clause: *Note the ready light, which is on the front panel.*

Table Headings

There has been a movement of late in technical writing, possibly stemming from the popularity of Information Mapping, a methodology for developing documentation that uses phrases in the headings of tables to introduce the elements in the

TABLE 9.2: Sample Table Headings That Are Difficult to Translate

IF THE USER ASKS...	THEN YOU MUST RESPOND BY...
"How do I do this?"	Showing the user how to perform the task.

TABLE 9.3: Sample Table Headings That Are Easily Translated

QUESTIONS	RESPONSES
"How do I do this?"	Show the user how to perform the task.

cells beneath them. This kind of table, an example of which is shown in Table 9.2, uses English syntax in a way that is similar to that of a formatted, bulleted list.

Jon Lavine, a Senior Editor at Berlitz Translation Services, notes that constructing table headings in this way makes translation particularly difficult. Each heading is based on a part of a grammatical unit that may or may not exist in a target language. Note, too, that the grammatical structure of each cell is grammatically consistent with the heading above it. The entire table forms a complete English-language sentence. If the target language does not have a grammar that can replicate the grammar in the table, the translator must reconstruct the entire table in a way that makes sense in the target language. In some cases, the entire effect of forming tables in this way is lost. What is more important, the translator must stop and rewrite your table.

A table style that is better suited for translatability is shown in Table 9.3.

Elisa del Galdo, an independent consultant, mentions in her explanation of how to treat online messages that grammars are not universal. Some programmers like to break up online messages into English phrases that become complete sentences after some action, which could be initiated by the system or by a user. Imagine how tedious it is for a translator, and even the programmer, who must reconstruct each of these sentences, of which there are typically over 50, so that they make sense in the target language? Hopefully the programmer is more willing to redesign the message construction so that it relies on a larger grammatical unit like a sentence or a paragraph, and not on a phrase based on English grammar.[22]

Word Order

The rules for ordering parts of speech in a sentence differ among the languages of the world. In *An Introduction to Language,* Victoria Fromkin and Robert Rodman, both university professors, offer this information about word order and how languages differ:

We find in all languages that sentences contain a noun-phrase subject (S), a verb or predicate (V), and possibly a noun-phrase object (O). In some languages the basic or "preferred" order of these elements is subject–verb–object (SVO). Many familiar languages, such as French, Spanish, and English, are examples. Other languages, such as Japanese and Korean, have the preferred order subject–object–verb (SOV). Others, such as classical Hebrew and Welsh, are VSO languages; and, rarely, one finds a language like Malagasy (spoken on Madagascar), which is VOS, or Dyirbal, an Australian language, which is OSV. No language has been discovered which has the preferred word order OVS.[23]

In a handout for his *Translatability Seminar*, Crum calls attention to the importance of word order for cover art, which, after translation, may require additional production. Table 9.4 provides an example.

Be aware of design elements (logos, company names, glyphs, and so on) that are affected by translation. The affect on design and production may be so great that translation would introduce more problems than it solves. Conversely, a better design that is more flexible may be the best solution of all.

Semantics

Semantics is the study of meaning in language.

Words in English

Of all the complaints with English and writing for translation, word choice and use is the number one complaint. Specifically, translators state that technical writers frequently use the same word to mean different things (*homophones*), or they use synonyms to refer to the same thing. In either case, translators strongly recommend that we apply the phrase, "One thing, one name, consistently." Translators read every word you write. If they come across a word or phrase that is used differently in another part of a manual, they wonder whether you meant to say something different. If you restate an idea in a different way, translators

TABLE 9.4: **The Effect of Translation on Word Order**

Language	Translation
English	*Marvolink* Communication Systems
German	*Marvolink*-Kommunikationssysteme
Swedish	*Marvolink* kommunikationssystem
French	Systèmes de communication *Marvolink*
Italian	Sistemi di comunicazione *Marvolink*

also wonder whether you are saying something different. We can think of this as a one-to-many semantic relationship of a word in English to other words in English.

For example, *homographs* are words that are spelled the same but have different meanings. In English, you have flexibility to do word play on grammatical constructions. Homographs are often used in short phrases that stand alone, and can be very confusing to non-native speakers of English. A homograph can be more than one part of speech, depending on its desired meaning. Sometimes the intended meaning of a homograph is not clear, as in this example.

> *Empty file.*

Is *empty* a verb or an adjective? Crum suggests that to lose the ambiguity, make the phrase a complete sentence or use omitted words like articles to identify the word's part of speech. Some possible solutions to *Empty file* include:

1. Empty this file.

2. This file is empty.

3. An empty file.[24]

Additional examples of words that are homographs include: *display, time, document, address,* and *use.*[25]

Controlled languages adamantly impose this rule of one thing, one name. Every source you ever consult about any kind of controlled language will tell you that consistent use of terminology is mandatory.

A now classic example of usage is in the *Digital Guide to Developing International User Information.*

> *A display at a trade show*
>
> *Change the scroll rate on the display.*
>
> *Display it on the screen.*
>
> *A spreadsheet display*[26]

The word *display* is used differently each time. In languages other than English, *display* may translate differently in each of these instances. But, in the *display* example, a translator would have to keep track of four or more non-English equivalents for the word *display,* since its part of speech and meaning is different in four cases.

O'Donnell, author of *Programming for the World,* offers the list shown in Table 9.5 of synonyms and a term that a formal version of restricted English might choose.[27]

TABLE 9.5: **Synonyms and Suggested Terms for Consistent Use**

SYNONYMS	APPROVED TERMS
collate, order, sort	sort
command, utility	utility
display, monitor, screen, tube	screen
display, demonstrate, show	show
delete, erase, remove, strip	delete
documentation, text	text
flag, option, switch	flag

Just as there are one-to-many relationships of English words in English, there are sometimes many-to-one relationships of words in other languages to words in English. This creates the problems of appropriateness and accuracy of translating these special words from other languages into English.

For example, Inuit has many words for types of *snow*, but not just one all-encompassing word for *snow*. Finnish has many words for types of *reindeer*, but not just one generic word for *reindeer*. French also has "a half-dozen different words equivalent to the English *valve*, depending on size, shape and function. Faced with the lonely 'valve' on a parts list, the French translator is stalemated."[28]

Harris and Moran suggest that you become aware of alternate spellings of English words like these British-English and American-English spellings: cheque/check, colour/color, organisation/organization, centre/center.[29] O'Donnell offers some solutions to these variant problems, which can also be used to address the problems of synonymous words.

1. Include all variants in the index to the book. For example, a main index entry of *removing* would have synonyms of *deleting* and *erasing*. You could include these index entries: *deleting* (see *removing*) and *erasing* (see *removing*).

2. When you introduce a word in your native language that has an alternate spelling in another country, include in parentheses its alternate spelling. This solution is similar to what you do when you first introduce acronyms.

3. Add more words to the glossary.[30]

4. You could also address these variants in a *Preface* or in a section about "Conventions Used in This Manual."

Here are some specific words whose meanings are of particular importance to technical communicators who work in the software industry.

- **Bytes versus Characters.** Internationalization affects the use of the words *byte* and *character*. With internationalization and the need to find ways to represent the many characters in alphabets around the world, the software industry has had to find ways of encoding characters. Each character in the ASCII code set, for example, occupies one physical byte of space. In other character sets, like those for Japanese, Korean, and Chinese, a single character can occupy multiple bytes.

    O'Donnell notes that it may be technically inaccurate for you to refer to characters, especially if you are describing a software system that has been internationalized. In these instances, she recommends that you replace the word *character* with the word *byte*.[31] She offers this example:

    Before internationalization: *A path name can contain up to 1024 characters. . . .*

    After internationalization: *A path name can contain up to 1024 bytes. . . .*

- **ASCII versus Text.** ASCII is an acronym for American Standard Code for Information Interchange. It is a character set (also called a *code set* or *code page*) that represents a total of 256 control codes, which consist of various hardware and proprietary control codes, punctuation marks, symbols, the Roman alphabet, and numbers. ASCII is limited by the number of graphic symbols, a total of 256, that it can possibly represent from a given alphabet. Considering the number of graphic symbols in some alphabets, like Japanese and Chinese, ASCII is limiting.

    With the push for internationalization, there are now many, many character sets that are specific to certain languages. Many of these are now ISO standards. The *Digital Guide to Developing International Software* contains a table that lists the character sets by country and language.[32] The ISO Latin-1 character set, for example, can be used in 24 of the countries in which Digital did business in 1991 because of its support of internationalization.

    For all these reasons, the term *ASCII* may not be technically accurate in some software documentation. It had become habit for many years among technical writers to use the terms *ASCII* and *text* synonymously to describe characters. However, as O'Donnell points out, internationalization has changed all that. "An internationalized system is capable of handling many code sets and encoding methods. For such a system, ASCII is wrong. . . ."[33]

Her recommendation is that you verify the technical accuracy of any references to *ASCII*, and that the word *text* is accurate in all cases. Here is an example.

Before internationalization: *Use **lpr** to send ASCII files.* . . .

After internationalization: *Use **lpr** to send* text *files.* . . .

How English words are handled in other languages can pose a problem. Dick Crum, a Senior Editor for Berlitz Translation Services, a speaker of over ten languages, and a linguist for over three decades, noted in a telephone interview that some cultures have different responses to using English words. The French, he comments, strongly discourage the use of English words in official government documents; terminology is strictly regulated by the l'Académie française. The French insist on creating French words for English ones. Canadians are similarly strict about the use of French-Canadian and monitor official French terminology; the Canadian terminology authority is the Terminology and Linguistic Services Directorate of the Translation Bureau, which are both run by the Department of State. The Germans, Italians, and Japanese, on the other hand, often do not bother creating new words for new English ones. He describes an article he read in German during a flight to Germany from the U.S. About 50 percent of the article consisted of English words.[34]

Because of all the translation issues related to terminology, there is an ongoing international effort at standardizing terminology for many disciplines in many languages. Ask your translators for suggestions on industry-standard terminology in your source language.

Slang, Idioms, and Jargon

Most technical writers do not include slang, idioms, and jargon in their writing. Formal versions of restricted English forbid their use. Be aware that slang and idioms are difficult, if not impossible, to translate.

O'Donnell offers this sensible advice regarding jargon, "Despite the advice to reduce jargon, the nature of technical documentation means that it must include new terms or use old ones in ways the dictionary never intended."[35] Most style guides recommend that you avoid using jargon because someone who is not familiar with the subject will not recognize the word or phrase. But, if you introduce the jargon, define it, and then include it in a glossary of terms, you have supplied sufficient information to introduce a reader to a new word or phrase.

In Berlitz's "Tech Writer's Translatability Checklist," the authors offer this interesting twist to jargon and its effect on translation, "A subcategory of undefined technical terms, jargon words develop within a specific industry, company, or even department. Translators sometimes play Trivial Pursuit games with them on coffee breaks. Try your luck with: *gladhand, headache bar, kick-down box*."

If and When Precision

Both words, *if* and *when*, take on very different meanings when writing procedures. Tuthill suggests that you use *if* when an event depends on some other event. Use *when* only if the event is inevitable.[36]

If you see the message . . .

When you see the message . . .

Humor

Betty Champagne and Kendrea Justice, in a paper presented at the 39th Annual Conference of the Society for Technical Communication, provide a quotation that seems to summarize the use of humor rather well:

> When someone blushes with embarrassment . . . , when someone carries away an ache . . . , when something sacred is made to appear common . . . , when someone's weakness provides the laughter . . . , when profanity is required to make it funny . . . , when a child is brought to tears . . . or when everyone can't join in the laughter . . . , it's a poor joke![37]

Humor is often very culture bound and may be very difficult to translate.

Puns, Metaphors, Similes

Puns are language-specific creations and are also culture bound. Metaphors and similes can introduce culture-specific, industry-specific, or company-specific references that may make no sense to your target audience. Metaphors and similes are very helpful literary devices, so to avoid them is to avoid a useful communication vehicle. When creating them, give serious thought to their global appeal and effectiveness.

Telegraphic Writing

Telegraphic writing is a very abbreviated, terse way of writing sentences in English. Telegraphic writing is characterized by its typical omission of articles, some simple verbs, pronouns, and prepositions. This reduces a sentence to its bare minimum for conveying an idea, but this does not mean that the sentence is a legal one according to the rules of English syntax. Native English speakers can usually derive the meaning of a telegraphic English sentence, because they do not need to rely on "syntactic cues," to borrow Kohl's phrase, to interpret the sentence. For everyone else, telegraphic English is more difficult to understand, let alone to translate.

Some typical words that are omitted from English sentences to create the telegraphic style include:

a, an, the, is, are, of, this, these, all.

Places where telegraphic English is often used include:

- Online Help systems
- Prompts displayed on a computer monitor
- Error messages and status messages from a software program
- Labels on hardware or equipment
- Forms
- Computer-generated voice instructions
- Callouts in illustrations, flowcharts, or diagrams
- Cautions, warnings, and danger messages in technical manuals
- Quick reference cards that supply steps for performing tasks
- Signs

The *Digital Guide to Developing International User Information* offers these examples of telegraphic English:

Label in an illustration of piece of equipment: *Close Cover.*

Prompt displayed on a computer monitor: *File: file.nam, delete? [N]:*

Error messages from a software program: *Wildcard required* or *Insufficient privilege.*[38]

Short Sentences

There are three reasons why short sentences are recommended by sources on writing for translation.

1. Short sentences are easier for non-native readers to understand.

2. Short sentences are easier for machine-translation software to parse.

3. Short sentences can conceivably reduce the number of words to translate; this saves money, because translation is priced on a per-word-translated basis.

Once again, you need to consider the effect that short sentences have on the response a native-English reader has to your writing. Will it sound overly simplified? Will your reader be offended?

Related to this topic of short sentences are all the readability formulas available to those of us who write in English. The Coleman-Liau and Bormuth readability formulas, for example, use sentence length as a criterion in determining the grade level of someone who can understand your text. How relevant are these readability formulas when you write for a multicultural and multilinguistic audience? Can these readability formulas assist in creating more translatable text? How applicable is the grade level a readability formula calculates when writing for a multicultural and multilinguistic audience? These are just some questions that are probably more interesting to ask than are the answers that might come from them.

Redundancy

Always edit your technical writing for redundancy. There is little need for it when you are being charged by the word or line for translation, when it adds no value to your writing, and when it might mislead a translator.

Informal Style

Brockmann suggests that using the pronoun *you* in technical writing may be perceived as too informal in Great Britain. He offers these examples:

U.S. style: *First,* you *should make a backup of your program disk.*

British style: *First,* the user *should make a backup of their program disk.*[39]

EXAMPLES OF LANGUAGE MEDIA AND PROBLEMS IN ENGLISH TECHNICAL WRITING

Here are many examples of language media problems that translators find in English technical writing.

ENGLISH AS AN ALPHABETIC WRITING SYSTEM

Alphabets seem to have less in common than they share. Many technical reference manuals that are written in the U.S. organize their content alphabetically. When these manuals are translated, the key words need to be translated and then sorted according to the sorting order for the target language. As a result, the entire manual gets completely reorganized for each target language. This is not a very efficient way of organizing a manual that is going to be translated. However, most Americans seem to prefer having information ordered alphabetically.

References to alphabetic ranges, examples that show users how to search for character strings, and any language-specific examples will need to be completely changed, repeatedly, if a technical manual is translated and exported to many target countries.

EXPRESSIONS OF WRITTEN ENGLISH IN PRINT AND ONLINE

Expressions of written English in print and online relate to the ways that the English language can be expressed in writing as compared to the ways that other languages can be expressed in writing. Note that this list is not complete. It identifies some common expressions of written English in technical writing about high technology.

Shortened Words

Shortened words include acronymns, initialisms, abbreviations, and contractions.

When I worked at the World Health Organization in Geneva, Switzerland, I referred to the organization as WHO when I spoke to colleagues in English. I had to remember to refer to the same organization as OMS (Organisation Mondiale de la Santé) when I spoke to colleagues in French. This was true for everything. I had to keep track of acronyms for all sorts of things in two languages. It was very confusing, and I am certain that I confused my listeners at least once as a result.

Del Galdo states that, "When translated, an acronym may no longer be as effective or as concise as in its original language. The acronym in its original language may have negative associations in a different language. . . . Abbreviations of words, if being used to save space, may not decrease to the same number of letters in other languages or there may not be an abbreviation available."[40]

Most sources recommend that if you do use abbreviations and acronyms, you should include a list of all of them and their meanings in all publications that use them. You should always provide your translators with a copy of this list prior to translation.

Most of the companies that I have done writing for discourage the use of contractions whether they export their documentation or not. Contractions are considered too informal and may not be understood by non-native speakers. Note that contractions are often forbidden in controlled languages.

Uppercase and Lowercase Characters

Rules for uppercase and lowercase characters vary. Some writing systems, like Hebrew, Arabic, Japanese, and Chinese do not recognize changes in case, since they do not use a Roman alphabet. German uses an initial capital letter for all nouns. In short, be wary of using uppercase and lowercase characters as distinguishing typographic conventions in your writing. They may not get translated.

Punctuation

Many translators and non-native readers encourage over-punctuating. Harris and Moran offer these thoughts about the comma, "Maximum punctuation should be used, e.g., commas that help clarify the meaning, but could technically be omitted, should be retained."[41]

Kohl describes the hyphen as "a translator's best friend." Hyphens, he states, eliminate the problems associated with modifier strings.

file sharing mode flags

Rewritten for clarity using hyphens:

file-sharing-mode flags[42]

Note, though, that the rules of punctuation differ among writing systems, and even differ within the same writing system, as is the case in British English and American English.

Symbols

Symbols are characters like the slash (/), the pound sign or number sign (#), the at sign (@), the single quotation mark ('), the double quotation mark ("), and the and sign (&). In English, these characters are used to mean a variety of things.

Bill Tuthill, author of the *Solaris International Developer's Guide*, documents the possible meanings of the slash (/).

Does / mean: and? or? and/or? with? divide by? root? path-name divider?

Tuthill also states that American technical writers should avoid using the symbols #, ', and " to indicate the units of measurement pound or the number sign, foot, and inch, respectively, since these symbols are usually recognized only in the U.S. The symbols @ and & may also have the meanings "at" and "and," respectively, in the U.S.[43]

Time of Day

Like measurements and currencies, expressions of time should be given using both the source format and the target format. Americans typically do not use a

TABLE 9.6: **Examples of Time Formats for Four Countries**

	U.S.	FRANCE	DENMARK	ITALY
Time	9:45 P.M.	21:45	21.45	21.45
Time	9:45 A.M.	09:45	09.45	9.45

24–hour notation for time; in the U.S., 24–hour time is sometimes referred to as "military time," since the military always uses a 24–hour notation to express time.

Many countries in the world use 24–hour notation to express time. However, the notation for expressing time differs. Table 9.6 offers some examples.

There are some additional variations. For example, in France, you can write 21h45. In Germany you can write 09:45 Uhr. In Argentina, you can write 2145.[44]

Typography

Many technical writers use typography to distinguish words or phrases in their technical writing. In the *User's Guide* for Microsoft Word, Version 6.0, for example, there is a section called "Typographical Conventions." This section lists formatting conventions that are used throughout the user's guide. The **bold** type indicates words or characters that users type. *Italic* type indicates specialized terms, titles of books, and placeholders for items users have to provide. A `monospaced` font is used for field syntax and macro listings.

Used consistently throughout a document, typographic conventions aid translators. Used inconsistently throughout a document, typographic conventions confuse translators, who must find ways of emulating their use in the target language.[45]

Keyboards and Keycaps

Because languages are different, keyboards and keycaps, which are used to type words in English and all the other languages of the world, are also different. Many companies, like IBM, Apple, Hewlett-Packard, and Digital Equipment Corporation, include an appendix in their manuals that graphically depicts how keyboards and keycaps are mapped for the various countries to which they export their products.

The *Digital Guide* recommends that you address the differences with keyboards and keycaps by identifying the "parts of the keyboard with illustrations that use number or shading, rather than key cap letters."[46] Figure 9.3 illustrates such an approach.

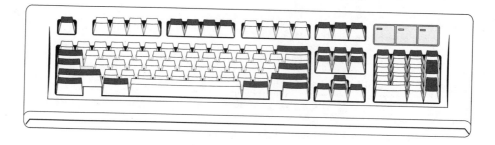

FIGURE 9.3: **How to address differences in keyboards and keycaps.**

If you are documenting a software product that maps functions to various keys or key combinations, you could spend pages and pages just documenting the different key combinations. This is a daunting task. The *Digital Guide* offers these suggestions:

- Document only the function names and not the keycap names.

- Document a default keyboard and develop a method for providing information about country-specific keyboards.

- Place most keyboard information online so that it can be customized more easily and less expensively.[47]

Dates

Dates and date formats are as diverse as time formats and time zones as compared around the world.

There are long date formats and short date formats. Table 9.7 offers some examples.

Use the alphanumeric characters to display the name of the month to avoid confusion with the order issue in date formats. Doing this for dates displayed at "information kiosks in airports or train stations" helps avoid the date-format problems in multinational environments.[48]

There are also different calendars that determine what year it is. Many countries, like the U.S. and the EU countries, use the Gregorian calendar.

In Japan, the Gregorian calendar is used, but so is the Imperial calendar, which is based on the number of years an emperor has been reigning. "In the Imperial calendar, 1992 is called *heisei 4*, the fourth year of the heisei reign (the reign of

TABLE 9.7: **Examples of Date Formats from Three Countries**[49]

	LONG DATE	SHORT DATE
U.S	Friday, September 9, 1999	9/09/99 (MDY)
	Friday, September 09, 1999	09/9/99
France	mardi le 9 septembre 1999	09.09.1999 (DMY)
Germany	Dienstag, 9. September 1999	9.9.99 (DMY)

the new emperor); 1988 is called *showa 64*, because the previous emperor's reign was called showa. Japanese Imperial dates are often written in year-month-day format without the name of the reign. For example, January 1, 1992, may be written 4.1.1."[50]

There is also a Buddhist calendar, two Islamic calendars, and a Hebrew calendar. There may be others.

In the U.S., the week begins with Sunday and ends on Saturday, which is illustrated in most calendars sold in the U.S. Throughout Europe, the week begins on Monday and ends on Sunday, as shown in most of the calendars sold in Europe.

The number of months in a year and the number of days in a month also differs from country to country. Saudi Arabia and Egypt have 354 or 355 days in a year, as compared to 365 or 366 days in the U.S. and Europe. The Hebrew calendar, during a leap year, has 13 months.[51]

Telephone Numbers

Some countries have toll-free numbers and others do not. If you include telephone numbers in any technical writing, make sure that the telephone number is valid for the target country. For example, an 800 number in the U.S. is often invalid if dialed outside the U.S., although it is sometimes valid when calling from Canada. The 900-number phenomenon in the U.S., which is used to charge callers a high rate per minute or increments of minutes, is not applicable in most other countries in the world.

All telephone numbers have an international part and a domestic part. The international part consists of an international access code followed by the country code. The international access code is usually not included when denoting a telephone number. The domestic part consists of the area code (U.S. only), city routing code, and the local telephone number.

TABLE 9.8: **Examples of Telephone Number Formats for Three Countries**

	TELEPHONE NUMBER
U.S	(603)878-4540
France	(16.1) 60.45.34.06
Germany	(089)3.59.44.11

TABLE 9.9: **Examples of Cardinal and Ordinal Number Formats in Three Countries**

	UNITED STATES	FRANCE	GERMANY
Cardinal numbers	1,107.61	1 107,61	1.107,61
Ordinal numbers	1st, 2nd, 3rd	1er, 2ème, 3ème	1., 2., 3.

The format of telephone numbers, as they would be printed on a business card, for example, is shown in Table 9.8. Be aware that, even within each country, there are often two or more telephone number formats that are acceptable.

Numbers

Numbers are represented differently around the world. Syntax, in particular, is what changes from country to country. It is critical that numbers be represented accurately.

There are two kinds of numbers considered here: *cardinal numbers* and *ordinal numbers*. Cardinal numbers are counting numbers. Ordinal numbers show the order of succession. Table 9.9 provides some examples of cardinal and ordinal number formats for the U.S., France, and Germany.

One additional difference regarding numbers is the definition of the word *billion*. In the U.S., one billion is one thousand million and is written like this: 1,000,000,000. Some countries, like Germany, England, and France, define *one billion* as one hundred thousand million, which is written like this: 1,000,000,000,000. This is a trillion in the U.S. The difference is not slight.

Everyone who has traveled beyond the borders of a country understands the significance of currency differences. Sometimes you profit and sometimes you lose.

Note that each country uses the same format for denoting the thousands separator, the radix point, and the decimal number as it does for denoting those for cardinal numbers. Table 9.10 provides some examples. Compare their format to the format of cardinal numbers in Table 9.9.

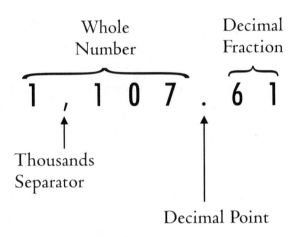

FIGURE 9.4: **Reviewing the format of cardinal numbers.**

Figure 9.4 diagrams the format of a cardinal number. Knowing the terms used to discuss a number's format helps when talking about numbers with translators.

Of additional interest relating to currencies is the amount itself. For example, if something costs $5.00 in the U.S., it might cost 8,437.95 Lira in Italy (L. 8.437 using Italian currency format). Quantitatively, both numbers seem totally unrelated, even though they are close equivalents when currency values are considered. If you use examples with currency in your technical writing, you should consider that:

1. The amounts you use in the source country need to be converted to the currency of the target country, and

2. The amounts are realistic given the economic condition of the target country.

Positive and negative numbers, which also affect currency values, are expressed differently in different written languages. The positive and negative signs can precede or trail the number itself. In the U.S., some accountants put negative

TABLE 9.10: **Examples of Currency Formats in Three Countries**

	UNITED STATES	FRANCE	GERMANY
CURRENCY	$1,107.61 USD	1 107,61 F	1.107,61 DM

numbers in parentheses or in angle brackets. If they have access to color printers, U.S. accountants print negative numbers in red to indicate debit.

Accounting practices differ around the world, too. So do the methods governments use to tax their citizenships. Be very wary of using examples that apply the

accounting principles that are in use in your country in technical manuals that will be exported to other countries. Consult the accounting department or the finance department in your company if you must use this kind of example. I recall being in a seminar on how to estimate the cost of technical communication that took place in the U.S. I spent about thirty minutes giving two Japanese participants an explanation of the meaning of the U.S. tax system, since this was the orientation of the seminar. Sales tax and Value Added Tax (VAT) are additional differences you should consider, especially if you create forms.

Conversions and the rounding of numbers are performed differently, which is important to understand if you convert numbers from the source value to the target value before translation to save money and control accuracy. Many sources recommend that you always include at least the U.S. measurement and its metric equivalent in all text to internationalize it. Internationally, this is most often accomplished by putting the non-domestic amount in parentheses right after the domestic amount.

Lavine recommends that you pay particular attention to the precision of the units of measurement: Inches, for example, are a much less precise unit of measurement than centimeters. Therefore, when converting from inches into centimeters or from centimeters into inches, round the result to an approximate number to compensate for the lack of equivalence in precision.[52]

Incorrect: *The bottom of the unit must have approximately 6 inches (15.14 cm.) of clearance from the floor.*

Correct: *The bottom of the unit must have approximately 6 inches (15 cm) of clearance from the floor.*

Rounding decimals is performed differently around the world. In the U.S., we look at the last digit of the decimal. If it is greater than five, we round it up by adding one to the previous digit and dropping the last digit.

11.07 rounded to the nearest whole number is 11.

11.07 rounded to the nearest decimal is 11.1.

In Argentina:

- if the last decimal digit is less than three, change it to 0 or drop it.

- if the last decimal digit is greater than two but less than eight, change it to five.

- if the last decimal digit is greater than eight, add one to the previous digit and change the last decimal digit to 0 or drop it.

For example:

123.452 rounded is 123.45.

123.456 rounded is 123.455.

123.459 is 123.46.[53]

Electronics (fuses, volts, plugs, amperages, wall sockets)

Electrical power ratings and their corresponding hardware vary around the world. The U.S. has its own electrical standards, Japan has its own electrical standards, and many countries in Europe have their own. Work with your engineering department to make sure that all information related to the electrical standards in a given country is absolutely accurate. References in text and illustrations that are affected by these variations include:

- Ilustrations of wall plugs, cords, and wall sockets

- Voltages

- Amperages

- Fuses

If you are unsure of the electrical standards in a target country, contact your national standards association, the national standards association in the target country, or a professional association like the IEEE. Inaccuracies in how electrical standards are indicated can damage equipment or seriously harm individuals, both of which can render your company liable for damages.

OTHER PROBLEMS IN ENGLISH TECHNICAL WRITING

- **Safety Labels.** Make safety labels a major concern as you write. Many countries now have product liability laws regarding the health and safety of workers who use the products about which you write. There may be requirements regarding the content of a safety label in a specific country, depending on the type of product and the risk of danger. Consult legal counsel regarding the specific laws and phrasing on all safety labels. In all cases, you should have safety information translated into the target language.

- Safety and warning labels should always be written in full.

- Cautions and notes should be placed before the action to which they refer and preferably on the same page.[54]

- **Names.** The order in which people list the parts of their names differs. In some countries, like Japan, a name is in the order family name, given name. In the U.S., names follow the order first name, middle initial or middle name, last name.

  The social rules for greeting people by name differ as well. In some countries it is common to address people by their last names only, preceded usually by a title (Dr.), or Mr. or Mrs., or some other socially distinguishing word. In other countries, as in the U.S., it is common to refer to people by their first names. Consider using names in your technical writing that reflect typical names and forms of address from the target countries. This helps internationalize your technical writing.

- **Sounds.** Elisa del Galdo offers this suggestion to those of you who write documentation about hardware devices. "If during installation the hardware makes particular noises, describe these in the documentation and use them as audio cues if appropriate."[55]

- **Geography.** O'Donnell suggests that when you refer to places, keep in mind that your readers may not know where they are on a map. In my travels to New Zealand, for example, I met few people who knew where the state in which I live, New Hampshire, was in the U.S. Most people asked me to provide them with the degrees of latitude and longitude so that they could find my state on a map.

  Use place names that are known, like Paris, France; or New York City, U.S.A.; Tokyo, Japan; Sydney, Australia; or London, England.

- **Time Zones.** There are many time zones in the world. A common way of denoting time differences is by expressing them with respect to Universal Time, coordinated (UTC), which used to be called Greenwich Mean Time (GMT). New York City, U.S., is -5 UTC. Tokyo, Japan is +9 UTC.

Each regional time zone has its own acronym, which might be the same as that of a time zone many thousands of miles away (Eastern Standard Time in North America and Eastern Summer Time in Australia).

Time zones tend to be in whole hour increments apart, but this is not always true. Some countries have time zones that are 30 minutes apart. In South America, Guyana's time zone is 45 minutes behind that of Suriname's time zone. Countries and even states in the U.S. can set their own time zones. Differences abound. In the U.S., most states have a Standard Time and a Daylight Time, which they use to move their clocks forward an hour or back an hour, respectively, twice a year. The U.S. state of Arizona, however, does not use Daylight Time.

- **Hemispheres.** There are hemisphere differences, too. The seasons for countries in the southern hemisphere are the opposite of the seasons for countries in the northern hemisphere. In examples that rely on geography and dates, consider the season of the target country at that time of year. Sometimes, too, the time zone will be different depending on the current season, as is the case in the U.S.[56]

GENERAL RECOMMENDATIONS

- Information on the topics of writing style for particular cultural groups and cultural rewriting is not included in this chapter. Marginal information on these topics does exist, but it is either very anecdotal or insufficiently conclusive to include in a list of suggestions. There is ample room for research in these areas.

- Hire trained professional writers. They can deliver source-information products that minimize language problems as much as can be expected.

- Because of diversity throughout the world, you are encouraged to internationalize as much as possible. The more you internationalize, the less you have to localize, or the easier it becomes to localize technical writing.

- There is no magic formula for generalizing cultural diversity. It exists. It can be frustratingly contradictory. Perform an international-user analysis. Edit your text for cultural bias. Use core information. Consider language problems. Work closely with your translation team. Open your mind to learning new ideas and new ways of thinking.

END NOTES

1 Here are the sources I consulted to create this map of the structure of language. David Crystal, *The Cambridge Encyclopedia of Language*, Cambridge University Press, New York, 1987. Apple Computer, *Guide to Macintosh Software Localization*, Addison-Wesley Publishing, Reading, Massachusetts, 1992. Victoria Fromkin and Robert Rodman, *An Introduction to Language*, 2nd Ed., Holt Rinehart and Winston, New York, 1978. Sandra Martin O'Donnell, *Programming for the World*, Prentice-Hall, Englewood Cliffs, New Jersey, 1994. Ken Lunde, *Understanding Japanese Information Processing*, O'Reilley & Associates, Sebastopol, California, 1993.

2 As a point of comparison, see Crystal, p. 200, and Apple Computer, p. 59.

3 R. John Brockmann, *Writing Better Computer User Documentation*, Version 2.0, John Wiley & Sons, New York, 1990, p. 112. For critical summaries of various forms of restricted English, see "Simplified English Roundup: Fait Accompli or Impossible Dream?" by Ralph Calistro, in *Proceedings*, 40th Annual Conference, Dallas, Texas (1993), pp. 158–161; "Simplified English—Is It Really Simple?" by Don E. Hinson, *Proceedings*, 38th International Technical Communication Conference, New York, New York (1991), pp. WE33–36; O'Donnell, pp. 301–304.

4 Crystal, p. 356.

5 Crystal, pp. 312–313.

6 John Kirkman, *Good Style*, E&FN Spon, New York, 1992, p. 154. The IMCO vocabulary could have helped in this instance: the headline of an article in the *Seattle Times* (Seattle, Washington, U.S.) in 1991 read "Lack of English may have lead to ships' collision." One of the ships was Chinese and the other was Japanese. Eric Nalder, *Seattle Times*, August 1, 1991, p. B4.

7 Kirkman, p. 149.

8 Ibid., p. 150.

9 Ibid.

10 Elisa del Galdo, "Internationalization and Translation: Some Guidelines for the Design of Human-Computer Interfaces," from *Designing User Interfaces for International Use*, ed. Jakob Nielson, Elsevier, New York, 1990, p. 8.

11 John R. Kohl, "A Procedure for Using Syntactic Cues," a handout at *Syntactic Cues Workshop*, 41st Annual Conference, Minneapolis, Minnesota, 1994, sponsored by the Society for Technical Communication.

12 John E. Warriner and Francis Griffith, *English Grammar and Composition*, Harcourt, Brace, Jovanovich, New York, 1973, p. 12.

13 Philip R. Harris and Robert T. Moran, *Managing Cultural Difference*, 3rd Ed., Gulf Publishing Company, Houston, TX, 1991, p. 46. This suggestion is one of a list of 20 propositions for internationalizing the use of English, which were originally printed in

the following source: Riddle, D. I., and Lanham, Z.D., "Internationalizing Written Business English: 20 Propositions for Native English Speakers," *The Journal of Language for International Business*, 1985.

[14] *Digital Guide to Developing International User Information*, Digital Press, Maynard, Massachusetts, 1992, p. 50.

[15] Ibid., pp. 50–51.

[16] H.W. Fowler, *Fowler's Modern English Usage*, 2nd Ed., Oxford University Press, New York, 1990.

[17] The Carnegie Group, handout at the LISA Forum Annual Meeting, April 21–22, 1994, Heidelberg, Germany.

[18] Kohl, handout, "A Procedure for Using Syntactic Cues."

[19] The Carnegie Group, handout, at the LISA Forum Annual Meeting, April 21–22, 1994, Heidelberg, Germany.

[20] Bill Tuthill, *Solaris International Developer's Guide*, Prentice-Hall, Englewood Cliffs, New Jersey, 1993, p. 114.

[21] Warriner and Griffith, p. 630.

[22] del Galdo, p. 9.

[23] Fromkin and Rodman, p. 335.

[24] Crum, handout for Berlitz's *Translatability Seminar*, given annually at the STC Annual conference.

[25] *Digital Guide to Developing International User Information*, pp. 42–43.

[26] Ibid., pp. 42–43.

[27] O'Donnell, p. 302.

[28] Berlitz's "Tech Writer's Translatability Checklist."

[29] Harris and Moran, p. 46.

[30] O'Donnell, pp. 296–297.

[31] Ibid., pp. 309–311.

[32] Cynthia Hartman Kennelly, *Digital Guide to Developing International Software*, Digital Press, 1991, Maynard, Massachusetts, pp. 256–258.

[33] O'Donnell, pp. 308–309.

[34] Telephone interview with Dick Crum, April 3, 1994.

[35] O'Donnell, p. 300.

[36] Tuthill, p. 113.

[37] Kendrea L. Justice and Betty Champagne, "Humor as a Defuser," *Proceedings*, 39th Annual Conference, Society for Technical Communication, Atlanta, Georgia (1992), p. 484.

[38] *Digital Guide to Developing International User Information*, pp. 54–55.

[39] Brockmann, p. 114.

[40] del Galdo, p. 8.

[41] Harris and Moran, p. 46.

[42] Kohl, "Improving Translatability and Readability with Syntactic Cues," a handout at *Syntactic Cues Workshop*, 41st Annual Conference, Minneapolis, Minnesota, 1994, sponsored by the Society for Technical Communication, p. 20.

[43] Tuthill, p. 114.

[44] O'Donnell, pp. 45–46.

[45] Berlitz's "TechWriter's Translatability Checklist."

[46] *Digital Guide to Developing International User Information*, p. 92.

[47] Ibid., p. 67.

[48] *The GUI Guide: International Terminology for the Windows Interface,* European Edition, Microsoft Press, Redmond, Washington, 1993, Appendix B.

[49] del Galdo, p. 4.

[50] *Localization for Japan*, Apple Computer, Inc., Cupertino, California, 1992, p. 44.

[51] O'Donnell, pp. 42–43.

[52] Jon Lavine, telephone interview, April 6, 1994.

[53] Emmanuel Uren, Robert Howard, and Tiziana Perinotti, *Software Internationalization and Localization: An Introduction,* Van Nostrand Reinhold, New York, 1993, p. 27.

[54] del Galdo, p. 65.

[55] del Galdo, p. 61.

[56] Much of this information was derived from O'Donnell, pp. 44–47. She covers this topic in much more detail than any other source I consulted. And it is a very confusing topic!

10

EXPRESSING WRITTEN LANGUAGE IN

ELECTRONIC FORM REQUIRES SOME TECHNICAL

KNOWLEDGE IN ADDITION TO LINGUISTIC

KNOWLEDGE AND CULTURAL AWARENESS.

Technical Issues
....

Cultural Concerns
....

ONLINE ISSUES

10

IBM introduced the phrase *machine-readable information* (MRI), which is particularly meaningful when discussing online issues as they relate to international technical communication. IBM defines MRI as "all the language-sensitive information passing between the user and a product" and provides this list of examples of what machine-readable information can be:[1]

- Messages
- Audio output
- Animations
- Windows
- Panels
- Helps
- Tutorials
- Diagnostics
- Clip Art
- Icons

To this list, I would add:

- README files
- Electronic books
- Computer-based training courses
- Hypermedia presentations
- Electronic mail

The principles that IBM describes as they relate to machine-readable information are the same or very similar to those recommended in every book written about software internationalization. These principles are discussed in the section on technical issues. You do need to understand these technical issues—if only in principle—if you are to internationalize and subsequently localize online information, as the technology to date is not sophisticated enough to make the technical issues transparent. I will keep the technical discussion to a minimum and focus mainly on concepts. If you want more information about the technical issues, see Appendix C, "Resources in International Technical Communication." Cultural issues as they relate to machine-readable information are discussed at the end of this chapter.

TECHNICAL ISSUES

Computers and the software that run them were created in the U.S. Because of this history, most software was written with English in mind. Many software programming languages, for example, still rely on English syntax. Most operating systems also have commands that are based on English syntax and semantics.

Software is now being written by programmers worldwide. New software is being written so that it can overcome the language barrier that is inherent in its history.

No more than four or five years ago, software internationalization was a difficult goal, because there were few software tools available that made internationalization systematic. Many software internationalization problems were solved with custom tools that were often created in house.

Today, software internationalization is significantly easier because most major software vendors provide internationalization toolkits with their products. All major computing platforms, like Windows, Macintosh, UNIX, and IBM platforms, have been internationalized to a large extent, and their internationalization continues to improve over time. Most computing platform vendors offer internationalization training to software developers, and teach them how to internationalize products that run on their platforms. They even offer training in setting up international distribution channels. Many software developers now know how to do software internationalization, and are getting better and better at making it easier and more efficient; they have systematized internationalization to a large extent.

Everyone is being trained in internationalization, it seems, except technical communicators. What follows, then, is a conceptual overview of software internationalization as it affects us, technical communicators, and the online information that we create, which is referred to here as machine-readable information.

EXPRESSING WRITTEN LANGUAGE ONLINE

The most visible difference between a software program that is created in the U.S. and one that is created in Japan is language. There are many technical problems that occur when you try to make a computer understand both the English and the Japanese software programs simultaneously, and all of them begin with the language problem. Remember that most computers and their software were created with English in mind, and their architectures reflect that in a major way. The exception is in Japan, where many proprietary hardware and software platforms exist, possibly made necessary by the prevalent English bias years ago. Figure 10.1 illustrates the language problems unique to the electronic expression of written language.

Media and Expressions of Written Language

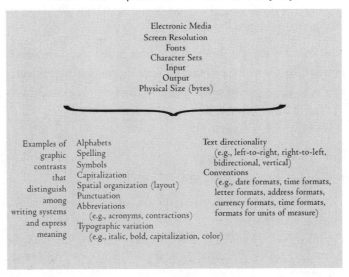

FIGURE 10.1: **Some language problems introduced by expressing written language in electronic form.**

A multilingual computer must be able to perform the following basic computing tasks:

1. Store characters on storage media, like floppy disks, hard drives, and CD-ROMs.

2. Accept characters as input from input devices like keyboards. (This discussion will not consider voice-input devices.)

3. Send characters as output to output devices like computer monitors and printers.

Storing Characters

Computers store information in bits and bytes using binary encoding (ones and zeros). One character—in English, that is—is physically stored in one byte of disk space. One byte of storage consists of 8 bits. If each character is 7 bits wide, then you have 2^7, or 128 possibilities for characters. If each character is 8 bits wide, then you have 2^8, or 256 possibilities for characters.

All computers use *character sets*, which in the DOS world are called *code pages*.[2] (I use both phrases interchangeably in this book.) A character set consists "of letters, ideographs, digits, symbols, and/or control functions used to construct words and concepts of natural or computer languages."[3] There are character sets for most alphabets in the world, and many are now ISO standards.

Character sets that support 256 characters are called *single-byte character sets*. All alphabets for the phonological writing systems can be represented in single-byte character sets. Examples of writing systems that are phonological include English, Cyrillic, Thai, Hebrew, Arabic, and Japanese kana. (See Figure 9.2 for an illustration of kinds of writing systems.)

Still, 256 characters is not enough to support the ideographic writing systems (Chinese, Japanese kanji, Korean) for two reasons:

1. The ideographic writing systems are too large to be represented with a single-byte character set; there are not enough characters in a single-byte character set, which has a 256-character limit. Basic literacy in Japanese, Chinese, and Korean makes use of approximately 2,000 ideographs.

2. Ideographs are complex pictures that can each require 30 or more strokes to build. A byte is too small to store all this graphical information. Ideographic writing systems, then, require two or more bytes in order to store a single ideograph.

A group of representatives from software companies like Apple Computer, Xerox Corporation, Digital Equipment Corporation, Microsoft, Hewlett Packard, and Sun Microsystems have been working on these issue for years as the Unicode Consortium. *Unicode* stands for universal code. It incorporates characters from many writing systems in the world. It does so by using what is called double-byte encoding, or a 16-bit (2^{16}) encoding system. Such an encoding allows for a character set or code page of 65,536 characters. Unicode is referred to as a *double-byte character set*.

There are some character sets that are called multibyte character sets, because they allow for 4-byte or even wider characters.

Unicode is able to support many writing systems simultaneously, including many of the characters in the ideographic writing systems, European writing systems, Cyrillic writing systems, and Arabic and Hebrew. Unicode is an ISO standard character set.[4]

Character sets and encoding get even more complicated. For example, many users often need to toggle from one writing system to another. A translator writing in Japanese might need to type words that are in English, German, Arabic, or Russian. Computer software needs to support this, as do keyboards. At present, there are no smooth solutions to these problems, but solutions *do* exist.

Inputting Characters

Input methods—how a user types characters on a keyboard, for example—are also a challenge for a multilingual computer. The more complex solutions are for the Asian writing systems. In some Asian writing systems, users have to build ideographs and words piece by piece, using key combinations. In some other Asian writing systems, users type a code that inserts an ideograph from a particular character set.

Typing Arabic, Hebrew, Thai, or one of the Indian dialects is as complex. The form of characters varies with the context in which they occur, for example, which characters they are next to or how they are pronounced.

In some writing systems, users also need to switch the direction of typing. Apple Computer splits the text insertion cursor in two, "one half indicating where new text can be added in the current writing direction and the other half marking the last place where the direction of writing changed."[5]

Users also need to select text to have the software perform actions on it. Apple Computer describes how users who type in Arabic and Hebrew highlight words:

A text selection may be highlighted in as many as three separate segments if it covers a continuous string of words written in both directions.[6]

Importing text from another source, like a different computing platform or a different file format introduces the problem of character-set conflict, which was mentioned previously. A special character in one character set may not produce the same character in a very similar character set.

Outputting Characters

There are two output methods that are considered here: displaying machine-readable information on a monitor and printing machine-readable information on paper.

Ideographic writing systems introduce the additional problem of displaying their complexity on computer monitors. You will need to research the technology to which your users have access to make informed decisions regarding design.

High-resolution monitors are the ideal solution to this problem, but you may not be able to enforce this. Apple Computer's analysis of the Japanese computing environment in 1992 showed that 50 percent of the computer hardware market belonged to NEC. The specifications of the typical computer monitor in Japan then were:

- 640 by 400 color graphics standard with 4 or 12 bits of color

- 16 by 16 pixel high-quality, fast, Japanese character generated display[7]

By comparison, IBM recommends a 24 by 24 pixel display.[8]

If the resolution is low, ideographic characters can be displayed in a larger point size, reducing the number of characters displayed. You can also make a larger monitor a requirement.

Printing capabilities as they relate to online documents may require that you do some font research on two issues: typographic conventions and system performance. Typographic conventions do vary around the world. If your online document is very simple, this may not be a problem. But a more complex typographic entity like a manual that is available online and offers demand printing can be a problem in some target writing systems. Be aware of the font family that is the default for the computing platform on which your online documentation is available.

Also be aware that some font families for ideographic writing systems are very large (over 6 megabytes in size). This will take up RAM. If your document requires a lot of RAM to print, especially if it contains a lot of graphics, then the effect on system performance may prevent your user from printing. It is always good practice to have someone test demand printing for the Asian versions, including Japanese, Chinese, and Korean.

Displaying Characters

Chapter 6, "Design Issues," presented text directionality. In English, words are typed and read from left to right. All European writing systems are left-to-right writing systems (LTR). Most computers can print characters based on LTR on a computer monitor with no problems.

Arabic and Hebrew, however, are typed and read from right to left. In a sentence in Arabic, though, a word in French might need to be typed. French is read from left to right. This dilemma is so common that Arabic and Hebrew are referred to as *bidirectional writing systems* (bidi). Clearly bidi is no simple technical feat for computers, and certainly not easy for anyone who is typing on a computer keyboard to master. You need to be able to switch into one text direction or another very easily.

Japanese, Chinese, and Korean can be typed vertically in addition to being acceptable as LTR writing systems. Even though most technical information is presented in LTR, computers need to support the vertical writing system.

General Solutions for Going Online

Making a computer multilingual is complicated. Machine-readable information that is localized for target countries will most definitely be affected by this technical complexity. Some software that you use to create machine-readable information may not support all the technical complexity that is required to export your product to all target countries.

If your machine-readable information is to be used across many computing platforms, the complexity only increases. Character sets might be different. A symbol you used in a Windows application might be displayed as a different symbol when it is used on a Macintosh or a UNIX platform, because character sets are not uniform.

To minimize this problem, follow these guidelines:

1. Choose a product for creating the machine-readable information from a software vendor that is committed to internationalization.

2. Verify with the software vendor that the software supports the computing platforms you need and the target writing systems you need.[9]

3. If your company exports its products simultaneously to many countries, choose a software vendor who does the same to ensure access to the writing system versions of the software product you need.

4. Know how to use your tools and be familiar with their capabilities.

5. Design your machine-readable information with the technical considerations expressed here in mind. For example, if you know that you will be exporting to countries where double-byte writing systems are used, research the results of creating the source information in a double-byte version of the software used to create the machine-readable information.[10]

ISOLATING MACHINE-READABLE INFORMATION

A key to minimizing the complexity of localizing machine-readable information is to isolate it from the software program. "Separating source code from user-interface text is the first and most basic requirement for internationalization."[11] This approach lets translators access and change the machine-readable information easily. "There is no need for the translator to see the logic or executable code of a product, since translation should not require a change in the logic flow. In addition, if the executable code is exposed to the translator there is a possibility that it will be changed, either inadvertently or through some misguided attempt to translate English-like keywords."[12]

Isolating machine-readable information is an approach that is typically called *enabling*, *national language enabling (NL-enabling)*, or *internationalization*. Here is how it works.

Machine-readable information is stored separately from the program logic (executable files) in *resource files*. Resource files can be grouped together in national databases. A resource file can be compiled separately from the executable files that make up a software application.[13]

> The core of each program is stripped of all hard-coded language and country-specific information. What is left is a generalized base product that makes no assumptions about the [user's cultural context or language]. In the meantime, the text and edits (dates, currency, and so on) needed to create a different language version are stored in an independent "national" database. This database can be accessed by the core program using generalized routines (many of which come with the localized versions of the operating system).[14]

Most standard computing platforms, like Macintosh and Windows, have anticipated the need for localization and make it easy for you to separate machine-readable information, help text and error messages, from the code. However, many companies that supply software applications that you might use to create machine-readable information are not so internationally aware. Like you, they are learning how to implement internationalization techniques.

A common problem that localization engineers and translators encounter in English source versions of machine-readable information is *text string concatenation*. A text string is concatenated with one of many possible sentence fragments after some action to form a complete sentence that is displayed for the user. Translators would have to re-create every possible action in order to determine what the sentence fragment should be in the target language. In addition to this often being difficult and time consuming, it opens up the opportunity for a bad translation or worse, re-engineering of the source code to accommodate the translated text strings. Unfortunately, these problems are often caught only during localization and not before, delaying the availability of localized product variants. When creating text strings, use only entire sentences and do not use sentence fragments that are dependent on the syntax of a particular language.

If the product for which you are creating machine-readable information is to be used on many computing platforms, consider this advice from ILE Corporation: "Sharing resource files across platforms requires conversion to the relevant character set prior to inclusion in the program."[15] Anticipate this and minimize your use of symbols, or, ideally, compare how different character sets map each character.

You need to research what internationalization techniques your software application can support when you create machine-readable information. Translators and localization engineers can help you choose a design methodology that is most suitable to internationalization if your software application does not explicitly recommend internationalization techniques.

TERMINOLOGY

The terminology that is employed in the user interface must be consistent with the terminology used in all help and documentation files. This also means that the translations of any terminology must be consistently used as well. Some localization companies have created tools that link terms utilized in the user interface with terms used in the online help. This linking forces terminology consistency throughout the entire product in its source language and in all target languages.

All major operating systems have terminology that is used to introduce their own user interfaces and software functionality. Glossaries exist for all major operating systems, and the terminology is used relatively consistently throughout the documentation describing the operating system. Wherever possible, take advantage of this platform-specific and standard terminology. M. Raymond Jason of ILE Corporation's project engineering department notes that by doing this, you eliminate a step in the process of translation and localization. He cites the example of Apple Guide text tags like Tip and Do This. Changing these deviates from the Apple standards and adds to the complexity of translation and localization.

All localization engineers and translators who specialize in computer software are familiar with platform-standard terms, and the glossaries are readily accessible in many languages; note, however, that not all language versions of these glossaries are equally thorough or even accurate in their choice of translations for the terms. If you choose to use a variant of a platform-standard term, document what the term is, why you chose a different term, and provide this information to the translator. Such information ensures a consistent and accurate translation of the variant terms in the target languages and throughout the product.

Choose words with care and be thorough if you create keyword lists that are used as search criteria for help topics. Be aware that synonyms in the source language could share the same translation in a target language. This reduces the list of keywords in the target language, which may pose design problems.

TEXT EXPANSION

Text expansion (discussed in Chapter 6, "Design Issues") occurs when translated text occupies more physical space than the text in the source language did. IBM reports a statistical average across many languages to be a 30 percent text expansion rate in technical manuals. However, in the online world, much of the text is very short, like a word or a phrase. Refer to Table 10.1, which is an adaptation of IBM's translation table, when choosing terminology and designing interfaces for machine-readable information.

Text expansion poses a few more problems in the online world than it does in the print world. The print world offers a lot more flexibility. Here is a list of some of the restrictions in the online world as they apply to text expansion and machine-readable information.

- In most cases, you cannot kern characters to accommodate text that expands.

- You cannot change the size of the font without sacrificing readability.

TABLE 10.1: **Text Expansion Factors for Contiguous Machine-Readable Information**[16]

TOTAL NUMBER OF CHARACTERS (INCLUDING SPACES AND PUNCTUATION)	TEXT EXPANSION FACTOR
Up to 10 (This is typical in a user interface, such as menu items, fields in an online form, text in an icon, labels for buttons in a dialog box, and so on.)	100 to 200%
11 to 20	80 to 100%
21 to 30	60 to 80%
31 to 50	40 to 60 %
51 to 70	31 to 40 %
Over 70 (This is typical of a normal text paragraph in a technical manual.)	30 %

- There are physical restrictions that are imposed by the operating system or the software application that you are using regarding the length of character strings and the size of the files that contain them. For example, balloon-help text strings on an Apple Computer platform allow a maximum of 255 characters. Because of text expansion, it is recommended that you limit text to 127 to 180 characters.[17]

- A character from a double-byte character set occupies twice as much physical space as a character from a single byte character set. "A full screen of English MRI may have 1200 characters encoded as 1200 bytes. The Japanese translation would be only 1560 characters according to [Table 10.1], but would be encoded as 3120 bytes."[18] For off-the-shelf PC software products, the amount of physical space that online documentation requires on the program disks is very important. Equally important is the amount of disk space that the user needs to have available to install the software. If the help files, for example, are too large, the user may not be able to load them, or, worse, may choose not to buy the product.

- If the file is larger because of a double-byte character set, text expansion, or if it uses more than one character set, and so on, it could degrade the performance of the machine-readable information, as in an tutorial. Going from page two to page three and waiting for the application to redraw the information could take an irritatingly long time.

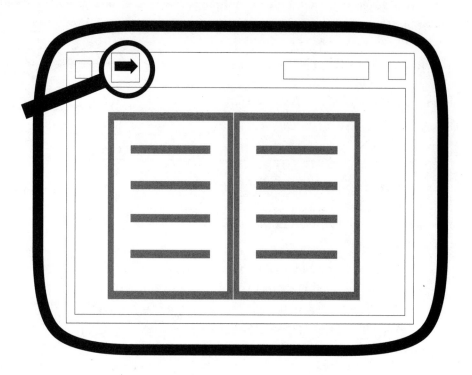

FIGURE 10.2: **Example of an online document with a navigational arrow that assumes an LTR writing system.**

TEXT DIRECTIONALITY

ILE Corporation provides the example of on-screen controls that allow users to scroll through an online document.[19] LTR and bidi writing systems would have the arrows in the opposite order from each other. Consider Figure 10.2. This application would need to be localized to accommodate a bidi writing system so that the reader could scroll through the document in the correct direction.

Localization engineers or translators need to be able to reverse these arrows for the appropriate writing systems. There may be other examples of text direction-ality problems in the machine-readable information as well. As with everything else, make this machine-readable information accessible by externalizing it from the program logic whenever possible.

SYNCHRONIZING AND LINKING MEDIA OBJECTS

Multimedia presentations (or productions) are not inherently a problem. It is the individual *media objects* that make up a multimedia presentation and their relationships to each other that pose the problem in internationalization and localization. These problems are aggravated when localized multimedia applications are accessed remotely and used to link to other computers on the worldwide web.

Media objects in a multimedia presentation can be text, graphics, animation, image, video, and audio objects. "Typically they are part of a larger object, such as a document, a spreadsheet, or a presentation. This higher-level object, or the *composite object*, is an object that is made up of other objects. These objects are not specific to multimedia products; however, they will be integrated into the user interfaces."[20]

Many media objects need to be localized because of their cultural content. Voice audio, for example, must be rerecorded in the target language. Text must be translated. And so on. (This is discussed in more detail in the section on "Cultural Issues" later in this chapter.) Creating a multimedia presentation that allows you to substitute localized media objects requires some forethought.

To date there is not much information on this subject, probably because few companies are creating composite objects and even fewer are localizing their media objects. However, there are some recommendations that can be made to facilitate the localization of media objects above and beyond the information presented thus far in this chapter.

To reemphasize the most important design principle of internationalization, you need to create media objects so that all machine-readable information is externalized from the program logic. This facilitates the localization of the machine-readable information. Not all machine-readable information associated with the different media objects needs to be localized. In this way you will be able to plug in localized information as necessary for a given target country or market. This lets you reuse information, minimizing the cost and time associated with localization. Refer to Chapter 7, "Creating a Core Product," for more information.

Applying this design philosophy to the creation of a composite object introduces synchronization problems. This is not a new concept; film has dealt with synchronization problems for decades. Consider the simple example in Figure 10.3. There are only three layers (also called *tracks*) in the time segment. The voice audio expands in the target variant because the information must be presented differently for the target audience or it takes longer to express a concept in the target language. (Both alternatives are possible.) The video layer and the music-audio layer do not need to be localized.

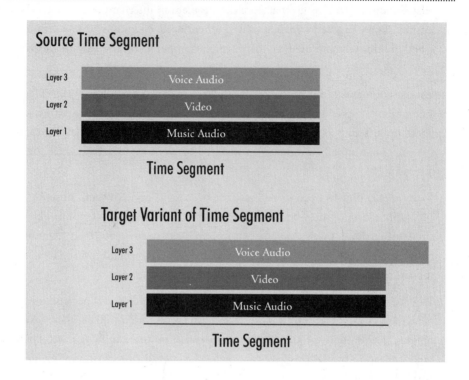

FIGURE 10.3: **A time segment in a composite object showing the levels of media objects before and after localization.**

Here are some possibilities for the synchronization of the media objects in this example. This is not an exhaustive list, and all possibilities are limited or enhanced by your multimedia toolset's capabilities.

- The voice audio can be compressed, but test (listen to) the result.[21]

- The voice layer can contain checkpoints every 20 to 30 seconds so that it can be synchronized with both the music and the voice audio tracks more easily.[22]

- The music audio can be expanded by adding spaces to it.

- The last frame of the video segment can be repeated, creating a still.

Synchronization problems become more challenging when you factor in the linking capabilities of a multimedia toolkit. A hypertext link connects an anchor node and to a destination node. If these nodes are layered, or if they are of different media object types (a graphic-media object and a video object both linking to an audio-media object), synchronization gets complicated.[23]

The only realistic solution to these problems is to anticipate them and try to design in anticipation of these problems. And, of course, choose tools that let you do sophisticated editing of the various media objects (see Chapter 12, "Tools Issues," for more information).

Linking requires a bit more discussion. There are not many tools available that make it easy to track hyperlinks. Many authors map links manually by drawing them or just taking good notes.[24] For translators and localization engineers, links become problematic for a few reasons.

- If a link is based on a keyword or a topic, the keyword or topic will change in translation. The keyword should be represented numerically in the source code so that it is not language dependent.[25] This is especially important when topics need to be listed in the sort order. Their sort order will change in target languages.

- All links need to be thoroughly tested in the source version of the composite object. If there are errors in the source version of the composite object, they will be replicated in each of the target versions if the translators and localization engineers are unable to catch them. One way to solve this problem is to provide the translators and localization engineers with a map of all the links. Testing links can then be integrated into the quality-assurance process more systematically.

DEMAND PRINTING

Demand printing, in this context, refers to the ability to print a page of an online document so that it can be read on paper. Paper sizes, as discussed in Chapter 6, "Design Issues," are different around the world. At a time when there is a growing trend to put printed manuals online, this becomes an important issue. Here are some questions you should consider.

- Can document margins accommodate the smallest possible standard paper size that a printer can accommodate, of all target audiences?

- If the machine-readable information was designed for custom page size because it was designed as a printed document, can it be printed at all on standard paper sizes?

- Is there a way to adjust the margins of the online document dynamically so that printer paper size can be configured by the user?

STYLE AND FORMATTING GUIDELINES

It is important to supply translators and localization engineers with the style guidelines and the formatting guidelines that you use to format machine-readable information, like online documents with hyperlinks. Examples of some formatting include displaying all hypertext links in green, and using 14-point Helvetica for all headings. To preserve your formatting, translators need to know the style and formatting guidelines that you used when creating the source version. In this way they can preserve the formatting in the target variants.

CULTURAL CONCERNS

There are some cultural concerns that are unique to the online world. These are in addition to all the international variables presented in Chapter 4, "Performing an International-User Analysis." It is assumed here that you have performed an international-user analysis and that you have a sense of the cultural context of all target audiences. Icons and color are discussed in Chapter 11, "Graphic Design's International Concerns."

TRANSLATION ACCURACY

Accurate translation is important both in machine-readable information and in printed information. However, in the online world, the translation of a single-word menu item, for example, becomes very significant, since users must comprehend it each time they use the product to perform a task. An inaccurate translation in machine-readable information, particularly text at the user-interface level, frustrates users, makes it difficult for them to intuit meaning independently, and may inhibit them from choosing the option out of fear of doing something wrong.

Jakob Nielsen cites this example of a misleading translation in the Danish variant of Apple Computer's product MacPaint. There is a dialog box in the English source version that has a button labeled *eject*, which, when chosen, ejects a diskette from a floppy drive on the PC. The dialog box also has two other buttons, one labeled *save*, which writes information to disk, and one labeled *cancel*, which does nothing except make the dialog box go away. In the Danish variant, the English word *eject* was translated to the Danish word *aflever*, which means *hand over*. One Danish user thought the command saved the file (handed over the file) to the diskette in the floppy drive. Apple Computer has since changed the translation to *skub ud*, which means *push out*. The difference has to do with connotation. *Aflever* did not connote a physical response by the computer.[26]

It is especially important to test the translation of terms in a user interface. These words are usually translated first, before the error messages, the online help, and the documentation, for this reason. The terms are used throughout all the machine-readable and printed information and are critical to the usability of the product. Think of how many times the terms in a user interface are used in the documentation alone. If the translations are inaccurate or misleading, this can cause many problems.

Nielsen cites an additional example. In Japan, the word *undo* had not been translated into kanji. Nielsen inquired about this, since *undo* was the only English word in the user interface. The Japanese explained that there were no accurate translations for *undo*, so they decided it was more important to use the English word than to risk a poor translation.[27]

Test all terms that are critical to the user interface with users who speak the target language, or preferably, with users who live in and are native to the target country.

MEDIA OBJECTS

Media objects can offer a rich sensory experience. Sensory experiences can communicate below the surface in the realm of the subconscious. They are also a matter of style and taste. In essence, they can be very personal. For these reasons, it is important that you give considerable thought to how your users' cultural context will influence how they respond to certain media objects. The media objects that are discussed here relate to sound. They are sound effects, voice, and music.

- **Sound Effects.** Sound can certainly add to the experience of using a computer. My modem software beeps when I have successfully connected to a remote computer. I can set the alarm on the calendar application so that it goes off when I need to make a telephone call or go to an appointment. And, certainly, all game software blasts me with sound every time I press a key on the keyboard or point to and click on a part of the screen with the mouse. Sound makes interaction more real.

  But choosing appropriate sounds and using them at appropriate times requires some cultural research. Reporting on Japanese preferences, Apple Computer notes that sounds software makes when a user makes an error can cause a user to lose face in Japan. Apple Computer also states that animal sounds and sounds that suggest violence are not recommended, since users in various countries have complained about their inappropriateness.[28]

- **Voice.** Media objects that use voice for narration, teaching, story telling, and so on require significant cultural research. It is important to investigate accents and dialects in the target countries and how they are perceived by your target audience. A good source for ideas is television programs in the target country. News programs usually are the most conservative in the U.S., while commercials use the broadest range of accents and dialects for effect. The British have been able to capitalize on the appeal of their accents in the U.S. A British accent often gives Americans the impression of aristocracy.

  When I studied Japanese, albeit for a very short time, I remember the instructor telling us about her experience in Japan, where she lived and worked for many years. She told us that Japanese women tend to speak in high-pitched voices and this was considered very appropriate and the proper way for women to speak in Japan.

  The choice of using a woman's voice or a man's voice is also very important. A voice of either sex elicits different responses depending on the context of the speech and depending on the cultural context of the listener.

- **Music.** Your choice of music in a media object is also a cultural concern. Certain composers may be symbolic of religious or political activities. John Philip Sousa's compositions usually evoke a response from many Americans, for example. His compositions are usually played during national and political holidays like July 4th, Independence Day.

END NOTES

[1] *National Language Design Guide: Designing Enabled Products,* Volume 1, Second Ed., January 1991, IBM, p. 2–1.

[2] Emmanuel Uren, Robert Howard, and Tiziana Perinotti, *Software Internationalization and Localization: An Introduction*, Van Nostrand Reinhold, New York, 1993, p. 276.

[3] Sandra Martin O'Donnell, *Programming for the World*, Prentice-Hall, Englewood Cliffs, New Jersey, 1994, p. 414.

[4] For more information about Unicode, see *The Unicode Standard: Worldwide Character Encoding*, Version 1.0, Addison-Wesley, Reading, Massachusetts, 1991.

[5] Apple Computer, *Guide to Macintosh Software Localization*, Addison-Wesley, Reading, Massachusetts, 1992, p. 14.

6 Ibid., p. 105.

7 *Localization for Japan*, Apple Computer, 1990, p. 35.

8 *Designing Enabled Products*, p. 7–4.

9 In Japan there are many computing platforms, many of which are not common any-where else in the world.

10 Telephone interview with Bernard Gateau, the president of ILE Corporation, September 16, 1994.

11 ILE Corporation, *Accent on Internationalization*, August 1994, Boulder, Colorado, p. 8.

12 *Designing Enabled Products*, p. 2–2.

13 Susan L. Fowler and Victor R. Stanwick, from a draft of their chapter "International Software," which was printed in *The GUI Style Guide*, Academic Press, Cambridge, Massachusetts, 1994, p. 15.

14 Ibid., p. 14.

15 ILE, p. 16.

16 *Designing Enabled Products*, p. 2–4.

17 ILE, p. 35.

18 *Designing Enabled Products*, p. 7–4.

19 ILE, pp. 32–33.

20 *CUA Guide to Multimedia User Interface Design*, 1st Ed., IBM Corporation, June 1992, p. 9.

21 Thanks to Bob Walker, an audio engineer from Temple, New Hampshire, who records, mixes, and edits news stories for Monitor Radio, which is the news and information branch of Public Radio International (formerly American Public Radio). Bob helped me understand the basics of audio and the possibilities for editing it.

22 *Designing Enabled Products*, p. 5–7.

23 Jakob Nielsen, *Hypertext and Hypermedia*, Academic Press Professional, Boston, 1993. See especially Chapter 6, "The Architecture of Hypertext Systems," pp. 107–120.

24 This is based on monitoring various newsgroups on the Internet that discussed this thread.

25 William Horton, *Designing and Writing Online Documentation: Help Files to Hypertext*, John Wiley & Sons, New York, 1990, p. 61

26 Ibid., pp. 42–43.

27 Ibid., p. 43.

28 *Guide to Macintosh Software Localization*, p. 128.

11

KNOW HOW TO ASSESS THE CULTURAL

APPROPRIATENESS OF IMAGERY AND COLOR.

LEARN HOW TO DEVELOP GRAPHICS THAT MAKE

LOCALIZATION AND TRANSLATION EASY.

GRAPHICS ISSUES

Graphic design issues as they relate to international technical communication are both technical and cultural. The technical issues are discussed here, as well as a few of the cultural topics. This chapter is not an exhaustive discussion about graphic design, internationalization, and localization. This chapter covers topics that are not readily accessible, rather than repeating what has been already stated many times in books about high technology and internationalization.

Topics covered in this chapter include:

- Imagery   ■ Color   ■ File formats   ■ Capturing screen images
- Callouts and labels   ■ Clip art

Most of what you need to know about graphic design for international audiences can be determined from performing an international-user analysis (see Chapter 4). Refer to Appendix C, "Resources in International Technical Communication," for additional references.

IMAGERY TO RESEARCH WELL OR AVOID

There is a standard list of imagery that requires significant cultural research or it should be avoided when illustrating manuals, newsletters, online help systems, media objects in multimedia presentations, and when designing icons. The reason is that these images are interpreted differently around the world. Some may be offensive, others sacred or simply inappropriate for the context, while others may not mean what you think they mean in a target country.

There are four general categories of imagery that can introduce cultural conflict. I merely call them to your attention here and encourage you strongly to include these categories as international variables when you perform an international user analysis. There is an abundance of information available on these categories.[1] Refer to Appendix C, "Resources in International Technical Communication," for more information.

- **People.** Areas of particular sensitivity include gender, gender relationships, ethnic dress, and hand gestures.

- **Animals.** Many cultures revere particular animals for religious reasons, have domesticated them as pets, or simply consider particular animals to be base, dirty creatures.

- **Everyday objects.** Many everyday objects have different shapes in different countries. Two examples include mailboxes and trashcans, which are often used in computer icons.

- **Religious symbols.** This category can vary from religious icons to particular numbers to specific animals that have religious significance.

COLOR

Here are some explanations for choosing color with care in a technical context:

- Illiteracy

- The level of a user's visual literacy

- The nature of the communication

ILLITERACY

If the target audience has a low literacy level, then color choices may have significant meaning. Edward T. Hall's research on culture provides examples of this. In *The Silent Language*, Hall describes how Americans "treat colors informally as a whole—that is, situationally." He compares the value Americans place on color with the value that the Navajo Indians in America place on color. "To the Navajo. . . colors are ranked just as we [Americans] rank [the value of the precious metals] gold and silver [to other metals, like iron or magnesium]—only more intensely."

Color was used in a particular situation because the Americans needed a method for helping them identify political candidates in this instance, since as Americans the Navajos could vote. The Americans chose colors without researching their cultural value and ended up "labeling" one of the candidates very negatively just because the color that represented him connoted bad things.[2]

V I S U A L   L I T E R A C Y   L E V E L S

Charlene R. Johnson did graduate research on "Communicating Health Care Issues to Nonreaders in Developing Countries." In her research, she notes that visual literacy levels vary around the world. Color is a facet of visual literacy. She provides an interesting example from Botswana in 1984. "When new traffic lights commonly used in the West were installed in the city of Gaborone, government officials soon discovered that motorists did not share the Western understanding of red as a signal for danger or stop, amber as a signal for caution, and green as a signal for go. Therefore, the officials had to have the new traffic lights covered until motorists were taught how to interpret the meanings of the traffic light colors."[3]

N A T U R E   O F   T H E   C O M M U N I C A T I O N

The choice of color is also important in packaging, marketing, and advertising. Consider the following anecdote from David Ricks's *Blunders in International Business*.

> In advertising as in production, choosing a color is another important consideration. At least two different firms encountered problems in Hong Kong marketing efforts when they decided to use green hats in commercials. One company attempted to sell its beer using the message that the beer was so good that even the Irish like it. The Irishman, of course, wore a green hat while drinking his beer. The other firm marketed cleaning agents and in its commercial featured individuals tossing hats at a male model. A green hat eventually landed on the man. In both cases, the color chosen was not appropriate; the green hat is a Chinese symbol used to identify a man as a cuckold. Understandably, consumers avoided both products.[4]

Most color is used in online communication, as in icons on a user interface or illustrations in a computer-based training module. There is certainly some cultural imagery that might be a cause for concern about color. Consider an image of a man handing a woman a white flower. If this is image is retained when a product is exported to Asian countries, it may send the message that the woman is mourning the death of a loved one.

GENERALIZING ABOUT COLOR

In many cases, the sources I consulted for information about culture and color do not give cultural reasons why a color is bad or good, but simply say that a color is interpreted well or poorly by the particular target audience; it is assumed that there are cultural reasons for these responses.

Note that there may also be regional and ethnic differences in cultural responses in some countries. These regional differences sometimes introduce contradictory interpretations of color.

As Johnson's research reflects, users can also be taught to interpret color in a particular way given a certain context. It is often difficult to separate what is learned because of cultural conditioning or more artificial education scenarios that often appear in advertisements and marketing materials. David Victor notes two additional examples of trained response that the U.S. Occupational Safety and Health Act (OSHA) has enforced. The color blue has been legislated to symbolize equipment for preventing and reducing hazards. Similarly, OSHA has made widespread in the United States the association of yellow—with physical danger and the need for caution."[5]

Another influence affecting color response is the association of color with particular objects. For instance, a white lily or a white carnation is often associated with mourning in France and Japan. In these cases, users may not have cultural responses to the color white, but they will have a cultural response if the color white is associated with a particular object like a flower.

Similarly, a color used in combination with one or more colors may induce responses. Red, white, and blue connote patriotism to Americans because they are the colors of the American flag. Alone, the color red, the color white, and the color blue may mean nothing in particular to Americans. The colors of the French flag are also red, white, and blue. Green and orange are politically charged in Ireland. And, red, white, and green are symbolic in Italy and Mexico. These colors are often on the covers of cookbooks about Italian and Mexican cuisine since they are the colors of the national flags in these countries.

For all these reasons, it is often dangerous to generalize about color and the reactions it is likely to induce.

C O L O R - T O - C U L T U R E   M A P S

Table 11.1 maps colors to their *possible* cultural interpretations taken from the anecdotal evidence as reported in many sources.[6] Consult this table if your imagery will be localized to the cultural context or literacy level (visual or otherwise) of the user, or if you are involved in making decisions about packaging design or marketing and advertising materials.

TABLE 11.1: **Colors and Their Possible Cultural Interpretations**

COLOR	TARGET COUNTRY OR AUDIENCE AND RESPONSE OR INTERPRETATION
Red	Thailand—most popular color
	China—prosperity, rebirth
	Malaysia—valor and might
	Ivory Coast—mourning (dark red)
	U.K.—first place
	France and the United Kingdom—masculinity
	U.S.—power, stop, danger
	India—procreation, life
	Many African countries—blasphemy or death
Green	Many countries—environmentally sound or safe
	Thailand—least favorite color
	Muslims—favorite color of the Prophet Mohammed
	U.S.—proceed, capitalism, envy
	Republic of Ireland—patriotism
	Countries that have dense and green jungles—disease
	France, the Netherlands, and Sweden—cosmetics
Black	Thailand—old age and death
	Malays of Malaysia—courage
	Malaysian Indians—evil
	Malaysians of Chinese descent—death
	U.S. and many European countries—death
Orange	Thailand—religion
	Northern Ireland—patriotism

Continued

TABLE 11.1: **Colors and Their Possible Cultural Interpretations** *Continued*

COLOR	TARGET COUNTRY OR AUDIENCE AND RESPONSE OR INTERPRETATION
White	Thailand—purity
	Muslim and Hindus—purity and peace
	Japan and many Asian countries—death and mourning
	Christians—purity, faith, innocence, virginity
Blue	Thailand—no meaning associated with color
	Malays—beauty and liberty
	Malays of Indian and Chinese descent—grief and sadness
	Ghana—joy
	Iran—negative connotations
	Egypt—truth
	U.S.—equipment that reduces the possibility of physical injury, first place (excellence)
	Many European countries—calming, sleep
	Hopi Indians—sacred religious significance
Yellow	China—joy and wealth, rank and authority
	Malaysia—royal color
	U.S.—caution, possibility of physical danger
	Many countries in the world—femininity
	Europe, Canada, Australia, and New Zealand—happiness and generally positive connotations
Purple	Latin America—death
	Europe and the Middle East—royalty
	China—barbarous
Pink	U.S.—femininity

Consider creating your own color-to-culture map as a part of an international-user analysis. Review the colors, their use, and their possible associations in your industry with in-country reviewers.

Remember, though, that there is little scientific evidence that supports the statement that color choice makes a difference.

Performing an international-user analysis should identify many trouble areas.

Clearly having the imagery and colors reviewed by in-country reviewers before the product is formally exported will identify any problems that remain.

FILE FORMATS

Most graphics software products have a proprietary, native file format. This file format is usually the only one the graphic image can be in if you want to edit the graphic using the source graphics software. Most word-processing or electronic-publishing software allows you to import only certain graphics file formats. These limitations become very important in the context of localization, since your translators may not be running the graphics software or the word-processing software on the same platform that you used to create the original graphics and text.

For example, most of the illustrations in this book were created in Corel Draw, Version 4.0 for Windows. The native file format of a Corel Draw file is .CDR. I used Microsoft Word 6.0 for Windows to create the chapter files in this book. Microsoft Word does not allow me to import .CDR files directly into my document. For this reason, I save the .CDR files as Windows bitmap files (.BMP), which I can then import to a chapter file in Microsoft Word. If I want to edit the graphic, I need the .CDR version of the graphic so that I can use Corel Draw. I then have to export it again as a .BMP file in order to use it in a chapter file.

Walter Smith, the manager of technical publications at ILE Corporation, recommends that you always supply your translation or localization company with both file formats so that they can edit the original graphic. This is especially important if the graphic must be edited so that text can be translated or when the graphic must be modified for cultural content. Always make the file format clear in the file name itself.[7] If the file is a Windows bitmap file, use the .BMP extension. If the file is a native Corel Draw file, use the .CDR file extension. If your tools restrict the length of file names, create a table in which you identify each file by name and content, or map each file name to its caption to provide meaning. For this book, for example, I created a spreadsheet that lists the file names of each figure in one column and provided their captions in another column. Marcia Sweezey, an internationalization consultant, suggests that you list any callouts in the spreadsheet or in a table.[8] In UNIX environments, where you can use almost any file name you want, choose something that is meaningful and that clearly indicates the file format.

For screen images, ILE also recommends: "Use standard, cross-platform-compatible graphics formats such as TIFF, EPS or HPGL [for CAD plotter files]."[9]

C A P T U R I N G   S C R E E N   I M A G E S

Technical documentation about software products often uses screen captures. In the non-PC environments in which I have done technical writing, screen captures were usually difficult to do. (There seems to be good screen-capture software for PC environments.) There was either no utility that could capture a screen image, or the screen-capture software did not let me edit the screen image once I captured it. There were also other problems, like the size of the resulting file if I captured a color screen image, or the lack of a utility that could translate color screen images into monochrome ones without degrading the resolution of the image. I confused myself many times in trying to remember the workarounds I had invented to capture twenty or more screen images. And the file formats of the screen images were often necessarily proprietary and I had to correct them once or twice to get them into a file format that I could import to the documentation, like encapsulated PostScript (.EPS).

Translators often must recapture the screen images from the translated software to insert into the technical documentation. To do so, they need to know how you captured the original screen images. They might even need to know how your computer was set up when you captured the screen image. Supply your translators with detailed notes as to how you capture your screen images. "Include factors such as color depth (black and white, gray scale, or color; 1 bit, 4 bit, 8 bit, etc.) and screen resolution. Note the software used."[10] The simpler the process for capturing screen images, the better.

Also supply the translators with a detailed listing of the file names, and, ideally, an image of the screen in the source language to make it easier for them to recognize them in the software product and associate them with file names. The file names should suggest where in the document the graphic should be inserted, and it should also suggest its file format, like .EPS. For example, the file name FIG10-2.EPS clearly indicates the chapter number, figure number, and the file format.

If you edited the screen image in a graphics editor after you captured it, you need to tell the translators how you did this, what you edited, and what software you used.

If translators do not have access to the software product, and the utilities you used to capture and edit the screen image, who will recapture the screen image? Can it be recaptured after translation? For example, if text in the screen image is translated into a double-byte language, is the screen-capture software able to run on a double-byte platform? You should investigate the answers to these questions early in the project.

Another way of including images from the software product is to draw them using a graphics software product. The problem with this method is that the character set you use to create the graphic might not be the character set used in a target language. If you use the graphic characters in a character set to draw lines and boxes, these can be mapped to letters or symbols in another character set. Translators usually know how to work around this problem, but it can be time consuming. Discuss this potential problem with the translators early in the project to avoid missing deadlines.

CALLOUTS AND LABELS

Digital Equipment Corporation did a study many years ago that analyzed hardware documentation. Digital wanted to determine the format for the hardware documentation that was best suited for translation issues, like text expansion. Their hardware documentation contained many illustrations with callouts that needed to be translated.

The study concluded that illustrations should use numbered callouts. The numbered areas in the illustrations are then explained in a legend where text is free to expand in target languages.[11]

All translation companies that I have interviewed concur with Digital's recommendations. See Figure 11.1 for an example.

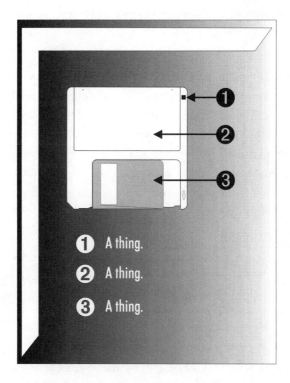

FIGURE 11.1: **Callout method that is best suited for translation.**

Sweezey adds that in an ideal situation, you should import the graphic file to the document so that translators do not need to manipulate the graphic. Enter callouts directly in the document, properly positioned to accommodate the graphic. Translators treat callouts as text.

Labels are also a source of some concern. Some industries have a standard set of graphics that are used in labels for machinery, chemicals, and so on. Some of these graphic images have been adopted by ISO, for example, ISO standard 3461, "Graphic Symbols, General Principles for Presentation," and ISO standard 4062, "Dictation Equipment Symbols." The International Electrotechnical Commission (IEC) has published standard 417K, "Graphical Symbols for Use on Equipment."

Verify whether standards exist for graphic images in your industry. If the products your company exports can in any way be misused to the extent that a person can be injured, there is a very good chance that standards exist, either national, industry, or international in scope, for warning a user about potential dangers. See Appendix C for the names and addresses of many standards associations.

CLIP ART

Most clip-art packages that I have used over the years are not internationalized. They often contain all kinds of culturally offensive graphic images, which are often touted as business graphics. They are also not sold in international versions as yet.

An international version of clip art might contain the common variations of electrical plugs in the world. It might contain many currency symbols. There would be many maps of the world that would each showcase a different continent as the center of the map. The office scenes would show realistic offices and spaces in different parts of the world. Text would not exist in any images, unless it was in the target language of the image depicted. There are many other items to add to a wish list for clip art that can help us make our technical communication more interesting. But, to date, companies that supply clip art have not answered this call.

Be aware that clip art containing images from around the world for technical material is very hard to find. Do your research early in the project. You may need to order special clip art that takes weeks to deliver, only to find out that it does not contain the images you thought it did.

END NOTES

[1] For an excellent compilation of imagery and the potential problems that can arise from them, organized culturally, see the *Guide to Macintosh Software Internationalization,* Apple

Computer, Addison-Wesley, Reading, Massachusetts, 1992. See also: Henry Dreyfuss, *Symbol Sourcebook: An Authoritative Guide to International Graphic Symbols*, Van Nostrand Reinhold, New York, 1972; William Horton, *Illustrating Computer Documentation: The Art of Presenting Information Graphically and Online*, John Wiley & Sons, New York, 1991, and also, *The Icon Book*, 1994.

[2] Edward T. Hall, *The Silent Language*, Anchor Books, New York, 1981, p. 108.

[3] Charlene R. Johnson, *Communicating Health Care Issues to Nonreaders in Developing Countries*, a thesis submitted in partial fulfillment of the requirements for the degree of Master of Science, University of Washington, 1991, p. 22.

[4] David Ricks, *Blunders in International Business*, Blackwell, Cambridge, Massachusetts, 1993, p. 62.

[5] David A. Victor, *International Business Communication*, Harper Collins Publishers, New York, 1992, p. 218.

[6] Sources consulted include: David Ricks, *Blunders in International Business,* Blackwell, Cambridge, Massachusetts, 1993; *Guide to Macintosh Software Localization*, Apple Computer, Cupertino, California, 1992; Philip R. Harris and Robert T. Moran, *Managing Cultural Differences*, 3rd Ed., Gulf Publishing, Houston, Texas, 1991; David A. Victor, *International Business Communication*, Harper Collins Publishers, New York, 1992; Charlene R. Johnson, *Communicating Health Care Issues to Nonreaders in Developing Countries*, a thesis submitted in partial fulfillment of the requirements for the degree of Master of Science, University of Washington, 1991. For sources on color research, Victor cites the works of M. Lüscher, who apparently developed a color test based on psychology. Lüscher's works are listed as being written in German, publisher Test-Verlag, Basel, Germany, throughout 1948–1961. Other sources include L. Cheskin, *How to Predict What People Will Buy*, Liveright, New York, 1957; H. Ketcham, *Color Planning for Business and Industry*, Harper, New York, 1958; and V. Packard, *The Hidden Persuaders*, McKay, New York, 1957.

For an interesting discussion of color from the perspective of symbolism and art, refer to *The Dictionary of Symbols*, J. E. Cirlot, translated from Spanish by Jack Sage, 2nd Edition, Philosophical Library, New York, 1982, pp. 52–60.

[7] Telephone interview with Walter Smith, International Language Engineering (ILE) Corporation, Boulder, Colorado, September 28, 1994.

[8] From review comments on a draft of this chapter, October 10, 1994.

[9] ILE Corporation, *An Accent on Internationalization*, ILE Corporation, Boulder, Colorado, 1994, p. 28.

[10] Ibid.

[11] Elisa del Galdo, "A European Evaluation of Three Document Formats for Hardware Installation Guides," *Designing User Interfaces for International Use*, Jakob Nielsen, Ed., Elsevier, 1990, pp. 45–69.

12 USE TOOLS THAT FACILITATE THE

DEVELOPMENT OF INTERNATIONAL TECHNICAL

COMMUNICATION. LEARN ABOUT THE FEATURES

THAT CAN ASSIST RATHER THAN HINDER.

Features and
Capabilities

Evaluating the
Tools Publisher

SGML

Commentary

T O O L S   I S S U E S

Technical communicators spend much of their professional lives explaining to people how to use tools and how to use them well. If anyone can appreciate why evaluating tools is important, it is most certainly a technical communicator.

This chapter does not offer a critique of tools, nor does it advocate one tool over another. Most companies that develop tools for creating technical communication are trying to provide solutions to the technical problems that internationalization introduces for all types of tools. This will understandably take some time. We are already seeing the fruits of their labors in all of the tools that most of us use every day.

Understand that there is a big void in the tools available for technical communicators whose product is technical information for export. There are many features and capabilities that are missing from the tools we use. These features would allow us to interface with translators more efficiently and effectively, and allow us to create internationalized source information that is better suited for localization. As we learn to streamline the process of creating international technical communication, we will influence the design of new tools to facilitate our goals.

F E A T U R E S   A N D   C A P A B I L I T I E S

The features and capabilities of the tools that you use should facilitate internationalization so that localization, which includes translation, is easy, painless, fast, and affordable. The list of features and capabilities presented here is not exhaustive, but they provide a strong starting point for your tools evaluation.

G L O S S A R Y   D E V E L O P M E N T

As stated throughout this book, one of the most important requirements of a quality translation is the consistent and accurate use of technical terms.

Translators must be familiar with the terminology used throughout a product. In this way, they can ensure consistency and obtain a higher quality translation.

In Chapter 8, "Working with Translators," I presented the concept of a glossary for translators that you should prepare, maintain, and provide to your translators. The glossary contains terms that are integral to the technical information you create for a product. It also provides information on the accepted usage of terms and their synonyms (if any are allowed).

There are some glossary-development tools available, but the ones with which I am familiar are essentially utilities that are integrated in computer-aided translation (CAT) tools. There are few technical communicators who want such a bundle.

Ideally, glossary tools would allow you to:

- Store the terms
- Define rules for their correct usage (noun, verb, adjective, and so on)
- Enforce usage dynamically as you create the source information (using some sort of fuzzy logic)
- Extract and port the terminology database to the CAT tools that your translators use

A glossary tool would also have to be an integral part of the publishing tools that you currently use. But such tools do not exist at present.

Some localization companies have developed internal terminology tools that they use to provide their clients with consistent terminology throughout a product and its accompanying documentation. Their tools link terms in the user interface with terms used in the online help systems. But, again, these are internal, proprietary tools.

While we are waiting for tools to help us create glossaries for translation that are integrated with our publishing tools, we can begin the process by creating a database of terms using whatever tools we have access to. Ideally, the database would support many languages so that as terms are translated into additional target languages, you can continue to build a multilingual glossary that is tailored to the needs of your company. The database should be portable in the sense that you should be able to provide translators with these terms in an electronic format that they can read, print, and use. Some publishing tools have features that you might be able to adapt for glossary development.

AUTOMATION

There are a variety of automation features that currently exist in most publishing tools. These features make it easier for translators and are a means by which to streamline the process of creating international technical communication. In general, use the full potential of all automation features that a publishing tool provides. But as Walter Smith, the manager of technical publications at ILE Corporation, points out, "If your publishing tool provides automation features, be sure to use them, and then be sure to use them well and wisely."[1]

Indexes

A translator does not want to re-create an index manually. A translator wants to generate an index in the target language automatically. If you do not use the index-automation features of a publishing tool, then you create a very expensive problem. The translator will have to create the index in the target language manually and verify the page numbers for each entry.

Having translators re-create index entries manually takes a lot of time. It also opens up the possibility for error. As technical communicators, you know the value of a good and accurate index. Provide translators with only a coded index that can be automatically generated, not a manually created one.

Consider, too, that an index in a target language will be completely different from an index in the source language. This is because the sorting orders for languages differ. The page numbers will also be different, because of text expansion or compression throughout the whole document.

It is possible that the source-language index will contain two synonyms that translate to the same word in the target language. In these cases, translators will either delete the redundancy, shortening the length of the index, or they will find a way in the target language to present the redundancy in a useful way. You need to tell the translators which method you prefer.

Jon Lavine, a senior editor at Berlitz Translation Services, adds this caution. "The worst thing of all is to edit a generated index." At the very least, you should provide the translators with notes that identify your edits if, for some reason, you cannot provide a non-edited index.

Table of Contents

Most tools generate a table of contents automatically based on the styles or formatting codes that you use. The result is an accurate page number and the text associated with each major heading.

If you manually edit the table of contents after it is generated by the publishing tool, you force the translators to do the same for every target language. Their goal is to provide accurate translations and an information product that looks exactly the same as the source version. If you must edit a table of contents, make sure that you document your changes for the translators.

Also, do a quality check of the generated table of contents before you hand it over to translators. Are the page numbers accurate, or do you need to regenerate the table of contents? Did you encounter problems when you generated the table of contents and have to do a manual workaround? If so, document what the problem is and how you fixed it and provide the translators with this information.

Headers and Footers

Most often, headers and footers contain page numbers, the date, the part number, the chapter title, and the name of the book if this is how you have designed them.

Many publishing tools now provide macros that you can use in headers and footers to let users know what section of the document they are currently reading. These macros read the value of the current section according to the formatting code use and print its title in place of the macro. Some publishing tools even let you define your own macros that can insert custom text or graphics that will be repeated in the header and footer of a document.

When you manually enter information into the header and footer, or when you change the header and footer of only a few pages to deviate from the pattern, document these instances and provide your translators with this information. If at all possible, use the automation capabilities of the publishing tools and avoid manual overrides. Each override takes time for translators to incorporate, and there may be many language versions affected.

Cross-References

Cross-referencing is a wonderful feature to have in a publishing tool, and most publishing tools do provide this feature. One problem with using this feature is that you have to make sure that it is accurate at all times, and doing so can be difficult in some tools.

The more powerful publishing tools and platforms use the concept of a book or a master document that contains many smaller documents, like chapters, and provide updating capabilities via these features. I have created books and master documents for some of the manuals that I have written. Many of these have referenced ten or more files. In order to keep cross-references updated, I needed to have a system that would let me open all of these documents. Depending on the tool, the documents needed to be open simultaneously or sequentially for the updating process to work. Sometimes I would bypass the automation of the update process and just type in the exact cross-reference because I did not have the computing resources to do otherwise.

In an internationalization environment, though, this should be discouraged. Tracing cross-references through a 200-page manual in seven or more languages is not something that is a cost-effective use of translators's time.

Another problem with cross-references is that you can create problems if you use them in a manner similar to text-string substitution, which concatenates text strings to form complete sentences. Use whole entities in the cross-references that are not dependent on a particular grammatical structure. The target language probably cannot accommodate the grammatical structure you assumed. This requires the translators to modify the sentences and the text of the cross-references in order to write grammatically correct sentences in the target languages.

Tables

Many vendors of publishing tools have really responded to the need for easy table generation. Not too long ago, creating tables was difficult, cumbersome, and required that you know all sorts of coding. Now tables can be created very easily so that you only have to focus on the text. Some tools will even format the tables automatically for you if this is what you specify. You should try to rely on automatic table generation features at all times. The alternative—to create tables manually—introduces all sorts of complexities in the context of internationalization.

To create tables manually, you insert character code sequences to draw vertical and horizontal lines and then use the space bar or the tab key to align text or numbers.

The resulting file is sent to the translator, who then might have to load a different character set in order to type in the target language. The character set maps the character-code sequences to completely different characters so that you no longer have horizontal and vertical lines.

Add to these problems the expansion of text in the target language. The alignment is now completely wrong. Words may break in strange places because the line length has increased overall. The hard spaces and tabs prohibit a more natural control of the column width.

The result is a mess. The translator now has to re-create the entire table manually. If this is a multipage table, and if there are many tables in the document, which is not unusual, the translation of the document will take longer. Once again, the translator is not translating but spending time formatting something that can be done automatically with the proper tool.

Using the automatic table feature of a publishing tool can have an additional benefit depending on the tool. Some table features dynamically size the width of a column depending on its content. Some even carry the column headings to the subsequent pages if the table is many pages long. These are great features for text that expands in the target language. If your documents contain a lot of tables, consider investing in tools that provide these capabilities. It will save a lot of time in the end.

Sidebars

Sidebars are quite popular in documentation, and are used for all sorts of information (graphics, quotations, tips, notes, summaries, media objects, and so on). These can suffer from the same problems that tables do, if they are created manually. Most publishing tools provide ways to automate the positioning of sidebars, and the methods vary widely. Some use anchored frames, others master pages that define the page layout. Still others rely on the formatting codes that you use. Whatever the method, use it and use it consistently.

Numbering

Automatic numbering is also a common feature in most publishing tools. You can use automatic numbering for figure numbering, table numbering, page numbering, heading and section numbering, chapter numbering, and so on. You can even use it to do hyphenated numbering based on the chapter number, like Figure 13.2, and page 7-30, and so on. Take advantage of these features.

Conditional Text

Some publishing tools allow you to define a conditional set of events so that certain information is visible or printed, but other text is not. This has the potential to be a fantastic feature for internationalization, but it is also dangerous.

Conditional text that inserts sentence fragments or anything else that is grammatically dependent is a very bad idea in an internationalization environment, since target languages do not share grammatical rules with the source language or each other.

Conditional text that inserts complete paragraphs is a much better idea. In this way, translators can translate text in an entire context and be able to render a better translation.

GLOBAL FORMATTING

Global formatting is formatting that is automated and therefore consistent and predictable. Publishing tools provide global-formatting control at four levels. The higher the level, the more you can control, the more automated the document, and the more global the formatting. Figure 12.1 illustrates the levels of global control.

1. The master document design defines an entire publication, including cover, front matter, chapter, and back matter design options. Very sophisticated publishing tools offer looseleaf publishing and magazine design features that make complex pagination issues relatively simple.

2. The page layout design defines one or more contiguous page layouts that affect one or more parts of a publication. Special page layouts that affect only one or two pages break the rhythm of the document and undermine automation.

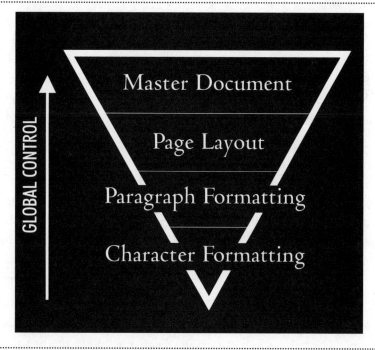

FIGURE 12.1: **Levels of global formatting control.**

3. Keep paragraph formatting to a minimum, but be thorough. Fifty or more paragraph formats make formatting very complex and can degrade the performance of publishing tool because too much information has to be stored in memory. Sacrifice some design decisions in favor of automation, assuming that this preserves usability.

4. Like paragraph formatting, keep character formats to a minimum. For most publishing tools, character formatting is very local; you highlight text and then apply the character format you want. Character formatting minimizes the automation of a document, although it can visually enhance its usability. Balance usability and automation. Try to incorporate character formatting at a higher level of formatting, like the paragraph-formatting level, if at all possible.

At all times, use these abilities. They make internationalization and localization significantly easier. Documents can be fully automated, given the proper publishing tool. Standardize formatting in your company and document it in the publications-standards guide. Provide this information to the translators so that they can replicate the look and feel of the publication.

FORMATTING CODES

Typically, translators can work more efficiently in text format. In this way, they can spend their time translating and not formatting or learning how to use a publishing tool to re-create the formatting you used. The other reason that translators prefer text format is that they can translate it on any platform or using any tool they want. Some also use it to take advantage of CAT tools, which can speed up translation if used by professional translators.

Most publishing tools are WYSIWYG tools. They hide the formatting codes so that you can focus on the document's design. Translators who translate documents by overtyping the text in the source language can inadvertently type over formatting and any hidden codes like index markers, cross-reference markers, and so on. Sometimes you can control this if the publishing tool lets you hide and freeze these hidden codes to prevent overtyping. All CAT tools facilitate hiding formatting codes in some form or another, and some localization companies have created internal tools that can do this. However, most translators still prefer to translate by overtyping text.

A workaround is to save the document in its markup format. A markup format is one that shows all the formatting codes, hidden and otherwise, plus the text.

Most markup formats are proprietary. Examples of proprietary markup formats are RTF (Microsoft Corporation) and MIF (Frame Technology). While these are not as clean as translators would like them, since there are so many codes that it becomes hard to find text to translate, they are sometimes the best alternative.

The additional problem with markup formats is that because they are proprietary, they cannot be ported to other computing platforms or other publishing tools without some loss of formatting.

Ideally, all publishers of publishing tools should agree on a standard markup language, like the Standardized General Markup Language (SGML, explained later), an international standard for describing documents, so that technical communicators and translators could avoid some of the problems discussed here. Some publishers do support SGML, but usually these are for large, expensive publishing tools.

When choosing tools, consider the file formats supported by the tool. They should optimize the time that a translator spends translating, which could be a critical factor if your company is pushing simultaneous release of its products.

TEXT EXPANSION

Text expansion has been discussed fairly exhaustively throughout this book. Consider the effects of text expansion on headings, tables, and callouts, and choose tools that allow for expansion. Tables are particularly problematic. Cells should grow dynamically with text. Text that is boxed, which is sometimes used for notes, warnings, cautions, or examples, should also be able to expand. The publishing tool should be able to support automatic expansion if this is a design element used in your technical information.

FONTS

What font support does the publishing tool provide in the target languages? Refer to Chapter 10, "Online Issues," for some technical background on this topic.

Here are some additional font and publishing tool issues that you should research.[2]

- Are all characters supported in a particular font for the target language? Asian languages are particularly problematic, as are Eastern European languages in another way, because some of the diacritics and glyphs are missing from the font.

- How much physical space will the font family occupy?

- Does the publishing tool and/or the operating system make it easy to switch among character sets?

- Is the font vendor established and committed to developing font families in many languages?

TEXT DIRECTIONALITY

This feature is important to consider if the translators will be using the publishing tool while translating into bi-directional languages.

FILE MANAGEMENT

File-management capabilities are critical if you intend to use core information to reuse text, graphics, and so on. At present, this capability is provided only in the more sophisticated publishing tools.

There is a tools void here. There are no good tools available for recognizing core information. Tools do exist, however, for storing core information in an intelligent database and then linking it dynamically to the document. (See Chapter 7 for more on reusing information and ideas for file structures and implementations.)

Some CAT tools provide a feature called *translation memory* that may have potential as a tool for implementing core information. Translation memory uses fuzzy logic to find exact and near matches of text in the source language and replaces it with equivalent text in the target language. Translation memory as it is today would require a great deal of modification to be used for core information, but it has some real potential. Again, most technical communicators do not want the extra features that come with a CAT tool. In addition, the capability would have to be integral to the source-language publishing tool.

EVALUATING THE TOOLS PUBLISHER

The tools publisher's business objectives should complement those of your company. Researching the business objectives of a tools publisher may be important to your satisfaction with the tool itself. If your target-language requirements include languages that use alphabets that are different from the alphabet of the source language—English to Japanese, for example—then your translators will need a localized version of the tool you used to create the source information. Be sure that the tools publisher supports the language pair.

You should consider tools publishers who can meet these two criteria:

1. The tools publisher is committed to simultaneous release of all language versions of the tool.

2. The tools publisher offers technical support worldwide for all language versions.

S G M L

As defined by an SGML guru . . .

> The Standard Generalized Markup Language (SGML) is the International Organization for Standardization (ISO) standard for document description (ISO 8879:1986 Information Processing—Text and office systems— Standard Generalized Markup Language (SGML) *Geneva*, 15 October 1986). It is designed to enable text interchange and is intended for use in the publishing field, but can also be applied in the office and engineering areas. SGML documents have a rigorously described structure that may be analyzed by computers and easily understood by humans.[3]

There is a lot of confusion about SGML. Many people think that it is a software product that you can buy at a computer store. Others know it only as an international standard. And still others think of it as a sort of programming language. It is none of the above.

This is not intended to be a primer on SGML. It is to alert you to the advantages of using it in the context of internationalization and localization. But first, some rudimentary explanation of SGML terminology and how it works.

A   B R I E F   I N T R O D U C T I O N   T O   S G M L

SGML allows you to create your own document markup language. A *markup* is "the process of adding formatting or other processing commands to a text."[4] A *markup language* is a set of rules that describe a markup. You can create an infinite number of markup languages, one for each type of document that you need. Examples of document types include memos, letters, reference manuals, and newsletters.

The elements of the markup language for the particular type of document are all defined in a master document called a *document type definition* (DTD). The elements describe and define each of the four levels illustrated in Figure 12.1. You can also describe and define other types of elements, but let us keep this discussion simple.

SGML requires that you purchase an SGML parser, which is an off-the-shelf software product. The SGML parser processes the text, which you format using elements in the DTD. The parser verifies that you have formatted the text correctly, as defined in the DTD.

Most companies purchase SGML editors (they all do parsing) since the SGML editor lets you apply the elements of a DTD to text in much the same way that you would use Microsoft Word, WordPerfect, FrameMaker, or Interleaf products.

Most SGML editors let you toggle your view of a document; one view is WYSI-WYG, the other lets you see the elements. Some editors let you see both views simultaneously.

SOME ADVANTAGES OF USING SGML

- SGML enforces consistent formatting. This is an excellent feature that eliminates the problems associated with character formatting and with not using a publishing tool to its full extent. This is also a quality check.

- The DTD is not language dependent. A DTD can be written in any language, as long as there are character sets to support the language and the SGML editor supports the target languages.

- Documents are portable to many computing platforms. All you need is an SGML editor that runs on the computing platform you need. Thus, translators do not have to use the same computing platform that you do.

- Formatting codes, called *elements*, are easy for translators to spot and ignore if they overtype the text.

SOME DISADVANTAGES OF USING SGML

- The creation of a DTD requires a significant investment in time and resources to perform a document analysis that studies and defines your document's structure.

- A DTD is difficult to write.

- A DTD may be difficult to use, depending on the SGML editor and on the complexity of the DTD.

COMMENTARY

- Standardize the toolset used to create international technical communication in your company and document these standards.

- Evaluate the design of your documents to determine the features that you will need in your tools.

- Invest in tools that work for you, not against you.

- Invest in tools that are compatible with translation tools.

- Invest in computing platforms and hardware that work for you, not against you.

- Invest in proper tools training so that you know the most effective and efficient way to use the features provided.

END NOTES

1 From telephone interviews with Walter Smith, manager of technical publications at ILE Corporation, throughout the month of September 1994.

2 Thanks go to Walter Smith for educating me on the complexity of choosing fonts.

3 Eric van Herwijnen, *Practical SGML*, 2nd Ed., Kluwer Academic Publishers, Boston, 1994, p. 3.

4 Ibid., p. 274.

13 LEVELS OF QUALITY FOR INTERNATIONAL TECHNICAL COMMUNICATION HAVE NOT BEEN FORMALLY ESTABLISHED BY ANY NATIONAL OR INTERNATIONAL STANDARDS BODY. USE ISO 9000 REGISTRATION AS AN OPPORTUNITY TO ESTABLISH CRITERIA THAT ENSURE THE USABILITY AND QUALITY OF INFORMATION PRODUCTS. LEARN ABOUT METHODS FOR ASSESSING AND MEASURING QUALITY.

Quality System Registration

....

Tools for Assessing Quality

....

Minimal Requirements— All Languages

....

Localization

....

Usability

....

Value

....

ASSESSING QUALITY

13

An important part of any project is quality assessment. Quality is relative, however, and you will first need to define criteria for assessing it.[1] This chapter identifies some criteria, but is not exhaustive. Consider these tips when you choose criteria for assessing quality.

- Obtain formal support from upper management for your definition of quality and the quality criteria you identify for quality assessment.

- Evaluate the skills required for defining quality criteria and assessing quality.

- Assess the time required.

- Estimate the cost.

QUALITY SYSTEM REGISTRATION

Many companies are interested in becoming formally registered as organizations that adhere to total quality management practices. The rewards for registration are:

- Business growth ▪ Profitability ▪ An increase in market share

- An increase in consumer confidence ▪ An increase in customer satisfaction[2]

THE HISTORY AND PURPOSE OF THE ISO 9000 STANDARDS SERIES

The most common registration is ISO 9000 registration. In September 1992, over 65 countries had adopted or were expected to adopt the ISO 9000 standards series as voluntary national standards.[3]

ISO 9000 is a series of standards published by the International Organization for Standardization that define what constitutes a *quality system*. A quality system provides guidelines for quality management and quality assurance. It tracks and manages evidence that these practices are instituted throughout the organization.[4]

Here is a description of the history and purpose of the ISO 9000 series from the U.S. Department of Commerce and the U.S. National Institute of Standards and Technology.

> The ISO 9000 standards were intended to be advisory in nature and were developed primarily for use in two-party contractual situations or for internal auditing. . . . In some cases, compliance with one of the ISO 9000 standards (or their equivalent) has been or will be mandated by a U.S., foreign national, or regional government body. Conformance to ISO 9000 standards is also being required in purchasing specifications with increasing frequency.[5]

Here are some of the regulated industries where ISO 9000 registration is mandatory in the European Union:

- Telecommunications terminal equipment
- Industrial lab equipment
- Gas appliances
- Medical devices
- Industrial safety equipment
- Commercial scales

How ISO 9000 Affects International Technical Communication

To become ISO 9000 registered, a company must be able to demonstrate that the quality system it has in place ensures the quality of its products and services. (ISO 9000 registration does not register individual products.) This is a problem for technical communicators, as Jean Jahnke, the supervisor of technical communications at Allen-Bradley Company, describes:

> Your involvement in the achievement of ISO certification will answer questions that have plagued technical writers everywhere. Questions such as . . .
>
> - process definition—How many times have you tried to explain to the project team what you need to create a document? Or how long it takes to create it?
> - documentation control—How many times have you sent a document out for review only to find the specifications changed . . . and you weren't

notified? How many times have your reviewers passed on a photocopy of your draft to someone else?

- corrective action—How many times have you come across an engineer's problem file on a manual just after the writer sent it out for final review?[6]

Given these assurances, you will be able to develop a quality-oriented development cycle for information products that are exported. At issue for international technical communication is the ISO 9000 requirement of being able to assess the quality of the information product. This becomes particularly complicated for information products that must be world ready. There are many variables, and being able to assess the quality of an information product that will be used by people from around the world who have different information needs is quite a challenge.

Sally Yeo, the manager of technical documentation at Computer People Unlimited, lists the deliverables that technical communicators must create and maintain in order to satisfy ISO 9000 requirements.[7]

- **Quality plan.** A quality manual must define the information-development cycle, its processes, quality controls, and the standards and guidelines that all technical communicators must adhere to.

- **Documentation control system.** An ISO 9000 requirement is that all information be current, and that obsolete information products be removed. This requires a sophisticated tracking and version control system.

- **Process control.** A project plan should track the information development cycle, maintain a file of all edits to information, and establish an editing cycle.

- **Measuring quality.** "If your company is going for ISO certification, you can make a good case for usability testing, for contact with real users, and for editing if these are not currently funded. Keep records of your quality assurance practices. Hire qualified people, train your staff, and keep records of that training."

The remainder of this chapter provides many ideas, tools, and methods for developing a quality system by implementing quality management and quality assurance practices.

TOOLS FOR ASSESSING QUALITY

It is up to the technical-communication department to determine the level of quality assessment for the information products that it creates, since there are no international standards (or national ones, for that matter) that define what a quality information product is. The only criterion that the ISO 9000 series offers is that information products, like all products and services that fall under the umbrella of ISO 9000, must "meet customer expectations."

There are a variety of tools you can create to make it easier to assess quality. These tools should be appropriate for the level of quality assessment you establish in your quality plan. The easier these tools are to use and the more accessible they are, the more frequently they will be used.

Consider offering training on how to use these tools. Integrate these tools into the publications process that your department follows. Written records are more effective than verbal suggestions, and are also an ISO 9000 requirement.

CHECKLISTS

Checklists are most appropriate for each defined phase of your information development cycle.

Benefits include:

- Checklists organize.

- Checklists identify everything that needs to be checked.

- Checklists serve as proof of quality assessment.

- Checklists are proof of due diligence.

- Checklists help trace problems that arise after an information product is exported.

- Checklists contribute to the development of good habits.

- Checklists enforce accountability.

- Checklists provide statistics.

Disadvantages:

- Checklists can be too detailed or too general.

- Checklists can require more effort to complete than the benefit derived from them.

- Checklists can be perceived as a means of policing staff.

- Checklists can be perceived as treating professionals like children.

- Checklists can be poorly designed. (Test them.)

INTERNAL STANDARDS AND CONVENTIONS

Internal standards and conventions specify criteria that you must use to assess quality. In this case, quality assessment is checking how well information products conform to the standards and conventions.

There are a variety of internal standards and conventions that you can create.

- Editorial standards and conventions
- Terminology standards and conventions
- Style standards and conventions
- Formatting standards and conventions
- File naming conventions
- Tools standards

Although standards and conventions are helpful for assessing quality, they can be flawed.

- Standards and conventions can be culturally biased.
- Standards and conventions can be too rigid and inflexible.
- Standards and conventions can stifle creativity.
- Standards and conventions can become obsolete and dated.
- Standards and conventions can be purposeless.

When creating standards and conventions, test them for their usability and the value that they add to the development of information products. Provide a means for technical communicators to participate in the development of standards. Be willing to sacrifice standards and conventions that are not working.

PROCESS CHECKPOINTS

Process checkpoints are a way to assess quality continuously. They identify places in the information-product-development cycle where you pause to perform quality assessments. Process checkpoints serve to minimize expensive and time-consuming problems late in the project.

Where you place process checkpoints is contingent on the degree of quality assessment you want. Documentation describing how to use medical life-support equipment necessarily requires a different degree of quality assessment than documentation describing how to use calendar-generating software.

Consider creating a timeline. Label the processes of your information-product-development cycle on the timeline. Then add checkpoints in relation to processes where appropriate. Describe the kind of quality assessment required for each process checkpoint.

FEEDBACK

There are many kinds of feedback tools that you can create and implement. You probably use many of them already.

- Individual and group technical reviews

- Formal inspections

- Peer reviews

- Reviews by subject-matter experts who are fluent in the source and one target language

- Editorial reviews

- Marketing reviews

- Management reviews

- Product defect reports

- Legal reviews

- Reader response forms

- Focus groups

- Interviews

- Surveys

Feedback can solicit a subjective response. Feedback can also be objective (identifying a typographical error or technical inaccuracy). It is not definitive and can be misleading. There must be a process for bringing all the feedback together to determine what the most important issues are.

TESTS

There are many testing methods you can use, too, to assess the quality of an information product. They can be as simple as performing a manual, random check of page references in the index to as complex as using a laboratory environment to measure the time it takes for a user to perform a task described in a user's manual.

As with all testing, have clear, quantitative goals. Research the testing methods available so that they are appropriate for what you want to learn and measure.[8]

MINIMAL REQUIREMENTS — ALL LANGUAGES

A professional information product must meet some minimal quality requirements. This is a list of the minimal requirements that I recommend for all information products—in the source and target languages.

TECHNICAL ACCURACY

Information that describes high technology must contain technically accurate information. The integrity of the information depends on it. In international technical communication, any inaccuracy in the source language is repeated in all target languages. Note that this affects both written and visual information. Illustrations must be accurate, too.

Typically, source information is reviewed by the developers, usually engineers, who created the high-technology product. They are responsible for verifying the technical accuracy of the information. In some cases I have been fortunate to work with testers (usually from a quality-assurance department), to whom I provide the information. Testers have much technical savvy and know the product well. Other groups I have used to test the technical accuracy of information are field service, customer service, and telephone support. All these people have practical knowledge of the product from a technical perspective. They always provide me with valuable information.

One way to formalize technical reviews is to require reviewers to sign their names to a review sheet indicating that they reviewed the information for technical accuracy.

It is possible that technical inaccuracies will be created in the target language because of poor translation. In this case, there are two ways to catch the inaccuracy before it reaches users:

1. The subject-matter expert who is fluent in the source and target language and who reviews the translation may notice the inaccuracy.

2. Users in the target country who test the translated information may notice the inaccuracy.

Chauncey Wilson, a human factors specialist, adds that reviews should have an impact on job performance. Being a technical reviewer should bring some reward.[9]

It continues to surprise me to hear professional technical translators describe source information that contains technical errors. Technical translators will call attention to any technical inaccuracies that they notice and they will rectify the inaccuracy in the translation. However, perhaps it is accidental that they notice the errors at all. Most technical translators do not often have access to the product, so they have no way of testing information.

Three common reasons why technical translators receive technically inaccurate source information:

1. The source information is written by individuals who are not professional technical writers. Professional technical writers rarely make this kind of mistake. If they do, it is often for reasons that are beyond their control, as in the next reason. Chauncey Wilson notes, "I have often noted technical inaccuracies from competent technical writers because the writers did not know about particular interactions or had not seen customers use the product in wild ways."[10]

2. The information is written in an environment where there is no freeze on the development of the high-technology product. Development continues until the last minute. Technical communicators cannot be expected to develop quality information in such an environment. I have worked in environments like this and it is impossible to do your job well. There has to be cooperation of the entire project team so that everyone's scheduling requirements are addressed fairly.

3. The technical reviewer is a poor reviewer, does not have time to do a thorough review, or is not as technical as you might have thought.

LANGUAGE

The spelling and the grammar of the information in the source language and the target languages must be correct. Again, the integrity of the information is jeopardized if these two criteria are not met. There are many methods you can use to ensure the proper use of language.

- Hire one or more professional editors to verify the grammatical correctness of the information in the source language.

- Require the translators to have their work reviewed by professional editors who are fluent in the target languages. Most translation companies do this, but it should be verified.

- Use spelling checkers. However, Robert Sprung, president of Harvard Translations, notes that many spelling checkers contain misspellings![11] Jon

Lavine, a senior editor at Berlitz Translation Services, states, "In addition to which, spelling checkers only catch misspellings, not cases where the wrong spelling is also a valid word."[12]

- Develop editorial standards. Provide them to source language writers, editors, and translators. Offer training to ensure that everyone knows how to use them.

Verify terminology in the source language early in the project, preferably as a part of the first review cycle. Use the glossary that you created for translators to assess consistency and usage. Make sure that all writers on a project use the same terms in the same way all the time. This greatly enhances the readability of the information in the source language. Consistent terminology ensures a higher quality translation of the source language. (See Chapter 8 for more information.)

CULTURAL BIAS

Assess the content's appropriateness for the target country. You can use the following channels to have content reviewed for cultural bias.

- **Translators.** They should be able to call attention to blatant bias, especially if they live in the target country. However, consider that translators are not cultural experts; they are language experts.

- **Subject-matter experts** who review the translated information. Again, they may not be the best choice, but they should be able to catch blatant bias.

- **International marketing professionals.** These people are excellent reviewers for cultural bias, especially if they live in the target country.

- **Distributors and salespeople** who sell the product in the target country. Another excellent choice for reviewers of cultural bias. They know their clients.

To focus a review of this kind, develop a sample list of questions that reviewers should use to assess the cultural appropriateness of the information. You can also prepare review guidelines in letter or memo form. Define cultural bias and explain why you believe the reviewer is qualified to evaluate cultural appropriateness.

In a recent project to develop a brochure that defined the purpose, mission, and activities of the International Technical Communication Professional Interest Committee (ITC PIC), Pat Gibbs, the copywriter for the brochure, sent a letter to eight people from around the world asking for their response to the brochure's content. Here is an extract from her letter, which offers good questions that reviewers can use for assessing cultural bias:

> . . .You are one of a select group of eight ITC PIC members who, collectively, provide an excellent representation of cultural, linguistic, and geographic diversity.

> We would very much appreciate your comments on this draft of the ITC PIC brochure. Please consider the following perspectives during your review:

> - Is there anything in the tone, wording, or graphics that is not appropriate for readers in your country or region of the world?

> - Is the language appropriate for readers whose native language is not English? If the language needs to be simplified, please suggest alternative phrasing.[13]

M E C H A N I C S

Mechanics refers to the mechanisms, like indexes, headers and footers, tables of contents, and cross-references, that users rely on to find or identify information.

Index Entries

Verify that index entries refer to the proper page in the document.

An automated index requires only a random spot check of index entries. Consider checking at least 25 percent of the total number of index entries. If the index has been manually generated, all index entries must be verified in the final version of the document.

Translators must verify all index entries, since text expansion or text compression affects pagination.

Headers and Footers

Sometimes writers put terms like *draft* and *last revised* in the header or footer of a draft document. Verify that these have been removed in the final version.

Also verify that any text in the header or footer is accurate. Did the name of the chapter change, for example?

Some headers change as they reflect headings throughout the chapter. This is often automated. Verify that the text is accurate. Consider the effect of text expansion on the header and footer text.

Translators should verify the same information.

Table of Contents

Verify the phrasing of chapter titles and headings. Verify page numbers. Have translators do the same.

Cross-References

Verify all cross-references as part of a final edit. If cross-references contain text and page numbers, verify both. In the target languages, it is common for pagination to change because of text expansion and compression. Translators or editors for the target languages should be required to verify cross-references, since it is likely that cross-references will be different from those in the source language. Some tools automate cross-references. If this is the case, insist on random checks. Automation features sometimes generate inaccurate cross-references, so manual checks are important.

Figures

Verify that all references to figures in text are accurate and they refer to the correct figure. Also make sure the correct figure is being used. Verify all callouts, especially if you are using a legend that identifies and describes each numbered callout.

If the information contains screen images of software, make sure that the screen images reflect the final version of software. Does the data in the screen images make sense?

A checklist can help ensure accuracy. The checklist:

- Identifies the file name of the figure
- Provides a description of the figure (the caption is usually sufficient)
- Indicates the figure's number in text (Figure 14.2)

Provide translators with this checklist so that they can verify the same information. Translators also need to verify that the screen images reflect translated software (if applicable) and that captions are translated.

Charts

Confirm all labels and data points along the axes of charts and that the chart type and format are appropriate for the target country. For example, U.S. stock charts use different symbols than are used in stock charts in Japan.[14]

Tables

Verify the numbering of tables, as in Table 4.6. Verify that all references in text to tables are accurate.

Create a checklist for tables. Include the table number (Table 4.6) and its caption.

Have translators verify the same.

Hypermedia Links

Confirm that all hypermedia links in an online document or multimedia presentation work and that they go to the correct destination.

The only tool that can really assist you here is a map of all links. It must be created as the links are created, unless you have access to a software tool that can trace all links for you.

Provide translators with the map of links. They will need to verify all links in the target language as well. Note that if any links are based on an alphabetic ordering of elements, they will be different in all language versions. For example, Microsoft Word for Windows, version 6.0, has an online index of help topics that are listed alphabetically. This index is re-created for all language versions of Microsoft Word.

Conversions and Units of Measure

All conversions of currency, temperature, distance, volume, height, weight, voltage, and other measurements must be checked in all languages. Verify the units of measure and their abbreviations.

Number, Date, and Time Formats

The accepted formats for many countries are easy to research and often easy to check yourself, even if you do not read or speak the target languages. Most technical translators will do this for you, but you should spot check important numbers, currency amounts, dates, and times yourself as a precaution. See Appendix C, "Resources in International Technical Communication."

- **Numbers.** The format for currency and numbers is different throughout the world. You can verify the format in the target language yourself if the numbers are recognizable. Make sure commas, decimal points, negative and positive signs, currency symbols, and the alignment of a list of numbers are accurately presented for the target audience. Verify the rounding methods preferred in target countries. Switzerland, for example, has a rounding method that differs from the rounding method used in the U.S.

- **Dates.** Verify the date format of all dates. Check the date itself, punctuation, and abbreviations. Consider that different calendars are used in some parts of the world. Verify that the correct calendar system was used for each target language variant exported. Remember the effect of the International Date Line.

- **Time.** Confirm the time format. Consider, too, that some countries move their clocks forward and back on a seasonal basis.

Addresses and Telephone and Fax Numbers

- **Addresses.** Check whether an address in source information should change for the target variants. For example, an address for customer service in France that is used in the source information may not be correct for information that is exported to Taiwan.

  Confirm the address format for all languages. This varies from country to country, so advise translators accordingly.

- **Telephone and Fax Numbers.** Verify whether a telephone and fax number in the source information is valid for the target variants. An 800-number for the U.S may not be valid for Canada or Mexico, for example, and certainly will not be valid elsewhere.

  Also verify the country code and the format of the telephone and fax numbers. If possible, indicate the time zone of the telephone and fax numbers. Have all abbreviations of the time zones verified in the target languages.

Names

Check the spelling of all names of products and people in all languages. Translators can help you. Also make sure that you use the correct form of address for all people. In some countries, an improper form of address is offensive. Research any ambiguities. For example, in Germany, it is proper to greet someone using their proper title. If someone has received a doctorate degree, he or she should be greeted as Doctor.

FORMATTING

Verify that formatting of information is consistent throughout the information, whether it is printed or online.

To ensure formatting consistency, first create formatting standards and conventions.

- Document all formatting standards and conventions.
- Name formatting styles clearly.
- Provide written typographic specifications for each formatting style.

- Provide a sample document that shows what each formatting style looks like when it is printed or displayed.

- Provide criteria that describe when to use each formatting style.

Verify that formatting standards and conventions are used correctly. Consider hiring a production editor or a desktop publisher to do this. This person should visually assess the design of each page in the document or each screen in an online document or multimedia presentation.

Provide translators with the formatting standards and conventions and have them verify formatting consistency of all language versions. However, the formatting used in the source information product may be impossible or undesirable to replicate in the target variant. Traditional typographic conventions in the target country or font limitations in the target language may require other formatting styles.

Consider limiting the number of formatting styles. They take a long time to learn, and an edit of format can be arduous. Also, many formatting styles can degrade the performance of an electronic document, causing significant scrolling delays.

CONFORMANCE TO LEGAL REQUIREMENTS

Legal content must be verified for all countries. Liability and misrepresentation are expensive, embarrassing, and dangerous mistakes. Also consider that laws vary from country to country and industry to industry. A corporate attorney or the legal firm that your company works with will be aware of this information, or is at least qualified to research it. At all times, have only attorneys (and not marketing) review the information for legal content or the lack thereof.

Trademarks and Copyrights

Trademarks and copyrights that belong to your company or to other companies must all be verified, especially if the information is to be exported. International intellectual-property laws as to what constitutes a trademark or copyright and how they must be labeled vary significantly throughout the world.

Prepare a listing of all proper names that are possible trademarks or copyrights. Include page references where they are found throughout the information. Provide corporate attorneys with a hard-copy version of documents and either access to online information or screen shots of relevant screens. They should also verify trademark and copyright notices for all packaging information.

For legal information in the target languages, have the corporate attorneys in the source country decide how to address this. Most companies should have legal counsel in the target country and usually fax translated legal information to the target country for legal review.

The corporate attorneys should indicate where registered trademarks and copyright notices belong and provide you with legally appropriate phrasing of any trademark and copyright information.

Licenses and Warranties

Laws governing licensing and warranties also vary considerably from country to country. At all times, consult your attorney for how to proceed. At the very least, ask, "Does this document require information about licenses and warranties?"

Seek an attorney's advice on who should translate the legal information and who should review it for accuracy and legal content, and advise translators accordingly.

Health, Personal Safety, and Environmental Requirements

There are many parts of the world where health, personal safety, and environment laws are strict. The European Union and the U.S., for example, have strict directives and laws that carry with them severe penalties for noncompliance.

Countries also have different requirements as to how warnings and cautions are phrased, what languages are required, and even the symbols and colors that are used to draw attention to them. Even environmental symbols differ worldwide.

While many high-technology products are not affected by health, personal safety, and environmental laws, many are. If, as you research the product itself, you sense that it could be used in such a way as to threaten the health or personal safety of the user, or if it poses any threat to the environment, you can assume that there are laws that affect your information. Penny Wilson, an intellectual property attorney for American Superconductor Corporation, adds, "If in doubt, assume at least that nearly all hardware products and some industrial or military software products are covered by these laws."[15]

Provide your attorney with early drafts of all chapters or screens. To make it easier for the attorney, consider supplementing the chapters and screens with an index of where warnings and cautions are located. It may take the attorney some time to research the information, which is why you should provide the early drafts.

The attorney should advise you of any changes needed to phrasing, color, symbols, and so on, and should also advise you as to who should perform the translation and who should review it.

This is very serious business. It is appropriate to be extremely careful, especially when a user's life could be threatened.

It is also strongly recommended that you have all cautions and warnings tested in the source and target languages. See "Usability" later in this chapter for more information about testing.

Labels on Machinery

There are strict laws regarding the labeling of machinery for safety, product liability, country of origin, and conformance to other local requirements, and they, too, vary worldwide. Again, consult a corporate attorney in all matters related to labeling.

LOCALIZATION

You can assess the quality of all localization for cultural appropriateness. Apple Computer offers this guideline for assessing the quality of localization:

> In short, every localized version of the original product looks and feels as if it had been designed in the user's home country for local distribution.[16]

There are a variety of tools that you can create and use to assess localization.

- Use a model of culture to evaluate look and feel. Create your own, or use an existing model of culture. (See Chapter 4, "Performing an International-User Analysis," for more information.)

- Have your information evaluated by cultural anthropologists or cross-cultural communication consultants who specialize in the target country. They will provide mostly subjective, but informed, feedback. If they are native to the source country, they are probably familiar with the most common cultural mistakes. Note that these people may not know much about high-technology products, so their input might be limited.

- Hire test participants in the target countries and have them use the localized information and provide feedback.

- Hire subject-matter experts in the target country to evaluate the localized information.

- Work with the sales staff to identify customers who can provide useful criticism.

- If your company has an office in the target country, arrange to have some staff (marketing, sales, and customer service staff are good choices) review the localized information.

- Have the distributor for the target country critique the localized information.

- Hire a human factors consultant in the target country to design test and evaluation criteria and methods for you. (See Appendix C, "Resources in Intentional Technical Communication.")

USABILITY

Jakob Nielsen, a human factors and usability specialist, defines usability in terms of five components and their effect on a user's ability to use the product.[17] They are:

- **Learnability.** How long does it take to learn the product?

- **Efficiency.** After learning a product, how productive is the user? Ease of navigation is often a key to efficiency.

- **Memorability.** How well can the user remember important information?

- **Errors.** How many errors does the user make during specified tasks?

- **Satisfaction.** How much does the user enjoy working with the product?[18]

When you assess the usability of an information product in the source and target languages, you should set usability goals for these basic components as well as other usability attributes. Usability goals include:

- an attribute

- a measuring task

- a measuring method

- a criterion

Chauncey Wilson defines usability goals in Table 13.1.[19]

This chapter does not discuss usability testing methods. This chapter does identify some peculiarities that you should be aware of when performing or arranging usability testing on international technical communication.

In all cases, you need to test all language versions of an information product. The usability of an information product in the source language is in no way a guarantee that it is as usable or usable at all in the target language.

FEEDBACK

When you use feedback methods like questionnaires, surveys, and reader reply forms, consider the following:

TABLE 13.1: **Wilson's Usability Goals for Information Products**

ATTRIBUTE	MEASURING CONCEPT	MEASURING METHOD	CRITERION
Initial learning	Two-part learning task	Number of successful interactions in the first half hour of the task versus the second half hour of the task	Participant's score in the second half of the task is at least 50 percent better than the second half
Ease of navigation	Read and locate task	Number of correct answers out of 20 questions	At least 15 correct answers must be found
Error rate after training	Basic set of tasks	Number of errors made during the basic set of tasks	No critical errors (errors that could cause irreparable damage)

- Use a return address in the user's country. Many companies that I have consulted with claim that the return rate is higher when they do this.

- Have the feedback method translated in the target language.

- Test the feedback method in the target country before you use it. Questions might seem awkward or unnecessarily probing to the user. For example, telemarketing and direct mail are common feedback methods in the U.S., but not in Japan.

- Review feedback methods used by companies in the user's country for ideas. The companies can be competitors or a company in a similar industry.

- Review trade magazines in the target country. Trade magazines often use feedback methods.

TESTING

Here are some ideas for testing that are unique to international technical communication.

- Test the intuitiveness of graphics and translated terminology.[20]

- Experiment with cultural rewriting.[21]

- Experiment with cross-cultural performance testing.

- Test the efficiency and usability of the information development cycle that you created to form world-ready information products.

Chauncey Wilson offers these additional comments about international usability testing from his experience as a human factors and usability specialist at Dun and Bradstreet Software and other companies:[22]

1. Make sure that you have the complete support of high-level management in the international group that you will be testing.

2. Should a native speaker administer the usability test? Some participants may feel uncomfortable with an interpreter and the results may be skewed by the interpreter's interpretations.

3. Make sure that you get more than yes or no answers, whether you are an interpreter or not.

4. Keep in mind that in some cultures (like Japan) people may not want to embarrass others. This fear of embarrassing others may affect the outcome of your usability evaluations.

HEALTH, SAFETY, AND ENVIRONMENTAL REQUIREMENTS

Many countries have strict laws about the effect a product has on the health and personal safety of users and on the environment. You should implement testing methods that address these liabilities.

Consult usability engineers who specialize in your industry for ideas on how to proceed, given the type of information product and its content. Insist that all language versions be tested thoroughly. Make sure that you keep excellent documentation of all testing, since it might later serve as legal defense material. Depending on the severity of the liability, consider having all testing objectives and methods reviewed and approved by the appropriate upper management before testing begins.

VALUE

JoAnn Hackos, author of *Managing Documentation Projects*, states that a quality information product is one that adds value for both the customer and your company. She demonstrates eight ways that information products add value. They are:

- Information products make information more accessible.

- Information products make customers productive more quickly.

- Information products reduce training costs.

- Information products lower the barriers for discretionary and infrequent users.

- Information products foster use by diverse user communities.

- Information products reduce the cost of customer support.

- Information products reduce the cost of field maintenance.

- Information products increase sales.[23]

Some additional ways that information products add value that are unique to international technical communication are:

- Internationalizing technical communication reduces the cost of translation and localization of the information product.

- Localizing technical communication embraces cultural differences.

Find ways to measure the value that your information products add. Track them over time to demonstrate your continuous quest for quality.

....

END NOTES

[1] JoAnn Hackos, *Managing Your Documentation Project*, John Wiley & Sons, Inc., 1994, p. 10.

[2] From a handout of a presentation on ISO 9000 by John Fluke Manufacturing Company, Inc., July 1992, Chelmsford, Massachusetts.

[3] Maureen Breitenberg, *ISO 9000*, "More Questions and Answers on the ISO 9000 Standard Series and Related Issues," U.S. Department of Commerce and the National Institute of Standards and Technology, NISTIR 5122, April 1993, p. 4.

[4] Ibid., "Questions and Answers on Quality, ISO 9000 Standard Series, Quality System Registration, and Related Issues," NISTIR 4721, pp. 1–2.

[5] Ibid., p. 2.

[6] Jean M. Jahnke, "Quality Time Well Spent," *Proceedings*, 40th Annual Conference, Society for Technical Communication, Dallas, Texas, June 1993, p. 495.

[7] Sally Yeo, "Quality Time Well Spent," *Proceedings*, 40th Annual Conference, Society for Technical Communication, Dallas, Texas, June 1993, p. 496.

[8] Here are some good resources for learning more about different testing methods. Thanks go to Chauncey Wilson, a human factors consultant in Wayland, Massachusetts, who introduced me to many of these sources. *Usability Inspection Methods*, Jakob Nielsen and Robert L. Mack, Eds., John Wiley & Sons, Inc., New York, 1994. JoAnn T. Hackos, *Managing Your Documentation Projects*, John Wiley & Sons Inc., New York, 1994

(see especially Chapter 20, "Introducing Usability Assessment"). *Usability Engineering*, Jakob Nielsen, Academic Press, Cambridge, Massachusetts, 1993. *Cost-Justifying Usability*, Randolph G. Bias and Deborah J. Mayhew, Eds., Academic Press, Cambridge, Massachusetts, 1994. Jeffrey Rubin, *Handbook of Usability Testing*, John Wiley & Sons, Inc., New York, 1994.

[9] From comments on an earlier draft of this chapter, October 24, 1994.

[10] Ibid.

[11] From notes taken at a meeting of the International Special Interest Group, sponsored by the Boston and Northern New England chapters of the Society for Technical Communication, Chelmsford, Massachusetts, October 20, 1994. Robert Sprung spoke on "Localization for the European Community."

[12] Jon Lavine, from review comments on a draft of this chapter, October 29, 1994.

[13] From a letter to reviewers from Pat Gibbs, dated October 25, 1994. The ITC PIC, of which I was the manager at the time Gibbs wrote this letter, is part of the Society for Technical Communication.

[14] Robert Sprung, "Two Faces of America: Polyglot and Tongue-Tied," *Designing User Interfaces for International Use*, Jakob Nielsen, Ed., Elsevier, 1990, p. 95.

[15] From comments made on an earlier version of this chapter, October 24, 1994.

[16] Apple Computer, Inc., *Guide to Macintosh Software Localization*, Addison-Wesley Publishing Company, Reading, Massachusetts, 1992, p. 5.

[17] Chauncey Wilson, a human factors specialist, provided the definitions of each component on a draft of this chapter.

[18] Jakob Nielsen, *Usability Engineering*, Academic Press, Cambridge, Massachusetts, 1993, p. 26.

[19] Chauncey Wilson provided this table in his review of a draft of this chapter, October 24, 1994.

[20] See Jakob Nielsen, "Usability Testing of International Interfaces," *Designing User Interfaces for International Use*, Jakob Nielsen, Ed., Elsevier, New York, 1990.

[21] See Jan M. Ulijn and Judith B. Strother, *Communicating in Business and Technology: From Psycholinguistic Theory to International Practice*, Peter Lang Publishing, 1995; Jan M. Ulijn, "Is Cultural Rewriting of American Technical Documents Needed for the European Market: Some Experimental Evidence from French and Dutch Technical Documents," *International Dimensions of Technical Communication*, D. Andrews, Ed., Society for Technical Communication, 1995.

[22] From review comments of a draft of this chapter, October 24, 1994.

[23] Hackos, pp. 12–14.

14

THE DEVELOPMENT OF WORLD-READY PRODUCTS REQUIRES A NEW PRODUCT-DEVELOPMENT MODEL, A NEW MINDSET, NEW TOOLS, AND NEW PROCESSES. CONCURRENCE OFFERS THESE GIFTS FOR THE TRULY GLOBAL ENTERPRISE. IT IS IN SUCH AN ARENA THAT WORLD-READY INFORMATION PRODUCTS CAN BE DEVELOPED TO INTUIT THE DIVERSE NEEDS OF A GLOBAL AUDIENCE.

Implement a Quality System

Implement an Information Library

Interact with Users

Insist on Continuous Training

Develop Localization Cookbooks

Cultivate Partnerships

Automate Information Development

Infiltrate the Corporation

TOWARD CONCURRENCE

International technical communication is the next generation of technical communication. Effective international technical communication requires a new approach to balance user needs and business needs. The new approach is concurrence.

Concurrence is the simultaneous occurrence of processes with shared goals that operate at an enterprise level.

Concurrence addresses these interests:

- **Concurrence addresses user needs.** Concurrence operates at a very high level in a corporation. It creates channels for information flow and encourages their use. Information flow is necessary for the successful development of world-ready products. There is such wide diversity among cultures that it requires the integrated effort of the whole product team at all levels in a corporation to gather cultural data and organize them to perceive the needs of global users with any accuracy. Multifunctional, multilingual, and multicultural teams are representative of global users. These teams, therefore, create products that address the needs of global users more accurately and perceptively. Intuitive, world-ready product interfaces are possible with such a team.

- **Concurrence addresses business needs.** Concurrence focuses on minimizing the redundancy of localization throughout the corporation and maximizing the economy of internationalization. Team members throughout the corporation need access to the same information and the same tools when creating world-ready products. Concurrence provides tools for accessing core information and cultural variants. Concurrence creates an environment where reusing internationalized and localized information is possible, easy to do, and routine. Recycling information contributes to an overall level of efficiency. Concurrence offers mechanisms for imposing a product-development environment that tracks and maintains scheduling and metrics for the team.

- **Concurrence addresses the need to maintain a high level of quality.** Quality checkpoints are built into a concurrent environment. These checkpoints and the tasks that are associated with them are defined by the team. The tasks focus on ensuring usability, safety, and the recurrent achievement of these goals.

The remainder of this chapter offers methods and ideas to implement concurrence.[1]

IMPLEMENT A QUALITY SYSTEM

The International Organization for Standardization, ISO, defines a quality system in its ISO 9000 series of standards in this way:

> The organizational structure, responsibilities, procedures, processes and resources for implementing quality management.[2]

A quality system provides the means, methods, and mechanisms for addressing user needs using business processes that focus on corporate goals and strategies. A quality system relies on your ability to perceive corporate goals, to design processes and methodologies to help attain them, and to create tools that implement your quality system's design.

A quality system for international technical communication:

- builds teams that are multifunctional, multicultural, and multilingual

- provides mechanisms for sharing information

- integrates user requirements, business and market requirements, national requirements, and industry requirements

- implements and automates processes that ensure high value and high quality, low cost, and timely information products[3]

Refer to the ISO 9000 series of standards for inspiration. Also refer to the national standards in your country for information about developing quality systems if such exist.

INTERACT WITH USERS

You need to interact with users from around the world if you are to address their needs with perception. If you cannot do so directly, you can take advantage of indirect methods.

- Monitor online forums and news groups, and attend user-group meetings, conferences, and seminars.

- Participate in focus groups, issue questionnaires, perform usability testing, and attend classes at your company that users attend.

- Contact team members in other countries to learn about the needs of users in their countries.

- Read customer-support logs, interview people in marketing and sales in your company.

- Develop alliances with individuals and departments throughout your company who interact with users regularly.

DEVELOP LOCALIZATION COOKBOOKS

A *localization cookbook* provides cultural, linguistic, technical, marketing, sales, training, and legal information about a specific target country and the users who live and work there. There should be a localization cookbook for every target country to which your company exports. The first I heard of this idea was at a seminar on global opportunities for the software industry in 1991. At this seminar, Jeremy Butler, the vice president of International and OEM Sales at Microsoft Corporation at that time, described how Microsoft creates localization cookbooks for each of its target markets.[4]

Localization cookbooks are used and maintained by every member of a multi-functional team. Localization cookbooks should be very accessible, easy to read, use, and maintain. Localization cookbooks should be living documents that change as new intelligence is introduced to or created by the team.

The closest example that I have seen of localization cookbooks is the International Business Series by Ernst & Young. These books are entitled *Doing Business In....* Here is a description from the preface of the book for Australia: "[This book] was written to give the busy executive a quick overview of the investment climate, taxation, forms of business, organisation, and business and accounting practices in Australia."[5] Each Ernst & Young firm throughout the world has created a similar guide for its country using the same generic structure to organize information.

On a lesser scale, but more applicable to high-technology companies, is a book from Apple Computer called *Localization for Japan* (1992). This is a wonderful guide for "software developers and publishers who wish to market their products in Japan. If you are interested in designing, programming, translating, marketing, or republishing software for the Japanese market, you will find valuable information in this book."[6] (And you *do* find valuable information in the book!) Here is a listing of the chapter titles to give you a sense of its scope.

- Demystifying the Japanese Market

- Marketing Application Programs in Japan

- The Japanese Computing Environment

- Localizing Your Application

- Testing Your Application

The book also provides information as to whom to contact for more information, a description of online services, a bibliography, and a glossary. The book lacks information about legal issues, training, sales, and technical communication, however.

Imagine a series of similar books in your company entitled *Localization for. . . .* The contributors to the book should be all the team members, preferably from around the world. They should be fluent in at least the official language of the corporation, and preferably also in the second most common language of the corporation. Additional language versions should be created based on a need to integrate other employees in other countries into the processes of concurrence.

Imagine again, if you will, having access to these localization cookbooks through a wide-area network. The localization cookbooks are hypermedia presentations that use video, animation, sound, text, music, and graphics, to take you to the target country.

There are demonstrations of the techniques for localization that are used by all members of the multifunctional teams—encapsulations explaining and demonstrating the challenges and goals of each team member. The localization cookbook uses the capabilities of multimedia to prove and demonstrate all the information contained within it. The bibliography has live links to the actual information so that you can read the source immediately. Wow! What an invaluable learning tool.

Note that if your company develops computing platforms, like Apple Computer, consider the value of a localization cookbook if it is available to all companies who create products that run on your computing platform. This approach makes it so much easier to have a strong worldwide presence, because it is your customers who are marketing your platform, not necessarily your company.

Technical communicators are the ideal candidates for designing localization cookbooks, whether they are printed guides or multimedia presentations.

AUTOMATE INFORMATION DEVELOPMENT

The development of international technical communication can be automated to a large degree. There are two levels of automation discussed here: the automation of an information product for worldwide use and the automation of the processes required to develop international technical communication.

THE INFORMATION PRODUCT

The automation of an information product requires the following:

- You need to start with a fully internationalized information map, a core product of sorts.

- You need generous information database capabilities. The database must be able to store, manage, and track versions of information in all forms: video, audio, animation, digitized imagery, CAD drawings, conceptual designs, charts, text, music, and so on. The information databases could access information in the localization cookbooks. The information databases could also store information in the source language and in all the target languages. Note that the physical storage requirements for such capabilities are enormous: many gigabytes of data.

- You need one or more tools that allow you to orchestrate the integration of localized information of all kinds with the internationalized information map.

- You need additional tools to recognize the potential for core information, interface with translation tools, and output to a variety of media types automatically.

THE PROCESSES

The automation of processes for developing international technical communication requires the following:

- You need to start with a comprehensive and established information development cycle.

- You need access to an enterprise-wide tool that concurrently monitors, guides, and tracks the product-development cycle from a multifunctional perspective. This tool is the manifestation of project management and quality assurance, and is indeed a quality system of concurrence.

- You need access to tools for conferencing capabilities that allow you to interact with other members of the team throughout the world.

- You need a tool that is designed to prompt you for and collect data for statistical purposes to track the effectiveness and efficiency of all processes and results. This tool should choose the most appropriate metric for you based on criteria that you enter describing what you want to measure. This tool should integrate the data from other departments throughout the world so that the entire enterprise becomes a quality system.

- You need access to a usability database that helps you select the proper test or tests to measure the usability of any given process or collection of information.

- You need access to an electronic mail alias that users from around the world can use to address their feedback on information and products.

IMPLEMENT AN INFORMATION LIBRARY

An information library is a collection of information databases that record the developmental history of all projects. Consider the following description.

The ultimate enabler of tool and data integration is the interoperable approach, where multiple tools have access to the original data, not copies of the data. And when you make a change to data in one tool, the change automatically occurs in the data used by all other tools. These tools can reside both on single computers and be shared through a network. To have integrated tools is important, but so is the level of integration. Without integration or interoperability, you create barriers where people have to re-enter data at various stages in the process.[7]

The implementation of an online information library extends the idea of automation to its fullest.

INSIST ON CONTINUOUS TRAINING

Training is required on a variety of levels. You need training to learn:

- How to use new tools
- How to present information most effectively from a palette of media choices
- How to design processes
- How to create world-ready information
- How to develop culturally specific information
- How to work in multifunctional, multilingual, and multicultural teams
- How to work concurrently
- How to assess, measure, and improve quality

Consider the following prediction.

It's quite clear that the success of a company's investment in technology depends on the ability of employees to quickly learn new technologies. This makes it imperative that companies stress and promote useful skills that translate into a good foundation for the continued training of employees.[8]

This prediction should come as no surprise to many of you, but it is important to convince your management that the investment in your training allows you to add even more value to the enterprise. It is truly discouraging to learn of companies that do not support continuing education.

If this is the case in your company, realize that it is in your best interest to take the initiative. There are many ideas you can implement so that many people in your company can benefit even during hard economic times.

- Invite professionals to your company to speak on new technologies, methodologies, and processes. They can speak after work hours or during lunch or some other break during the day.

- Invite professionals from within your company to speak to your department about their specialized knowledge.

- Read trade magazines and professional journals and newsletters that are in your corporate library. These sources can provide you with quite an education. Borrow sources from colleagues if your company does not have a corporate library.

And you can also finance your continued education yourself.

- Join a professional association.

- Set an annual goal to learn how to use a new tool, another language, or develop a new skill.

- Focus on developing subspecialties that will not become obsolete for at least five years.

Do not wait for your company to change its mind about financing your continued education. Take matters into your hands. It is, after all, your career.

CULTIVATE PARTNERSHIPS

Learn how to cultivate beneficial and compatible partnerships. Most companies are focusing on core competencies and are hiring companies from outside to manage and implement various facets of internationalization and localization. It is likely that you will work with one or more partners during an international project.

Partners include:

- Technical translators

- Localization and internationalization consultants

- Printers

- Distributors

- Usability engineers

- Cross-cultural communication consultants

- Cultural anthropologists

- Linguists

Niell Irwin, the director of Partnership Sourcing, describes the characteristics of a healthy and beneficial partnership.

- There must be a commitment to the partnership at a high level in the enterprise.

- There must be openness and trust.

- There must be clear objectives for each partner.

- There must be the promise and commitment to a long-term relationship.

- There must be a mutual commitment to total-quality management.

- There must be proof of the ability to work well together.

- There must be the willingness to be flexible.

- There must be involvement by all relevant disciplines throughout the enterprise and the relationship.[9]

Embrace these words of advice when working with or choosing partners.

INFILTRATE THE CORPORATION

All the ideas presented in this chapter provide you with ways to infiltrate your corporation. Why is this desirable? Consider the following description.

> An idea from R&D should be like a wave that ripples through the product development environment, and as it reaches production, marketing, and other areas, that wave creates secondary waves of information that change the original wave. Actually, each person, each tool, and each area that lives in the product development environment is constantly generating waves of ideas and receiving them in return as transformed reflections. The most successful companies understand and nurture this process.[10]

This description depicts an organic, living collection of natural processes, which too many corporations somehow stifle. It is a required collection of processes in a global enterprise, because there is too much diversity to filter, manage, and channel.

You cannot work in a vacuum and expect to be successful and effective. International technical communication demands access to information, tools, and talent from throughout the enterprise. If processes do not exist to provide this access, create processes that do.

Use the methods that are described in this chapter and throughout this book to create alliances all over the enterprise. Develop information tools that everyone needs, wants, and uses. Infiltrate the corporation. Aim for concurrence. Be a wave.

END NOTES

[1] There are many excellent resources available today to learn more about concurrence, which is most often referred to as *concurrent engineering* in the high-technology industries.

[2] ISO 9000, *Quality Management and Quality Assurance Standards—Guidelines for Use*, first ed., March 15, 1987, p. 2.

[3] Inspired by Donald E. Carter and Barbara Stilwell Baker, *Concurrent Engineering: The Product Development Environment for the 1990s*, Addison-Wesley Publishing, Reading, Massachusetts, 1992, pp. 35–36.

[4] Presented by Jeremy Butler at *Global Opportunities*, a two-day seminar sponsored by the Washington Software Association, Monday, April 8, 1991, Stouffer Madison Hotel, Seattle, Washington.

[5] *Doing Business in Australia*, Ernst & Young's International Business Series, New South Wales, Australia, June 1, 1994.

[6] *Localization for Japan*, Apple Computer, Inc., Cupertino, California, 1992, p. vii.

[7] Carter and Baker, p. 14.

[8] Ibid., p. 10.

[9] From a presentation handout for Niell Irwin, director, Partnership Sourcing, from a presentation made to the Localization Industry Standards Association (LISA), Boston, Massachusetts, August 25, 1994.

[10] Carter and Baker, p. 10.

WORKSHEETS

These are worksheets that you can use to begin organizing and managing international projects and collecting cultural data about target users. The worksheets are explained in chapters in this book. Consider using these worksheets as templates for a table, spreadsheet, or database that you create electronically. Maintain an archive of the data you collect as you replace the data with more current information. The evolution of this information can be valuable data by itself.

These worksheets are suggestions and may not be as thorough as you want them to be. You may find that you need to modify them for your particular situation, or even on a project basis.

The worksheets provided here include:

- Snapshot of Your Current Situation

- Scheduling Checklist

- International Variables Worksheet: Surface Level

- International Variables Worksheet: Unspoken and Unconscious Levels

- A Map of a Target Audience's Cultural Context

- Core Information Worksheet

- Glossary for Translators

- Checklist for Translation

- Color-to-Culture Map

- List of Figures for Translators

SNAPSHOT OF YOUR CURRENT SITUATION

Use this worksheet to collect data about your current situation. You may already have some of this information collected in separate documents or files. If this is the case, identify the title of the document or provide the full pathname or instructions on how to access and display the electronic document. This worksheet is based on Table 3.1.

TOOLS

Hardware	
Computing platform	
Graphics	
Word processing	
Publishing	
Online	

ROLES AND RESPONSIBILITIES

Roles	Responsibilities

EDITORIAL GUIDELINES

Preferred dictionaries	
Preferred published style guide (e.g., *Chicago Manual of Style*)	
Proofreading marks	
Punctuation conventions	
Assumptions about audience	
Information product types and their purposes	
List of accepted acronyms	
Preferred terminology	
Writing style and tone	

FORMATTING GUIDELINES

Master document level	
Templates, style sheets, catalogs	
Page layout level	
Paragraph level	
Character level	
Context-sensitive help	
Online documents	
Multimedia presentations	
Training modules	
Proposals	

REVIEW CYCLE

Review cycle	
Review criteria	
Review duration	

SCHEDULING CHECKLIST

Use this worksheet to identify the steps in each phase of the localization process you define in your information development cycle. Think about this worksheet as a master to-do list for all the tasks that you define for localization. This worksheet is based on Table 3.2.

PHASES	STEPS AND THEIR DESCRIPTION
Phase 0 Planning and preparation	
Phase 1 First review cycle	
Phase 2 Final review cycle	

INTERNATIONAL VARIABLES WORKSHEET: SURFACE LEVEL

Use the International Variables worksheet to write down the cultural data that you collect as they relate to the surface level of the Iceberg Model. Consider tailoring the names and number of international variables to suit your situation. This worksheet is based on Table 4.1.

		Politics	Economics	Social Organization	Religion	Education	Language	Technology
Similarities								
Differences								

TARGET COUNTRY:

TARGET LANGUAGE:

LAST REVISED:

INTERNATIONAL VARIABLES

INTERNATIONAL VARIABLES WORKSHEET: UNSPOKEN AND UNCONSCIOUS LEVELS

Use the International Variables worksheet to write down the cultural data that you collect as they relate to the unspoken and unconscious level of the Iceberg Model. This worksheet does not list the names of international variables, because you might want to use some of the international variables from the models of culture explained in Chapter 4. This worksheet is based on Table 4.1.

LAST REVISED:

INTERNATIONAL VARIABLES

TARGET COUNTRY:
TARGET LANGUAGE:

Similarities

Differences

A MAP OF A TARGET AUDIENCE'S CULTURAL CONTEXT

Use this diagram to plot the cultural data you have collected when researching the different levels of international variables for a particular target country. This map is helpful in determining the level of localization that is necessary. However, knowing that the level of localization is usually a marketing decision, I include this map because you may find it interesting and helpful to understand your target audience's cultural context.

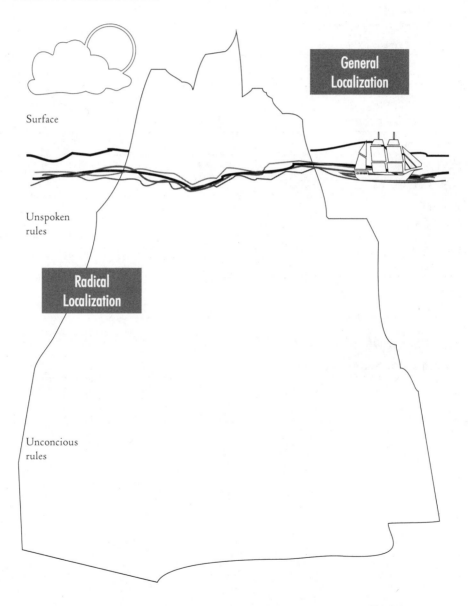

CORE INFORMATION WORKSHEET

Use this worksheet to identify, describe, and track the use of core information. This is based on Figures 7.2 and 7.3 and Table 7.1.

DESIGNATED AUTHORITY	
CATEGORY (*E.G., TRAINING MODULE, USER-GUIDE INFORMATION, PRODUCT FEATURES*)	
TYPE (*E.G., GRAPHIC, TEXT, VIDEOCLIP, TABLES, CODE EXAMPLES*)	
DESCRIPTION	
PREFERRED CONTEXT OR USE	
TEMPLATES AVAILABLE	
PHYSICAL LOCATION	
LANGUAGE VERSIONS	
USED IN THESE PUBLISHED INFORMATION PRODUCTS	

GLOSSARY FOR TRANSLATORS

Use this worksheet as a template for creating a project glossary for translators. Note that the Reference category should refer to page numbers in specific documents, references to specific screens, menus, or help topics in a software product, or specific labels for hardware products. This worksheet is based on Table 8.2.

TERM	
PART OF SPEECH	
DEFINITION	
REFERENCE	
ACCEPTABLE SYNONYMS	
UNACCEPTABLE SYNONYMS	
TARGET TRANSLATIONS	
LANGUAGE 1:	
LANGUAGE 2:	
LANGUAGE 3:	

C H E C K L I S T   F O R   T R A N S L A T I O N

Use this worksheet to help plan and organize the translation of information products on a project basis. This worksheet is based on Table 8.3.

PROJECT	
TECHNICAL COMMUNICATION TEAM	
SOURCE LANGUAGE	
TARGET LANGUAGES	
NAME OF TRANSLATION COORDINATOR	
NAME OF TRANSLATION COMPANY OR TRANSLATION COMPANIES	
TRANSLATION SCHEDULE PHASE 0: PLANNING AND PREPARATION PHASE 1: FIRST REVIEW CYCLE PHASE 2: FINAL REVIEW CYCLE	
TOOLS AND FILE FORMATS	
INFORMATION SUPPLIED TO TRANSLATION COMPANY	
TRANSLATION REVIEWERS	
EDITS	
QUALITY ASSURANCE METHODS AND SCHEDULE	

COLOR-TO-CULTURE MAP

Use this template as a part of your international user analysis to keep track of colors and their possible interpretations in the target countries. This worksheet is based on Table 11.1.

COLOR	TARGET COUNTRY OR AUDIENCE AND RESPONSE OR INTERPRETATION
Red	
Green	
Black	
Orange	
White	
Blue	
Yellow	
Purple	
Brown	
Pink	

COLOR COMBINATIONS	

LIST OF FIGURES FOR TRANSLATORS

Use this worksheet to identify all figures (screens, illustrations, CAD drawings), their captions, and filenames in a document for translators. This worksheet is based on information in Chapter 11 and Figure 11.1.

INFORMATION PRODUCT:

FIGURE NUMBER	CAPTION	FILE NAME AND LOCATION

SAMPLE INTERNATIONAL-USER ANALYSES

This appendix provides brief samples of how to collect and apply cultural data. I focus on gathering cultural data on Germans and Japanese from an American perspective using Edward Hall's cultural model and Fon Trompenaars's model of culture. I chose to provide an American perspective because this is the cultural context with which I am most familiar.

Hall's model focuses on finding out how to release the right response. Trompenaars's model focuses on problem-solving methodologies.

I provide a brief analysis of the cultural data with respect to international technical communication. Note that an analysis is more meaningful when performed in the context of a specific company and a specific product and based on formal research methods. However, the analyses here can serve as a beginning. The analyses focus on the information needs of the target culture and speculate on how the information might be presented to communicate most effectively. They are based on my observations of and research on both cultures, cultural data from Hall and Trompenaars, and informal analyses of German and Japanese information products.

ASSUMPTIONS ABOUT AMERICANS

In my experience as a technical communicator in the U.S. for over a decade, the preferences of American readers of information products about high technology have these characteristics:

- immediate gratification
- present and short-term future orientation

- direct and simple

- minimalistic

- organized

- individualistic

- time conscious, schedule driven

- contractual

These characteristics are assumptions about the source information that forms the basis for the following analyses.

USING HALL'S MODEL TO ANALYZE GERMANS

Note that within Germany, there are many subcultures. There continue to be significant cultural differences between the old West Germany and East Germany, for example. The cultural information presented here is typical of industrial centers, like Frankfurt and Bonn, but should not be interpreted as true for every individual in these cities.

INTERNATIONAL VARIABLES

Edward T. Hall identifies six international variables that can be used to understand how to release the right response from a German, for example. Table B.1 lists the name of the international variable and provides cultural data on each variable for Germans. I called the cultural data from Hall's writings about Germans.[1]

TABLE B.1: **International Variables in Hall's Model of Culture Applied to Germans**

INTERNATIONAL VARIABLE	CULTURAL DATA FOR GERMANS
Speed of messages	Slow is preferred. Prefer a lot of detailed historical and technical information.
Context	Low context. Very structured and organized information. Need a lot of information for communication to be successful. Very skeptical. Need proof of information and sources of information before trusting its credibility.

TABLE B.1: *Continued*

Space	Extremely compartmentalized. Private. Doors metaphor important for separating private and public space. Spatial boundaries include all five senses.
Time	Monochronic time. Valued highly. Precision. Value historical context.
Information flow	Very sequential. Orderly. Slow flow of information. High value placed on following prescribed order.
Action chains	Very important to finish all tasks in the prescribed order.

ANALYSIS

Like information on the historical development of a product or idea. Like technical detail and background. Prefer very orderly procedures. Like more academic style, research approach. Prose is very valuable. Exercises and examples helpful. User friendliness is less important than detail and thoroughness of information. Anticipate skepticism. Organizers like introductions, summaries, conclusions helpful. Orderly and logical presentation of topics and very clear and obvious organization of the information product appreciated and helpful. Footnotes, endnotes, and related crediting ensure trust in the integrity of the information. Integrity and credibility of information extremely important for communication to be successful. Glossy, marketing-type presentation of information is very successful. Color, contemporary page design and fonts, high-quality paper, binding methods are important. Concern about the environment suggests using recyclable materials.

German documentation tends to begin with the history of its subject and proceed through a wealth of technical detail to produce specific recipes that can be followed literally. German technical writers often use scholarly footnotes and references to other literature, as well as detailed summaries as each point is made. Their sentences tend to be long, full of compound words and subordinate clauses. Prose that is simple and concise may be judged to represent a technology that is trivial.[2]

USING TROMPENAARS'S MODEL TO ANALYZE THE JAPANESE

Fons Trompenaars identifies seven international variables that can be used to understand a target culture. Table B.2 lists the name of the international variable and provides cultural data on each variable for Japanese. I culled the cultural data from Trompenaars's writings about Japanese.[3] Note that these cultural data are general, since they were not collected in the context of a particular company or for a particular purpose. Your international-user analysis should provide more specific data. Refer to Chapter 4 for more information on Trompenaars and his model
of culture.

INTERNATIONAL VARIABLES

Table B.2 identifies Trompenaars's seven international variables that can be used to understand how a target culture solves problems.

TABLE B.2: **International Variables in Trompenaars's Model of Culture Applied to Japanese**

INTERNATIONAL VARIABLE	CULTURAL DATA FOR JAPANESE
Universalism versus particularism	Loyalty to the broader context, like their country, their company, even in an ethical dilemma. The Japanese are particularists. They solve ethical problems with others by focusing on the quality of the relationship and potential that relationship offers in the broader context of things.
Individualism versus collectivism	Are collectivists. Individual contributions are important to the success and continued improvement of the collective effort and goals. Calling attention to an individual is cause for great embarrassment. Each element, each individual, is self-transforming and developmental.
Neutral or emotional	Japanese are emotionally neutral. Expressing emotion is discouraged strongly in a work environment.

TABLE B.2: *Continued*

Specific versus diffuse	Very diffuse. General to specific. Characterized by circling around to feel out the quality of the relationship. Partially ritualistic. Focus on discovering and learning about the attributes of the relationship. Focus on integrating details into whole patterns, relationships, and wider contexts.
Achievement versus ascription	Very ascriptive. Managers and supervisors are teachers who are concerned with nurturing the learning process.
Attitudes to time	Natural cycles. Sequential, but synchronizing the past, present, and future. Harmony. Integration.
Attitudes to the environment	You cannot control your own destiny. You are a part of a larger context.

ANALYSIS

Your role is that of a teacher, not a provider of encyclopedic technical information. Trust that Japanese readers can read between the lines. Create a comfortable learning environment. Consider the physical environment in which learning takes place. Space is at a premium. Small is better. Multimedia may offer real potential, contingent on level of dependent technology. Develop a comfortable emotional environment through the tone and style of your writing. Tone and writing style should be empathetic and concerned with nurturing the learning process. Content tends to be successful if it contains 50 percent graphics and 50 percent text. Cartoons are successful. Teaching by example and offering a number of perspectives that build on past knowledge preferred. Consider including group exercises. Overall organization should focus on the general and move gradually into the specific. A modular approach that uses montage to connect information might prove successful. Understatement is preferred. Use the writing style and tone to project your company's eternal commitment to continual quality improvement and to addressing users' needs. Overt enthusiasm focused on the reader is discouraged. Indirect expression of emotionally charged messages is more successful. High-quality materials (paper, binding methods) are very important. High-gloss, marketing-type approach is discouraged. Provide information on specific people they can contact for more help and information.

Japanese documentation . . . tends to approach its subject elliptically. It often begins with a story that creates a setting, then examines the subject from differing perspectives. Japanese writers often use cartoons or sayings to make their point, and usually avoid summaries. Their basic aim is to create a mood in which the reader can absorb the subject most comfortably. It is expected that the customer will read the entire manual at least once before trying to use the product.[4]

END NOTES

[1] These are the books by Edward T. Hall that I referred to: *Beyond Culture* (Anchor Books, New York, 1981), *The Hidden Dimension* (Anchor Books, New York, 1982), *The Silent Language* (Anchor Books, New York, 1981), *The Dance of Life* (Anchor Books, New York, 1983), *Understanding Cultural Differences: Germans, French, and Americans*, with Mildred Reed Hall (Intercultural Press, Yarmouth, Maine, 1990).

[2] Apple Computer, *Guide to Macintosh Software Localization*, Addison-Wesley, Reading, Massachusetts, 1992,
p. 48.

[3] These are the books by Fons Trompenaars that I referred to: *Riding the Waves of Culture: Understanding Cultural Diversity in Business* (Nicholas Brealey Publishing, London, 1993), *The Seven Dimensions of Capitalism: Value Systems for Creating Wealth in the United States, Britain, Japan, Germany, France, Sweden, and The Netherlands*, with Charles Hampden-Turner (Piatkus, London, 1993).

[4] Apple Computer, p. 48.

RESOURCES FOR INTERNATIONAL TECHNICAL COMMUNICATION

SOME STANDARDIZATION BODIES

Here are the names and addresses of some standardization bodies. The standardization bodies can provide you with contact information on certification bodies for various countries. If you need information on standards in countries not represented here, inquire at one of these organizations for more information.

EUROPE

Each country in Europe has its own national standards organization. National standards organizations for Europe are not included here. Information on them can be obtained through your national standards organization, or through any of the following European resources.

- International Organization for Standardization (ISO)
  1, rue de Verambe
  Postal box 56
  CH-1211 Geneva 20
  Switzerland

- European Community Official Publications Office
  2, rue Mercier
  L-2985 Luxembourg

- Consultative Committee for International Telephone and Telegraph (CCITT)
  2, rue de Verembe
  CH-1211 Geneva 20
  Switzerland

- European Computer Manufacturers Association (ECMA)
  114 Rue du Rhône
  CH-1204 Geneva
  Switzerland

- International Electrotechnical Commission
  3, rue de Verambe
  CH-1211, Geneva 20
  Switzerland

UNITED STATES

- American National Standards Institute
  11 West 42nd Street
  13th Floor
  New York, NY 10036 USA

- National Center for Standards and Certification Information (NCSCI)
  National Institute for Standards and Technology
  TRF Building, Room A163
  Gaithersburg, MD 20899 USA

JAPAN

- Japanese Standards Association
  4-1-24 Akasaka, Minato-ku
  Tokyo 107 Japan

- Standards Information Service
  First International Organizations Division
  Economic Affairs Bureau
  Ministry of Foreign Affairs (MOFA)
  2-2-1 Kasumigaseki, Chiyoda-ku
  Tokyo 100 Japan

Note that many standards are written in Japanese.

CANADA

- Canadian Standards Association
  178 Rexdale Boulevard
  Rexdale, Ontario M9W 1R3
  Canada

- Standards Council of Canada
  International Standardizations Branch
  2000 Argentina Road, Suite 2-401
  Missassauga, Ontario L5N 1V8
  Canada

CHINA

- China Association for Standards
  P.O. Box 820
  Beijing
  China

INTERNATIONAL ORGANIZATIONS

International organizations were created to foster international peace and welfare, among other international goals. Most of these organizations are based in Geneva, Switzerland, but have branch offices throughout the world. Here are some international organizations that can provide you with information about a target country. Note that each organization is made up of representatives from member countries. Each organization focuses on a specific goal or industry. Since each organization publishes extensively, it can supply you with data that is both current and interculturally representative. Contact information for these organizations is available through your government, a library, or through a representative branch of these organizations in your country or in a neighboring country.

- United Nations (UN)

- United Nations Educational, Scientific, and Cultural Organization (UNESCO)

- World Health Organization (WHO)

- General Agreement on Tariffs and Trade (GATT)

- International Telecommunication Union (ITU)

- World Intellectual Property Organization (WIPO)

- International Organization for Standardization (ISO)

- International Labor Organization (ILO)

- International Trade Organization (ITO)

CONSULATES AND EMBASSIES

Consulates are representative bodies of the target countries, and are established for international trade, immigration, emigration, and tourism. Consulates are often located in a nation's capital. In larger countries like the U.S., consulates are located in cities that do a high volume of international trade (New York, for example). Consulates are repositories of all sorts of information about the target country. When you contact a consulate, be as specific as possible regarding the kind of information you seek.

Embassies are the official government representatives of the source country to the target country. The ambassador to a country and affiliated staff concern themselves with political and economic relations between the source country and the target country. Embassies can share the functions of a consulate, but, through the ambassador, they act as the official voice of the source country to the target country. As with a consulate, you need to be specific about the kind of information you seek. Communication with the staff at most embassies tends to be quite serious and formal.

GOVERNMENT OFFICES

All governments have offices that specialize in international trade. Start with the offices in the source country to find out what services they offer you. Ask if they provide information on target countries and obtain any relevant information. Do these offices offer courses on these topics? Get contact information for similar offices in the target countries and see what kind of information they can provide you with about the target country. Some key areas to obtain information on are certification, standards generally and by product, business culture, import and export statistics by industry, and demographics.

In the U.S., for example, the U.S. Department of Commerce has many programs that assist American businesses that export. Its International Trade Administration program has country-specific and industry-specific specialists who provide information by regular mail, fax, or electronic mail to U.S. businesses about laws, regulations, and export requirements to specific countries and specific industries. They also provide contact information for the target country (standardization bodies, government offices of the target country, customs).

In addition, the International Trade Administration has offices throughout the country and is very active in training businesses on the basics of exporting. Its educational offerings can range from half- or full-day classes through the Small Business Administration, or full day seminars in major U.S. cities. It also provides consulting services to businesses.

CHAMBERS OF COMMERCE

Most countries have a chamber of commerce. There are also multinational chambers of commerce, for example, a U.S.-Dutch chamber of commerce, or a Chinese-French chamber of commerce. In the U.S., there is a U.S. Chamber of Commerce and there are chambers of commerce in most large towns in the country. A chamber of commerce is usually a non-profit organization that is supported by members, mostly small businesses. A chamber of commerce is a marketing and networking vehicle for member companies.

The kind of information that you can get from a chamber of commerce includes the names of companies that offer translation and printing services, for example. You can also get some statistics like demographics and export and import data from these sources, along with cultural information.

PROFESSIONAL AND TRADE ASSOCIATIONS

WORLD TRADE CENTERS (WTCs)

There are World Trade Centers in more than 60 countries throughout the world. World Trade Centers sponsor trade missions, provide many educational opportunities, and host dignitaries and trade delegations. They can supply trade information and a huge network of trade contacts throughout the world via their WTC NETWORK, a satellite-based communications and market trading system. The main WTC is in New York City.

THE INSTITUTE FOR ELECTRICAL AND ELECTRONICS ENGINEERS (IEEE)

The IEEE has been very active in defining standards for hardware, software, and network interoperability.

IEEE
345 East 47th Street
New York, NY 10017 USA

ASSOCIATION FOR COMPUTING MACHINERY (ACM)

The ACM, as its name suggests, focuses on the computer industry. It has a special interest group on systems documentation, called *SIGDOC*, that has an annual conference and publishes its own journal. It is a good resource for information on online documentation. It also has a special interest group on computer-human interaction, called *SIGCHI*.

ACM
11 West 42nd Street
New York, New York 10036 USA

SOCIETY FOR TECHNICAL COMMUNICATION (STC)

The STC has an International Professional Interest Committee that offers networking and educational opportunities for technical communicators who are interested in internationalization and localization. STC also has an annual conference at which speakers from around the world discuss issues relating to technical communication, among them international technical communication. The STC also has many professional interest committees (PICs), which publish their own newsletters. Some PICs include international technical communication, marketing, usability, quality, research and education, and management.

STC
901 North Stuart Street, Suite 904
Arlington, VA 22203-1854 USA

THE INTERNATIONAL COUNCIL FOR TECHNICAL COMMUNICATION (INTECOM)

INTECOM is a consortium of technical-communication societies from around the world. Every five years, INTECOM sponsors FORUM, which is a conference that is attended by members of many technical-communication societies from around the world.

INTECOM
Dr. Thomas L. Warren
Department of English, Morrill 205
Oklahoma State University
Stillwater, OK 74078 USA

HUMAN FACTORS AND ERGONOMICS SOCIETY

The Human Factors and Ergonomics Society (HFES) is an international organization dedicated to the human–machine interface. The HFES promotes research and the application of human factors and ergonomics to the design, development, and evaluation of machines, user environments, and devices.

Human Factors and Ergonomics Society (HFES)
P.O. Box 1369
Santa Monica, CA 90406 USA

USABILITY PROFESSIONALS ASSOCIATION

The Usability Professionals Association (UPA) is an organization of more than 1500 usability practitioners. The focus of this organization is on practical techniques for improving the usability of software, hardware, and documentation. The UPA publishes a quarterly newsletter called *Common Ground*. This newsletter occasionally carries articles on international design issues.

> Usability Professionals Association
> 108755 Plano Road
> Suite 115
> Dallas, TX 75238
> USA

INTERNATIONAL ASSOCIATION OF BUSINESS COMMUNICATORS (IABC)

The IABC focuses on various facets of business communication (marketing, public relations, publishing, media, for example). Its literature emphasizes its members' interest in multiculturalism.

> IABC Membership
> One Hallidie Plaza, Suite 600
> San Francisco, CA 94102 USA

ASSOCIATION FOR BUSINESS COMMUNICATION (ABC)

The majority of ABC's membership is from academia. Much of its material focuses on academic research and teaching methods for professors of business communication and technical communication.

> Dr. Richard Meyers
> Interim Executive Director, ABC
> Department of Speech
> Baruch College - C.U.N.Y.
> 17 Lexington Avenue
> New York, NY 10010 USA

INTERNATIONAL SOCIETY FOR INTERCULTURAL EDUCATION, TRAINING AND RESEARCH (SIETAR)

SIETAR is an international organization devoted to intercultural communication and research. SIETAR has a journal, a newsletter, and an annual conference. They also publish a directory of intercultural specialists and consultants.

SIETAR International
808 17th Street NW, Suite 200
Washington, DC 20006 USA

AMERICAN SOCIETY FOR TRAINING AND DEVELOPMENT (ASTD)

ASTD is a very large American-based organization of trainers and human-resource specialists. Of particular interest is its collection of publications, several of which are on topics relating to global training, intercultural communication, international management, and diversity in the workforce. They also have professional practice areas, one of which is devoted to international training and development.

ASTD
1640 Kind Street
Box 1443
Alexandria, Virginia 22313 USA

AMERICAN TRANSLATORS ASSOCIATION (ATA)

The ATA tests and certifies professional translators. ATA also offers several publications, one of which is entitled *A Consumer Guide to Good Translation*.

ATA
1735 Jefferson Davis Highway, Suite 903
Arlington, VA 22203 USA

THE LOCALIZATION INDUSTRY STANDARDS ASSOCIATION (LISA)

LISA is an international non-profit organization whose primary goal is to cooperate with industry partners to create the right conditions for the development of standards and professional support. These conditions should facilitate the creation of multilingual software, technical documentation, and the multimedia process at the highest possible quality levels to meet the needs of the end users.

LISA
2bis, rue Ad-Fontanel
CH-1227 Carouge
Switzerland

GLOSSASOFT

GLOSSASOFT is a consortium of organizations and companies that are producing guidelines and methods and specifying tools for the localization of internationalized software applications. The consortium defines the localization process as combining "the four skill areas of translation, publishing, software engineering and project management, with the objective of creating a quality local version of the product at a minimum cost and time."

Dr. Costas Spyropoulos
National Centre for Scientific Research "DEMOKRITOS"
Institute of Informatics and Telecommunications
15310 Aghia Paraskevi
Attiki, Greece

or

Professor Pat Hall
The Open University
Walton Hall
Milton Keynes MK7 6AA
England

SOFTWARE GLOBALIZATION COMMITTEE (SHARE)

SHARE helps users of IBM equipment deal with internationalization issues.

SHARE Europe Headquarters
17, rue Pierres-du-Niton
CH-1207 Geneva
Switzerland

TRADE SHOWS

In general, watch the trade show and exhibit calendar for your industry. Trade shows are excellent vehicles for networking and for determining what the competition is doing and are held in most countries throughout the world. You can usually get schedules for trade shows in your country from your government, national chamber of commerce, or a particular trade association. Trade shows also have an educational focus, which allows you to learn what other companies are doing. Most professional and trade organizations have an annual conference, many of which include a trade show. The STC, for example, has an annual conference and trade show. Here are two noteworthy trade shows in the computer industry.

- **CeBit** is held every year in Hannover, Germany at the Hannover Messe. It is the world's largest computer trade show. Software, hardware, and telecommunications companies dominate CeBit's 24 exhibit halls. This is an excellent resource if you need to develop alliances with computer and telecommunications companies in Europe. It is also an excellent resource for seeing how software is localized for the German market. In addition, you can meet many European distributors and translation companies.

- **Comdex** is not as big as CeBit, but it is just as influential. It is held twice every year in the U.S., its biggest show being in the fall, held in Las Vegas, Nevada. Similar to CeBit, the show focuses on computer hardware, software, and telecommunications and networking companies.

UNIVERSITIES AND COLLEGES

A university or college offers printed as well as people resources. School libraries, especially those that offer advanced degrees in technical communication, international business, international communication, and cultural anthropology stock hard-to-find resources, like theses for advanced degrees, obscure journals, newspapers from other countries, and publications in other languages.

Professors, graduate students, and students from other countries can supply you with the most current information on cultural and business issues. University professors who consult on international issues can offer advice based on the latest research. Undergraduate students might be interested in doing internships for college credit at your company that involves compiling cultural and business data for your international user analysis. Students from the target country might be interested in taking part in usability tests for your technical communication products.

Universities with technical-communication programs might even have usability labs that you can rent.

ETHNIC AND SOCIAL GROUPS

Immigrant populations in a country tend to band together. This is particularly noticeable in the U.S. in cities like New York and San Francisco. In such cities, there are usually sections of the city in which people from similar ethnic backgrounds congregate. Ethnic restaurants and shops offer a glimpse into the ways of life in other countries.

Immigrant populations also tend to establish ethnic and social groups to maintain their cultural heritage. These groups are often open to outsiders who want to learn more about the culture. The ethnic and social groups hold dances, invite speakers from a country to discuss current events, and congregate to share a language that might not be common in the source country.

One example of an ethnic and social group is the Japan-America Society. From the statement of purpose in the brochure from the Japan-America Society of New Hampshire: "The Society's primary purpose is to further mutual understanding between the peoples of New Hampshire and Japan—each other's society, history, economy and culture—and to promote the U.S.–Japan relationship in general." The Japan-America Society has branches throughout the U.S. Its events range from trips in Japan to attending art exhibits of Japanese artists to learning Japanese to attending performing arts presentations by Japanese artists.

Ethnic and social groups are excellent ways to learn about a target culture in your own country. Often you meet people who know people in your country or in the target country who can help you in creating effective international technical communication. The cost of membership in an ethnic and social group is often very reasonable, too.

LIBRARIES

Libraries are a resource for many different kinds of information. They offer periodicals, books, videos, statistics, and, more recently, compact discs and computer software. Most reference librarians can do a computer search by subject, author, or title, often for free. In the U.S., interlibrary agreements make it possible for one library to borrow books from another library, even if the libraries are on opposite sides of the country.

Some topics that you might consider researching include:

- cross-cultural communication
- international technical communication, generally, and human factors, graphics, usability, and writing for translation, specifically
- translation, machine translation (MT), and *computer-assisted translation* (CAT)
- international business communication
- cultural anthropology
- international business
- international negotiation
- psycholinguistics
- introductory material on learning a particular language

- cultural and business information specific to the target country
- localization, internationalization, globalization, and concurrent engineering, which are most often discussed in computer science
- international, national, and industry-specific standards and standards organizations

AIRLINES AND TRAVEL AGENCIES

Airlines and travel agencies that cater to businesses often produce publications that list business resources in their source countries. Both resources often have extensive business resources of their own, especially people resources.

Lufthansa German Airlines, for example, publishes many brochures and guides to doing business in Germany. These brochures and guides describe German culture in general and German business culture specifically. They also provide various statistics and descriptions of major industries. The airline will even arrange delegations. A delegation, which can consist of people from one or more companies, tours the country and meets with key German business contacts in a chosen industry.

ELECTRONIC COMMUNICATION

The modem and a myriad of communications protocols and communications devices are clearly making international communication easier. Electronic communication also minimizes the common-language problem by relying on the written word, which gives people more time to read and understand a message.

More and more people travel with laptop or notebook computers that have modem capabilities, which makes it easier for them to maintain communication when they travel. Now that cellular technology is maturing, people can communicate electronically without having to worry about differences in phone jacks or poor telecommunications capabilities in countries that are not as developed as their own. "Use this resource!" is really the message.

There are four electronic communication resources that deserve some attention:

- Electronic mail
- Internet
- Commercial information services
- Bulletin boards

ELECTRONIC MAIL

Most companies now offer their employees electronic mail capabilities for communication within the company. As mentioned in the section "Corporate International Resources," you can use electronic mail to query employees in your company to determine who is knowledgeable about a target country or a target audience.

Another common use of electronic mail is communicating with translation companies. Many companies send files electronically to translation companies around the world. The translation companies then send the translated files back to the company electronically, which greatly speeds up the process. Electronic mail is also used for dialogs between translators and members of the international team when the translator needs a concept explained or a technical question answered. Electronic communication, then, becomes a means for ensuring quality.

Some companies, like Chautauqua Communications of Seattle, Washington, offer electronic-conferencing services. Electronic conferencing is analogous to telephone conferences where three or more parties are able to communicate simultaneously, even when they are all in different locations. Electronic conferencing allows many—even hundreds—of people to communicate simultaneously via a modem. This is a clearly more cost-effective way of communicating.

Many Internet providers and online services like CompuServe offer similar electronic conferencing capabilities.

INTERNET

Internet use is increasing around the world rapidly. The World Wide Web (WWW) is contributing to this mass accessibility. The Internet is very much an international communication device. It offers listservers (devices that send a message to a list of subscribers) and newsgroups for discussion among people with common interests (music, literature, foreign languages, computer software, computer networking), and even library search capabilities (U.S. Library of Congress and many university and private libraries). For example, if you are writing about medical devices or medicine in general, you can access the World Health Organization in Geneva to find out about their activities and publications. There are so many services and information resources on the Internet that you would be best served by purchasing a book on the Internet and its resources.

Some Internet listservers that discuss international technical communication and related topics include:

- **TECHWR-L** is a listserver for all technical communication issues. Its membership is growing daily, and includes people from all over the world. To subscribe, send mail to LISTSERV@VM1.UCC.OKSTATE.EDU and include the message SUBSCRIBE TECHWR-L firstname lastname.

- **BIZCOM** is a listserver for all business communication issues. It is sponsored by the Association for Business Communication. To subscribe, send mail to listproc@ebbs.english.vt.edu and include the message SUBSCRIBE BIZCOM firstname lastname.

- **INSOFT-L** is a listserver that focuses on international technical communication topics and on software internationalization. The listserver also supports an anonymous FTP login so that you can download various files, one of which is a bibliography. To subscribe send mail to majordomo@magellan.iquest.com and include the message SUBSCRIBE INSOFT-L your@address.

C O M M E R C I A L   I N F O R M A T I O N   S E R V I C E S

Perhaps the most successful of these is CompuServe. CompuServe offers services similar to those of the Internet. Just recently, CompuServe went global, which means that they changed their software, making it possible for people in other countries to type in languages that require the use of extended character sets (letters with accent marks).

There are several forums and information search services that can help you research a target country, target market, or target audience. Use of these services is billed by the hour, unlike those on the Internet, which are free. Note that many information technology companies have their own forums. If your company has its own forum, you should monitor it for comments from users in target countries. If your company's product relies on technology from another company, see if the other company has a forum and monitor that forum.

Some services of interest include:

- European Forum, GO EUROFORUM.

- Federation of International Distributors Forum, GO FEDERATION.

- Computer Training Forum, GO DPTRAIN.

- International Trade Forum, GO TRADE.

In addition, access to over 10 reference library sources for doing literature searches and data searches for sources in the U.S. and in Europe is available.

BULLETIN BOARDS

Many of the professional and trade organizations listed above have their own bulletin boards or Internet addresses. Here are some:

- Society for Technical Communication (STC). Bulletin Board telephone number in the U.S.: 703.522.3299. Internet Address: stc@tmn.com.

- International Society for Intercultural Education, Training, and Research (SIETAR). Internet Address: 75250.1275@compuserve.com; CompuServe Address: 75250,1275.

- Localization Industry Standards Association (LISA). Contact the Director, Michael Anobile, at this Internet address: Manobile@divsun.unige.ch.

Contact the other individual organizations for more information.

MISCELLANEOUS MEDIA

A variety of resources exist in different media that can assist you in creating effective international technical communication. Media to consider include:

- Television specials

- Videos

- Cassette tapes

- Compact discs (Multimedia)

TELEVISION

If you are localizing for France, scan the television programming guide to see if there are any special programs about France and French culture. National Geographic specials sometimes feature cultural issues in various countries. Public broadcasting networks and cable companies often offer programs on the culture and language of other countries, as well as offering shows geared at that country's immigrant population in your area.

VIDEO

Companies that specialize in selling business videos may offer topics on cross-cultural communication, language, international business communication, and international negotiation. One publisher of note is the Intercultural Press (P.O. Box 700, Yarmouth, Maine 04096 USA). Some recent video titles include: *Going International*®, *Valuing Diversity*®, *Working with Japan*, and *New Skills for Global Management*.

Consider renting travel videos, too. These may teach you about the lifestyles and culture of a country.

Some professional and trade organizations videotape conferences and seminars that they sponsor. Contact specific organizations to find out if they do this and if they sell or rent the videotapes.

AUDIO CASSETTES

The recent popularity of listening to books recorded on audio cassettes in the U.S. has made many business books available for people who do not have time to read. Contact distributors of recorded books for a listing of business titles.

Audio cassettes for learning another language are also very popular. While not critical to creating effective international technical communication, knowing how to communicate in other languages can only help broaden your skills.

COMPACT DISCS (MULTIMEDIA)

Compact discs with multimedia presentations are now widely available. Multimedia presentations let you learn a new language; watch, listen, and interact with a travelogue to another country; and view any part of the world and read and watch short films about it. Multimedia products seem to become more useful and interesting every day.

INDEX

A

A4 and A5 page sizes, 153
Achievement-oriented cultures, 91
Action chains, 83
Adaptation. *See* Localization
Addresses, in source information, 301
Adverbs, 217
AECMA Simplified English, 214
Aerospace industry, version of English, 214
Africa
  color, cultural interpretations, 267
  high-power distances, 85
Airline publications, 352
Air Transport Association of America (ATA), 214
Aldus Corporation
  analyzing the competition, 92
  experience with technological differences, 76–77
  globalization experiments, 25
  glossary, 192
  graphics in documentation, 147–149
  localization, 14
  solution to enabling problem, 26–27
Algeria, French-speaking, 12
Alphabetic reference manual, 139–140
Alphabetic writing system, 210, 227–228
Alphabets
  collating sequence, 11–12
  graphic symbols and, 209–210

translation considerations, 227–228
American English
  nuances of, 132
  punctuation, 229
  spelling, 222
American National Standards Institute, 342
American National Standards Institute (ANSI), 26
American Society for Training and Development, 348
American Translators Association (ATA), 348
American Translators International (ATI), 185, 187, 198, 199
Americans
  assumptions about, 335–336
  low-context culture, 79
  readers, preferences, 335–336
  spelling, 12
Analysis
  current situation, 35–38, 325–326
  German cultural data, 337
  Japanese cultural data, 339–340
Apple Computer, *Localization for Japan*, 314
Arabic
  alphabet, 17
  alphabetic writing system, 210
  characters, typing, 247
  phonological writing system, 246
  text directionality, 76
  Unicode support, 247

uppercase and lowercase characters, 229
Argentina
  number formats, 236
  time, expressing, 230
Asia
  color, cultural interpretations, 268
  high-power distances, 85
  how-to books, 141
  localization considerations, 13
  translation costs, 179
  writing systems, 247
Asian languages, 26, 247
Association for Business Communication (ABC), 347
Association for Computing Machinery (ACM), 345
AT&T, Global Information Solutions, 185
Audio, synchronizing, 255, 256
Auditing existing information, 167–169, 170
Australia
  business considerations, 95
  localization considerations, 13
  short-term orientation, 88
  specific value orientation, 90
Australian English, 132
Authority conception, 84
Automation, 277
  conditional text, 280–281
  cross-referencing, 278–279
  file management, 284
  fonts, 283–284
  formatting codes, 282–283